SECRETS OF A CYBER SECURITY ARCHITECT

SECRETS OF A CYBER SECURITY ARCHITECT

Brook S. E. Schoenfield

CRC Press

Taylor & Francis Group

Boca Raton London New York

CRC Press is an imprint of the
Taylor & Francis Group, an **informa** business

AN AUERBACH BOOK

CRC Press
Taylor & Francis Group
6000 Broken Sound Parkway NW, Suite 300
Boca Raton, FL 33487-2742

First issued in paperback 2022

© 2020 by Brook S. E. Schoenfield
CRC Press is an imprint of Taylor & Francis Group, an Informa business

No claim to original U.S. Government works

ISBN 13: 978-1-03-247502-8 (pbk)
ISBN 13: 978-1-4987-4199-6 (hbk)

DOI: 10.1201/9781315369167

Visit the Taylor & Francis Web site at
http://www.taylorandfrancis.com

and the CRC Press Web site at
http://www.crcpress.com

Author Note

All references to *Securing Systems* throughout the book are from:

Schoenfield, B. (2015). *Securing Systems: Applied Security Architecture and Threat Models.* Boca Raton, FL: CRC Press.

All references to *Core System Security* throughout the book are from:

Schoenfield, B. (2014). Applying the SDL Framework to the Real World. In Ransome, J. and Misra, A. *Core Software Security: Security at the Source,* Ch. 9, pp. 255–324. Boca Raton, FL: CRC Press.

Trademarks Covered in This Book

Cisco and Infosec are registered trademarks of Cisco Systems, Inc. and/or its affiliates in the United States and certain other countries.

FACEBOOK is a registered trademark of FACEBOOK in Menlo Park, CA.

LinkedIn is a registered trademark of LinkedIn Corporation in Sunnyvale, CA.

IOActive is a registered trademark of IOActive, Inc., in Seattle, WA.

ISO is a registered trademark of the International Organization for Standardization in Geneva, Switzerland.

Linux is a trademark of Torvalds, Linus in Boston, MA.

Microsoft and Windows are trademarks of Microsoft Corporation in Redmond, WA.

MITRE is a registered trademark and ATT&CK is a trademark of MITRE Corporation in Bedford, MA.

SOC 2 is a registered trademark of the American Institute of Certified Public Accountants in New York, NY.

Dedication

This book is dedicated to the many security architects with whom I've worked and from whom I've learned: mentors, mentees, peers, students, comrades, friends. The InfoSec architecture team at Cisco (circa 2000–2011) and McAfee's Product Security Champions (2012–2018) deserve my special gratitude. Collectively, we've contributed to a discipline known now as "security architecture." Herein lie the many fruits harvested from our discussions, speculation, and philosophizing; the trials and successes we've shared; and your many insights. Thank you.

Contents

List of Figures and Tables

Foreword

This week's news includes that indicted Iranian hackers are still hard at work, a disruptive cyber event impacted the US power grid, and a high-school dropout hacked a million devices. It included brand-name companies in the headlines for security failures. And it looked very much like other weeks.

Many of the systems whose security failed had compliance checklists. Products were subjected to penetration testing, or ethical hacking, or dynamic testing. And they still failed, because the security approach their creators used didn't address the unique requirements of the systems being built and deployed.

Security architecture is a set of structures for thinking about what we're working on, what can go wrong, and, most importantly, what are we doing about them? We're infusing security into the things we work on. We're building features and worrying about the properties. The distinction is like this: a deadbolt is a security feature, and the steel it's made from has properties. If the steel of the deadbolt is brittle; if the receiver isn't well mounted; if the doorframe is weak, then the deadbolt will not deliver on the security goals for the door. (Incidentally, my book on threat modeling is largely focused on what can go wrong, and as such complements this one.)

Our software, like other things we build, has many interfaces to the world, and attackers can pick and choose which ones to examine or attack.

For years, security has shown up as designs are finalized, and then complained about those designs. It hasn't delivered the security that our society needs, and it hasn't led to effective collaboration.

Architecture, like security, has a bit of a bad name amongst software engineers. Too often, it's people who can't code, won't make tradeoffs, and don't ship, but do object—endlessly. Like any aspect of software, architecture and security can be done well or poorly.

The book that you hold in your hands is about doing it well, but that's not quite right. I don't care much about doing it well, in and of itself, and I don't think Brook does either. I care about helping the people I'm working with make better products, which includes shipping and includes shipping with appropriate security. Let me be clear about what *appropriate* means here: it means that the folks who make product decisions have the information they need to make those decisions. Sometimes you're happy with the result, other times not, but you shouldn't be surprised by the security problems systems have once they ship.

Of course, I prefer to make things I can be proud of, and so I want to do things well, and I hope you want the same. This book is about how to do that for security.

Adam Shostack
September 17, 2019
Seattle, WA

Preface

Context

As I wrote in *Securing Systems*, *"It is a plain fact that as of this writing, we are engaged in a cyber arms race of extraordinary size, composition, complexity, and velocity." Securing Systems*, p. 5

There are more than three billion[*] people who use the Internet and whose lives are intertwined with their digital devices. These connected people's medical, financial, and other personal data is spread out over hundreds if not thousands of systems run by a multitude of organizations, many of whom do not necessarily have the data owners' best interest at heart. Pandora's[†] cyber box has long since been opened, and the box's "demons" have been loosed upon the digital world. Indeed, most of us participants are attempting to get on with our lives, making our way through the digital battle zone. A few of you readers may actually be engaged in the cyber war in some professional or other capacity. But for the vast majority of us cyber-citizens, we are the collateral damage to conflict that has little to do with us on a personal level.

Like most war zones, in addition to the combatants, there always seem to be those out to make a profit amid the chaos. There be pirates and warlords on these Internet seas, Matey. I think that the current state of affairs may be comparable to the 300 or so years when international commerce was highly dependent upon sea trade, approximately from the late 1500s to the middle of the 19th century, the so-called "golden age of piracy."

Not that we don't have sea pirates today; of course we do. But, during the golden age of piracy, shipping, which, as the main form of transport underpinning international commerce, was never safe from marauding pirates. City states were funded through piracy; piracy made significant contributions to the tax basis of several nations. Piracy, or more properly, the

---

[*] According to the United Nations population estimates, in 2020, there will be near to 7.8 billion people on planet Earth. Please see https://population.un.org. Estimates of Internet users vary from 3.2 to 4.4. Please see https://en.wikipedia.org/wiki/Global_Internet_usage and https://internetworldstats.com/stats.htm for examples of estimates.

[†] Pandora, the Greek mythological character, not Pandora™, the music streaming company.

privateer, served as a way to fortify a nation's navy in times of war. At the same time, privateers provided a needed boost in state revenue at the expense of a nation's enemies.[*]

The age of piracy seems entirely analogous to the Internet Age's quasi-state "cyber armies" who attack, and sometimes plunder, digital commercial interests. As Dmitri Alperovitch so wryly noted in 2011,

> *"I divide the entire set of Fortune Global 2,000 firms into two categories: those that know they've been compromised and those that don't yet know."*[†]

In other words, any organization with valuable data has been and will be attacked, probably successfully, at some point and with some damage. And, don't all digitally connected organizations have at least some data that can be considered "valuable"? If the data is not intellectual property on which revenue is based, then the personal records of customers or employees will be valuable to digital attackers. For so-called non-governmental organizations (NGOs), strategic plans or the names of operatives in countries in which any disagreement with the local government raises suspicion or even sanction may be considered valuable to those charged with preventing dissent. Can we declare that in the Age of the Internet, no data is safe, no data is without value to attackers? On some days, this may seem to be close to a truism. Isn't this comparable to the golden age of piracy, when no ship in transit was safe?

There's a great deal of money to be made through theft and fraud of one kind or another on the Internet, which I liken to the great oceans of times past. And, there are large organizations and single actors who understand that "there's a sucker born every minute"[‡]—that is, a few billion unwitting potential victims to fleece. A great advantage for these attackers is that, mostly, the pirate does not have to come into physical contact with the victim. Many, if not most, successful attacks are relatively[§] anonymous. Which, one has to admit, is a big advantage for attackers.

We, the Internet connected,[¶] are the targets of all this cyber attack activity rather constantly and continuously.

Of course, government cyber armies practice defensive maneuvers. That is to be expected. Unfortunately, most government defense efforts are not focused on protecting you and me or the many independent or commercial organizations that hold our data as we blissfully go about our digital lives. In the USA, where I live, certainly the federal government is highly concerned about protecting not only its own resources, but also the nation's critical infrastructure. Still, despite the deep concern, most of that actual day-to-day protecting is done by the organizations, public and private, who run the infrastructure, not by the government. You may have

---

[*] This historical reference is drawn from my reading of historical analysis presented within *Pirate Utopias: Moorish Corsairs & European Renegadoes* (Wilson, 2004).

[†] Alperovitch, 2011.

[‡] Inconclusively attributed to P. T. Barnum.

[§] As of this writing, retrieving any identifying information from sophisticated attacks requires expert forensic analysis. The information retrieved is often quite piecemeal, at best. There may be pointers to the identities of attackers, but often there is no direct link from attack to person.

[¶] About half or so of Earth's human inhabitants do not use the Internet at the time of this writing. I always try to bear this in mind.

read newspaper accounts about the difficulties and gaps in those protections. Sadly, my professional opinion is that these media descriptions are more or (often) less accurate. I'm willing to bet that the USA's enemies are keenly aware of the situation. Many nations' infrastructure is equally at risk; the USA is not alone in this.

Cyber Defenders

To whom or what may a non-technical cyber-citizen turn?

During my 30+ year high-tech career, so called "computer security," "information security," or "cyber security" has grown from a fledgling group of interested amateurs who tried to squeeze in some security work alongside their busy, high-tech day jobs into a full-blown industry of thousands of professionals.

Many security companies have tried to steer clear of jingoistic association. The big vendors often have customers in any number of governments, some of whom at any particular moment will be in active cyber conflict with each other. It seems an interesting turn of events that security companies have to maintain a certain level of cyber neutrality in order to succeed. It turns out that refusing to take sides is just good security business.

Computer security companies offer a dizzying array of technologies, products, and services, many of which are marketed through some variation of "solves your security problems." Unfortunately, not.[*]

Part of the problem is that "security" is ill-defined and highly overloaded. Most security products handle some portion of the computer security challenge. No product I know of comes close to being a total package solution, taking care of all an organization's or person's computer security needs, soup to nuts. Why? Because security is a big, messy, multivariate, multidimensional arena. A reasonable "defense-in-depth" requires many technologies; smart, highly skilled people; and deep and broad analysis—all of which must come together into some sort of functioning whole, that whole often termed "a security architecture."

Why "Security Architecture"

Architecture:

1. The fundamental concepts or properties of a system in its environment embodied in its elements, relationships, and in the principles of its design and evolution.[†]
2. The structure of components, their inter-relationships, and the principles and guidelines governing their design and evolution over time.[‡]

---

[*] Full disclosure: As of this writing, I work for one of these "security companies." My comments do not represent the opinions of my employer.

[†] *Source:* ISO/IEC/IEEE 42010:2011

[‡] The Open Group, n.d.

"Traditionally, security architecture consists of some preventive, detective and corrective controls that are implemented to protect the enterprise infrastructure and applications."[*]

"It is not possible to build a space ship without vision, goals, and specific objectives, which are expressed in large-scale and also highly specific plans. Cyber security is much the same thing, which is where the practice of security architecture comes into play.

"One definition of security architecture might be, 'applied information security.' Or perhaps, more to the point of this work, security architecture applies the principles of security to system architectures." Securing Systems, p. 14

My previous definition probably assumes far too much to be useful unless one is already familiar with information security and the practice of architecture. By "system architectures" I meant to include any system that requires digital security, be it the architecture of a discrete application or program, a library or application programming interface (API), a global cloud, an organization's digital assets, etc. Though my definition may have sufficed for the purposes of a book on threat modeling, it still feels a bit too opaque, and I fear that it excludes some important aspects.

This book is about security architecture. My goal is to refrain from theory and focus instead on practice. You will not find much theory in this book. I hope that I have provided just enough theory to place the materials into sufficient context for full understanding. For a deeper explanation, I point the reader to any number of books on security architecture, including my own, *Securing Systems,* although that book was also intended to remain grounded in the practical and proven rather than being overly theoretical.

Good security architects have dozens of tricks of their trade in their kips. Herein, you will find my tips and tricks, as well as myriad tried and true bits of wisdom that my colleagues have been gracious enough to share with me.

I want to give these to you, the practitioner, to ease your way. This work can be hard, complex, certainly frustrating. Seasoned architects know how to surmount individual, team, and organizational resistance. They know how to express security requirements in ways that will make the requirements more palatable and, thus, get them accomplished.

Great security architects tend also to be masters of compromise, negotiation, and conflict management. In general, the people for whom I have the highest respect are consummate collaborators, as interested in understanding as providing their own solutions. The vast majority of practitioners with whom I've had the privilege and honor of working have been and continue to be high-integrity individuals who want the best for their organizations and typically, also, through their work, for the world at large. Of course, each of us gets to define "best" for ourselves.

Book Contents

The first chapter of the book is focused on what security architecture is and the areas of expertise a security architect will need in practice. The second chapter delves into the relationship

---

[*] Ghaznavi-Zadeh, 2017.

between attack methods and the art of building cyber defenses. Security people must become familiar with the many different ways that human actors attack systems. For some branches of digital security, the understanding of attack mechanisms must be deep and thorough. For other areas—say, people managers and executives—perhaps only a glancing understanding of attack methods is required, although often, these roles require a thorough understanding of the potential organizational harm that may result from successful attacks of one kind or another.

For the security architect, the level of understanding will be more holistic. Each class of attack involves a particular type of technical manipulation. Security architects typically must have enough computer science background to understand the basic mechanism of manipulation. Alongside this, an effective security architect will further have a command of the mechanisms that will thwart each class of relevant attack. Plus, the architect will understand both the effects of system attack on the system under attack and the potential repercussions to the organization.

Still—this is important, and we will delve into this in some detail—a security architect will typically not be required to hold the details of every variation of each class of attack, and not required to command the specific technical details by which a particular instance of a class of attacks will exercise a particular vulnerability. This level of detail is often irrelevant to implementing a defense.

This isn't to suggest that security architects cannot master the details of a particular attack; usually, they will have to have explored at least one example of each type of attack in order to understand its mechanism sufficiently. And, of course, people move around. There are plenty of security architects who were once penetration testers and penetration testers who are competent security architects. The point is, the exact assembler language to exploit each of a collection of particular heap overflows is not required for the memory be handled in a secure fashion by a programmer. The literature and other training is full of examples of how memory is to be handled correctly.

Importantly for this book's tips and tricks to make as much sense as possible, Chapter 3 (Architecture, Attacks, and Defences) will explore the required attack knowledge set in some detail—that is, why to use attacks and how to derive a set of mitigations and defenses.

Chapter 4, Culture Hacking, is a tour of the approaches, tricks, and yes, even a few manipulations that have proven successful for practicing security architecture in the face of the sorts of challenges most will meet. I also include bits about starting, maturing, and running effective security architecture programs. At least, these things have worked for me and quite a few of the people with whom I've worked. Your mileage, of course, may vary.

In Chapter 5 (Learning the Trade), the secrets of the trade revealed herein will be set out in a series of short snippets, each hopefully delivering a bit of wisdom that can be applied as you, the reader, practice security architecture.

Finally, in Chapter 6, I've tried to set down, as best that I can, a lot of the tricks that I've used to surmount typical problems. Lucky for me, I get to interact with a lot of practicing security architects. My network has provided me with strong anecdotal evidence that most programs will encounter many, if not all, of the challenges that I list in Chapter 6 as they mature. While not at all scientific, I've become convinced that there are milestone problems that crop up for nearly every program. I hope that it would be helpful if I listed these and then provided my methods for tackling them, for whatever worth you may get from these.

There are a few previously published pieces in the Appendices following the chapters that have been referenced during the text. I provide these to fill in any questions you may have, and for reference.

It is my sincere hope that *Secrets of a Cyber Security Architect* provides you a fun read, some insight, and also that it's organized well enough to be a desk reference as you proceed through your security architecture career and practice.

— Brook Schoenfield
August, 2019

Acknowledgments

Hopefully, *Secrets of a Cyber Security Architect* is *not* a work of fiction. The people mentioned herein by name are most assuredly actual people, though a few are sadly no longer living. This book concerns itself with practices that work versus practices that have proven counterproductive. The ideas, as Adam Shostack so wisely quips, "are abstract." As such, this is a human work, perhaps all to human? Unavoidably, the book is as much about people as technical matters.

There are, indeed, a number of fairly technical discussions here, as may be expected. Still, a great deal of the book is devoted to how people enact the abstract, how we move abstractions expressed through the practice of security architecture from ideas to working software that performs useful human functions and, at the same time, exhibits protective properties. With any luck, this book will help avoid adversary exploitation of software weaknesses that result in harm to the users and owners of the software. Make no mistake, adversaries are humans, too: adaptive, creative humans. Which brings us back to the very humanness that must underlie security architecture.

As I noted in the dedication to this work, hundreds of people at all skill levels contributed to this work. Without those who've tolerated me enough to try to learn from me, who've humored the many blind alleys that have eventually led to the teaching methods I employ today, this book would most certainly not exist. Whatever success my current methods have is due in large part to participants' patience, endurance, and persistence.

I arrived at Cisco in 2000 an extensively experienced software programmer, designer, and technical lead. Unfortunately, I was a rather less skilled security practitioner than I had believed about myself before I met people who were steeping themselves in cyber security. Thanks to Gil Daudistil and Doug Dexter for extending both their professional support and personal friendship, so that I survived that first year on Infosec's architecture team. The WebArch team, Steve Acheson, Laura Lindsey, Catherine Blackader Nelson, and Rakesh Bharania, may have hazed me a bit, yes. But they also pushed me to extend my skills. All remain treasured friends.

The Cisco Infosec identity management working group, circa 2001–2002, lead by Michele Guel, and including Steve Acheson, Steve Wright, Sergei Rousakov, and myself, grappled with what was at that time a huge paradigm shift: identity as an organization's "security perimeter."*

---

* At that time, cyber security defense focused on network protections.

It was through that effort that I began to find my feet as a security architect. We produced formative results that are just now gaining recognition close to 20 years later.

Having left the safety of a small software company to jump into the roiling waters of Big IT and Big Tech at Cisco, I was completely unprepared for the large number of highly skilled, highly motivated, high-integrity people with whom I've had the privilege to interact for the last 20 odd years. There is not space to name them all. That so many of my co-workers would become dear friends is the unexpected bonus of our shared passion to make people's digital lives just a wee bit safer. Or as John Stewart quipped one time when we were waiting for a plane to a conference at which we were both speaking, "Simply make the Internet work." Word!

John wrote one of the most lyric and beautiful Forwards I've ever read for my last book, *Securing Systems.* Thanks for your leadership. You guided what had been a dysfunctional organization to excellence. Thanks for your friendship. Obviously, thanks for being willing to stick your name onto my book. And, thanks for a few rides to the train, too. Those were important conversations, I think? At least, I carry them with me.

Without managers who see the value in playing a "long game," who've consistently seen the value of building a team first before focusing on delivery, much of what's in this book would not ever have been tried. Rob Rolfson, Michelle Koblas, Nasrin Rezai, the incomparable Dr. James Ransome, Scott "Chopper" Walker, Steve Mori.

Thanks are due to the first WebArch team that I led wherein we tried out the foundational concepts that through refinement blazed a trail to the material in this book. Vinay Bansal, Justin Tang, Ove Hanson each need to be acknowledged. Plus, there were a few project managers in that period who organized and supported the work: Caroline Thrasher, Ferris Jabri, Julian Soriano, and Dan Burke. Aaron Sierra helped me validate that the techniques also work for product security and cloud architectures.

The threat modeling exercises from which conclusions and suggestions herein are drawn have been greatly improved in collaboration with Damilare Fagbemi, who ran around Ireland and the United States co-teaching, and then incorporating class feedback into the class. A couple of other contributors to the class are Luis Servin, David Wheeler, Sun Lee, and Tania Skinner (though she may not realize the importance of her critique and validation).

James Ransome and I spent a couple of months in front of a whiteboard refining what we knew about software security and identifying that which we didn't. The proven ideas were then captured in *Core Software Security,* Chapter 9. Since publication of that book, we each keep honing those seminal concepts as well as finding new ones, a few of which are presented in this book, and most of which will be in our next.

No technical book should complete without technical review. The ideas presented here have received significant review from peers and then have been proven through practice; much of the practicing must be credited to the security architecture leaders of the programs I've led. There are too many peers to name: you know who you are.

Some of this work has been previously published in various forms: books, booklets, presentations, papers, posts. Along the way, specific technical reviews were provided by Jack Jones (risk), Izar Tarandach (security architecture and threat modeling), Blake E. Strom (unorthodox use of ATT&CK), Cedric Cochin and Raj Samani (posts covering various discreet subjects), Jon King and Celeste Fralick (continuing inspiration).

This book has been immeasurably improved through suggestions from Adam Shostack. Thanks to Adam for contributing his Forward, as well.

Thank you to the MITRE® Corporation for allowing me to reprint several of their copyrighted materials.

No book can move forward without the support of the publisher and publishing team: John Wyzalek for confidence in the concept. I apologize that the first draft took so long: sometimes the book I set out to write is not the book that emerges through my process. Thanks are due to Theron Shreve and his staff at Derryfield Publishing, with special acknowledgment for the diligence of copyeditor and typesetter Susan Culligan, who also provided significant project management.

Finally, but no less important is my daughter, Allison, who follows in Da's footsteps as a security architect. Dinner conversations invariably descend into technical discussions. She then continues to further prove these ideas through her work. My spouse, Cynthia, must lastly be mentioned. For one thing, she puts up with these technical discussions at the dining table. "It's the alien-speak, again." You have, with this one, suffered through the pain of writing five books about computer security. Without your humor, insight, and forbearance, none of this would unfold. Thank you.

About the Author

Brook S. E. Schoenfield is the author of *Securing Systems: Applied Security Architecture and Threat Models*[*] and Chapter 9: Applying the SDL Framework to the Real World, in *Core Software Security: Security at the Source.*[†] He has been published by CRC Press, SANS Institute, Cisco, SAFECode, and the IEEE. Occasionally, he even posts to his security architecture blog, brookschoenfield.com.

He is the Master Security Architect at a global cyber security consultancy, where he leads the company's secure design services. He has held security architecture leadership positions at high-tech enterprises for nearly 20 years, at which he has trained and coached hundreds of people in their journey to becoming security architects. Several thousand people have taken his participatory threat modeling classes.

Brook has presented and taught at conferences such as RSA, BSIMM, OWASP, and SANS What Works Summits on subjects within security architecture, including threat models, DevOps security, information security risk, and other aspects of secure design and software security.

Brook lives in Montana's Bitterroot Mountains. When he's not thinking about, practicing, writing about, and speaking on secure design and software security, he can be found telemark skiing, hiking, and fly fishing in his beloved mountains, exploring new cooking techniques, or playing various genres of guitar—from jazz to percussive fingerstyle.

---

[*] Schoenfield, 2015.
[†] Schoenfield, 2014.

Chapter 1

The Context of Security Architecture

1.1 Omnipresent Cyber War

At the time of this writing, those of us participating in the digital (online) world are living in an unprecedented age. Never before in human history have machines and the energy used to drive them performed so much of the labor required to sustain human life.

Consider for a moment mechanizations used for farming: tractors that pull tillers that can prepare hectares of soil for planting. Compare that to an 18th-century farmer who would hitch a draft animal to a plow, turning a single furrow at a time. Now even seed can be dispersed from a device pulled by the tractor.

What was once strictly the domain of human labor, perhaps including animal strength, can now be accomplished with the right equipment by one determined person.

That is not to say that farming cannot be accomplished by human labor alone, nor to say that it isn't by the many subsistence farmers still active on Planet Earth; certainly, people continue to farm with a stick or utilize animal power, if available and affordable.

I make this digression simply to illustrate the profound changes that have occurred over the last few hundred years in nearly every domain of human production, including information processing. The Computer Age (also called the Information Age and the Digital Age) has blossomed to magnify technology's reach and influence, for a computer can control a formally manual manufacturing process.

Lots of skilled and unskilled jobs have been replaced, and more are on the block. Perhaps truck/lorry drivers might be next? Anheuser-Busch has already delivered a load of beer with an automated truck.[*]

---

[*] Isaac, 2016.

In the context of farming, imagine that many (perhaps most?) farmers on the planet embed cheap moisture sensors in their soil, which they could monitor from their mobile phone. Since cell towers have long since leap-frogged land-line infrastructures in the Third World, there are mobile services available to many fairly remote areas. It is conceivable that even relatively poor people may have mobile phones in the near future.[*] This isn't idle speculation; I had this precise conversation with a principal of The Climate Corporation in 2015.

Computers are being adapted to either perform or assist with tasks, both new and old, at a dizzying and increasing rate; computers are everywhere surrounding us. Those of us living in the connected world are surrounded by an aura of radio frequencies the like of which has never been experienced, so far as we know. This bombardment with radio waves at many frequencies at the same time constitutes an unfolding experiment in human (and our animal companions') tolerance for radio transmissions. [Time will tell if we can actually tolerate the bombardment or what the effects may be. Perhaps evolution will step in with a genetic mutation for radio wave tolerance?]

I believe that we've really only scratched the surface in this transformation.[†] It is likely that computation capabilities will increase dramatically (quantum computation?) while at the same time size and power requirements will drop. Sensors of nearly everything sensible by computers will surround us, just as some futurists have imagined.[‡] It is quite likely that computers will start to write computer programs—at least, those parts of programs that are sufficiently deterministic and formulaic to be programmed algorithmically or heuristically (at least to start). [It is certainly within the realm of possibility that machine learning or artificial intelligence might be applied to the generation of software algorithms.]

I can imagine a digital world far more complex and rich than exists today, which is far beyond what I imagined possible 40 years ago, when I was introduced to programming. A great deal has changed. I think that far more is in front of us than behind. Our lives are incredibly dependent upon computers and the software that they run.

We also know that the software we depend upon is riddled with errors, whose correctness cannot be automatically proven (that is to say that at this moment, the Turing Proof still holds true). Which brings us squarely to the security problem those of us in the connected world must face, every day, sometimes many times a day: There be pirates on these digital waters, Matey.

> Our ability to develop complex software vastly exceeds our ability to prove its correctness or test it satisfactorily within reasonable fiscal constraints . . . complex software is difficult to write and to test, and will therefore contain numerous unintentional 'bugs'[.] It would be extremely difficult and expensive to determine with certainty that a piece of software is free of bugs[.] Given the relatively small amounts of funding allocated for developing and testing . . . software, we may safely consider it as effectively impossible.[§]

A couple of quotes from the Forwords to *Securing Systems* may help to illustrate our digital dependence:

---

[*] Ogundeji, 2015.
[†] Osborne, 2018.
[‡] For instance, the nano digital world imagined in Neal Stephenson's *Diamond Age* (Stephenson, 1995).
[§] Rivest and Wack, n.d., pp. 3–4.

"We are struggling as a security industry now, and the need to be successful is higher than it has ever been in my twenty-five years in it. It is not good enough just to build something and try and secure it, it must be architected from the bottom up with security in it, by professionally trained and skilled security architects, checked and validated by regular assessments for weakness, and through a learning system that learns from today to inform tomorrow. We must succeed." [*]

"Virtually every aspect of global civilization now depends on interconnected cyber systems to operate. A good portion of the money that was spent on offensive and defensive capabilities during the Cold War is now being spent on cyber offense and defense. Unlike the Cold War, where only governments were involved, this cyber challenge requires defensive measures for commercial enterprises, small businesses, NGOs, and individuals." [†]

Failure to understand that the dependence that we have not just on our obvious digital devices—smart phone, laptop, tablet, fancy fitness bling on your wrist—but also on a matrix of interconnection tying all these devices and billions more together will land you in the hot seat; consider what happened to THE HOME DEPOT®, whose management actively resisted understanding their business's interconnectivity.[‡] When THE HOME DEPOT's security folk pointed out the glaring weaknesses in the company's cyber defenses, an executive is quoted as declaring, "we sell hammers, not computers." The sad truth is that even a hammer and nail company must still account for its digital operations, which nearly always imply maintaining a cyber security defense posture. The breach occurred in 2014. By 2017, that breach had cost the company $179 million.[§] Not exactly chump change, even for a global corporation.

For more than three billion out of the seven billion people on this planet, we have long since passed the point at which we are isolated entities who act alone and in some measure of unconnected global anonymity. For most of us, our lives depend not just upon technology itself, but also on the capabilities of innumerable, faceless business entities and those entities' digital systems that act upon our digital behalf.

Consider the following common, but trivial, example: When I swipe my credit card at the pump to purchase petrol, that transaction passes through any number of computation devices and applications operated by a chain of business entities. The following is a typical scenario (an example flow—but not the only one, of course):

> My friend and former colleague Lucy McCoy wrote the communications code in the first generation of gas pump payment terminals. At that time, terminals communicated via modem and phone line. She was a serial communications wiz. I remember the point-of-sale terminal laid out in her lab area. Lucy has since passed away. She was a brilliant engineer; she gave my code the best testing that any code I've written has ever received.

- The point-of-sale device itself (likely supplied by a point-of-sale provider) (see inset)
- The networking equipment at the petrol station (see inset next page)

---

[*] John N. Stewart SVP, Chief Security & Trust Officer Cisco Systems, Inc.
[†] Dr. James F. Ransome, CISSP, CISM.
[‡] Please see brookschoenfield.com/?p=219 for more discussion on THE HOME DEPOT's large breach.
[§] WebTitan, 2017.

- The station's Internet provider's equipment (networking, security, applications—you have no idea!)
- One or more telecom company's networking infrastructure across the Internet backbone
- The point-of-sale company or their proxy
- More networking equipment and Internet providers
- A credit card payment processor
- The card issuer who must validate the card and agree to pay the transaction for me

> The transactions have to get from station to payment processing, right? Who runs those cable modems and routers at the station? Could be the Internet provider, or maybe not. I run my own modem/routers/switches at home to which I have sole admin access. An employee might easily slip a router under their control between terminals and provider; who's to know? You don't walk up to the payment kiosk and demand to see the routing gear, do you?

And so on . . . all just to fill my fuel tank. It's seamless and invisible—the communications between entities usually bring up an encrypted tunnel, although the protection offered is not as solid as you may hope; it is invisible and seamless, except when the processing is not so invisible, such as during a compromise and breach. [On a trip through Idaho several years ago, a fuel pump in a remote station from which I fueled had a card skimmer attached to it. My credit card was then used for fraudulent activity.]

Every one of these invisible players has to have good enough security to protect me, and you, if you also use some sort of payment card for your petrol.*

The foregoing is one of many examples:

- Medical gear and the networks that support them.
- Your financial institution's systems (where your "deposits" are really just digital data).
- The 100–200 processors in your car, with the stack of software that runs on them.
- Your Bluetooth headset—a Linux computer, as is that webcam watching your front door.
- Your smart TV—another Linux computer, as is your printer, the thermostat, Alexa, Echo; even your landline's handset may very well be another Linux system.

Is there nothing sacred? Probably not. And all of it is attack surface if there's anything worth stealing, learning, coercing, influencing, misusing, or disrupting to be found. Such has become the nature of the Connected World: it's all attackable given sufficient motivation.

The art of security architecture plays a part in the dance between adversaries and defenses. The security architect attempts to align defenses to expected attacks. As we shall see in Chapter 3, Attacks and Defenses, the security architect seeks to understand relevant attackers, their methods, and their goals. At the same time, they must also understand how particular types of attacks work such that appropriate defense mechanisms can be specified, implemented, and deployed.

Security architects may be thought of as software and system architects who specialize in attacks and defenses, who are proficient enough with architecture techniques to specify defenses as part of the structure of a system or software architecture.

I don't believe that our present and future digital security rests solely on this one discipline; that would be incredibly arrogant and also quite unfair to the many other disciplines that have emerged within the digital security space, such as:

---

* http://brookschoenfield.com/?p=219

- Exploit and vulnerability research
- Analysis of the dynamics of the threat landscape and human adversaries ("threat research")
- Malware analysis
- Incident response
- Risk analysis
- Defensive programming
- Vulnerability and error discovery tools and automation
- Constructing easier-to-secure programming languages and environments
- The defensive software industry
- Management of the problem space's complexity
- And so forth

Still, as was noted in NIST 800-14 in 1996,[*] if we cannot uncover appropriate security requirements during system design cycles, we have already lost an important—nay, key—opportunity. We leave ourselves with the difficult (and usually far more expensive) challenge to amend insecure software late in the game, perhaps even after deployment. That is the essence of this book: to add to a growing body of practice and, I hope, wisdom about what security architecture is, why it's important, and how to practice it successfully.

In the following chapters, sections, and pages, I hope by collecting some of the bits and pieces that I've found useful into one volume, I can contribute in some small way to the art and science, the practice of this thing that's become known as "security architecture," to which I've given some of the best of my professional life and quite a bit of my thinking.

Some of the following has been pulled from other works of mine. To that material, I've added additional thoughts and learnings derived since those publications. I've also tried to augment ideas that I've touched on in passing with greater depth. Let me know what you find useful, as always.

1.2 Know the Threat Actors

Attack and the subsequent "compromise"—that is, complete control of a system on the Internet—is utterly pervasive: constant and continual. And this has been true for quite a long time. Many attackers are intelligent and adaptive. If defenses improve, attackers will change their tactics to meet the new challenge. At the same time, attack methods that were once complex and technically challenging are routinely "weaponized": turned into point-and-click tools that the relatively technically unsophisticated can easily use.[†] This development has exponentially expanded the number of attackers. The result is a broad range of attackers, some highly ingenious alongside the many who can and will exploit well-known vulnerabilities if these are left without remediation.

The chance of an attempted attack of one kind or another is certain. The probability of a web attack is 100 percent; systems are being attacked and will be attacked regularly and continually. Most of those attacks will be "doorknob rattling"—reconnaissance probes and well-known,

---

[*] NIST, 1996.

[†] One recent example of such weaponization is SpookFlare 2.0, available from public GitHub servers for download at https://github.com/hlldz/SpookFlaref6e0>

Fifty million is a number given to me by intrusion analysts at a major high-tech company. At these levels, it doesn't really matter if the number is more like 30 million or even 100 million. The number of attacks overwhelm even the best staff unless they have significant automation.

easily defended exploit methods. But out of the fifty million attacks each week that most major websites must endure (see inset), something like one or two within the mountain of attack events will likely be highly sophisticated and tightly targeted at that particular set of systems. And the probability of a targeted attack goes up exponentially when the web systems employ well-known operating systems and execution environments.

A web server listening for connections from the Internet must remain open to all Internet traffic [unless IP address restrictions are put into place such that only some networks or even particular hosts can access the web server], which means that any attacker can probe the interface, at least at the network protocol level, if not deeper. The constant doorknob-rattling sweeps of the Internet will surely find and investigate whatever interfaces are open and available to unrestricted traffic.

Once an interested attacker finds and catalogs the open HTTP port, then the fun really begins. Like web vulnerability scanners, the attacker will probe every reachable page with every attack variation possible. These probes (and possibly downloads of portions of the site) will be unrelenting. To prevent restriction of the attacker's address, they may use multiple addresses or even shift attacking addresses on the fly (e.g., fast flux DNS).

In contrast, security architects must use their understanding of the currently active threat agents and their techniques in order to apply these appropriately to a particular system. Whether a particular threat agent will aim at a particular system is as much a matter of understanding, knowledge, and experience as it is cold hard fact. Considering the potential effects of threat agents and their capabilities to attack any particular system is an essential activity within the art of threat modeling. Hence, a security assessment of an architecture is an act of craft that wields engineering as the tool set.

Although in practice the order in which we consider different aspects of attacks and defenses doesn't materially affect the quality of the output, let's start with threat agents (actors, adversaries). The goals and capabilities of each *type* of actor profoundly affect how deep and thorough a defense must be. I explained this in *Securing Systems* at some length: some actors seek a quick return on effort. Others will work on a compromise until successful, no matter the time and cost. Some adversaries mean to cause harm, some mean to cause no harm, and some don't care about what harm may ensue, so long as a goal is achieved.

There are other dimensions to consider. I've settled on five areas:

1. Final goal of the attacker
2. Technical ability
3. Risk tolerance
4. Work factor
5. Activity level

There's nothing sacred about my categories. These threat actor attributes are the ones that allow me to set priorities when analyzing a system. If you don't like these or see holes in my thinking, then by all means use your own categories.

After years of refining the matrix, years of teaching threat modeling to diverse groups of people (from groups of a few individuals to 120 participants), and several years of having participants in my sessions build their own matrices, this set of categories seems to work fairly well. Still, I remain open to other approaches. There is probably a better way; if you find a system that works better for you, please let me know.

Below, I briefly explain each of these threat actor attributes or behavioral dimensions:

- **Goal.** Many successful compromises depend on the successful execution of a set of exploits, one after the other. From reconnaissance, to establishment of a presence, to privilege escalation, on through establishment of command-and-control and persistence, none of these is typically the ultimate goal of an adversary [except for vulnerability hunters and security researchers, who may be satisfied with establishing proof that an exploitable condition exists in isolation]. For real-world attackers, the adversary is after *something*; perhaps stealing credentials or controlling the host so that it may be employed as part of a botnet, stealing information, disrupting operations, or just plain and simple theft of money or other assets—attackers have many goals. In order to identify which assets may be valuable to the set of attackers who are likely adversaries, it helps to understand what results different classes of attackers expect to achieve.

- **Technical ability.** Not every class of attacker wishes to employ highly sophisticated, resource-intensive techniques. For a moment, ignore the potential for any attacker to be highly sophisticated and to have access to powerful compute resources; there are classes of attackers who, even if they had such resources at their disposal, might not bring them to bear simply because it's too expensive. For this reason, it's useful to understand the sorts of technical capabilities, the sort of exploits, that a particular class of adversary is likely to use.

- **Risk tolerance.** What I mean by this attribute is how willing or unwilling a particular attacker may be to getting caught or to having the attack discovered and when. Spies tend to be highly secretive. The best outcome is if the activity is never uncovered or, if discovered, that it is difficult to attribute to any particular group or state, and the goal of the action should certainly be obscured as much as possible. Cyber criminals without a doubt know that once your account has been drained, you will notice. The thief doesn't care that you find out, only that the thief doesn't get caught—or at least, only low-level participants in a crime organization get caught; the upper level management must be protected, usually at all costs. On the other hand, security researchers are generally not breaking any laws, so they expect to publish the results with no risk. Security researchers may then be thought of as having zero risk tolerance.

- **Work factor.** This attribute is an estimation of how hard a particular class of adversaries will work toward achieving their goal. For instance, the United States National Security Agency had, at one time, a $60 billion so-called "black budget." That seems to me to be an enormous amount of resources to apply to any particular cyber action. I assume that other major powers have similar budgets. Contrast this with a cybercrime business that needs to maximize the amount of profit from each operation. As I noted in *Securing Systems,* cyber criminals tend to focus on the poorly defended, spending as little on research and development of new techniques as possible. This is a vastly different approach than would be taken by a well-funded superpower's offensive cyber activities.

The foregoing categorization is entirely stereotypic. It must be understood that an individual actor can be an outlier; it is important to know that aggregating behaviors as I'm doing implies beyond any doubt that some threat agents in each group will not fit the profile in one manner or another.

The advantage of stereotyping and aggregating is to allow us to step away from a widely held fallacy of practice: that every actor is either a creative, innovating genius or a so-called "script kiddie" of no significant technical capability. There is a continuum of capabilities and clusters of attributes into which particular actors tend to fall. Even technically sophisticated actors may have very good reasons for using readily available, well-known, and understood exploits: new vulnerability discovery and subsequent exploit development for that vulnerability is expensive. When trying to maximize profit, businesspeople try to minimize research and development. As a profit-seeking business, cybercrime is no different from any other profit-seeking enterprise.

Along with the fallacy of either unlimited technical capability or zero knowledge comes another: it is widely believed that every vulnerability/exploit pair is equally valuable to every actor. As I demonstrated in a series of analyses published on McAfee's Securing Tomorrow blog in November 2017,[*] vulnerabilities first must offer an attacker something of attacker-value that will advance toward the attacker's ultimate goal.

> This is not a hypothetical example. I have entered into discussions many times with security professionals who didn't seem to understand the underlying lack of attacker value of additional memory manipulation after an attacker has gained full control of an operating system.

My classic example is a buffer overflow requiring high privileged access before it can be exercised (see inset). A buffer overflow allows the attacker to execute code of the attacker's choosing. However, having obtained high system privileges, attackers can already execute code of their choosing. They have no need to exploit yet another condition. With high privileges, not only can code be executed, but the attacker has access to all of the monitoring ....and logging capabilities on the system, such that their code can be hidden (with whatever facilities are available) and persisted through restarts of the operating system. There is no value to further exploitation of memory; the attacker already owns all memory on the system.

Once an attacker can insert her/him/themself into the kernel, it's "game over." The attacker has the run of the system to perform whatever actions and achieve whatever goals are intended by the attack. For system takeover, the kernel is the target. The highest operating system privileges typically allow access to the kernel. Hence, high privileges generally mean that the system's kernel is "owned"—or in the parlance, "pwned": compromised, under the control of the attacker.

The foregoing is basic risk analysis that every security practitioner ought to be able to perform. Still, I have seen precious few methodologies for including attacker value in the risk analysis equation. That's why I like the term "impact" vs. "loss." Impact is broader, such that it includes the possibility that an attacker has moved one step closer to their goal rather than focusing solely on the harm if the attacker should ultimately be successful.

Neither of these fallacies serve defense well, because they are both demonstrably untrue and create a situation (or mindset, unfortunately rather widely held) that implies that all issues must be defended against equally well (or worse, "fixed immediately"!).

---

[*]   Schoenfield and Quiroa, 2017.

Because few organizations and few systems can be successfully built and maintained to defend against every possible and imagined attack, the practitioner is thus rendered ineffective as a direct result of the two misconceptions expressed above. That is, smart engineers will see through "all or nothing" arguments as technically invalid and impossible. Smart engineers want to know where to place the most efficacious defenses; they want to have solid reasons for implementation *before* they will agree to implement anything. When a security practitioner insists upon defenses that seem unreasonable to those who must implement them, then security's influence has been squandered. I have seen it over and over again; once developers no longer trust security, they will evade security requirements as often as they can.

Please don't mistake my meaning. It is possible to make mistakes and then to admit error. In fact, doing so builds the required trust between security and developers. That is very different from insisting on defenses that have little chance of being tested by real attackers simply because it feels safer to a security practitioner or because some book or standard said that these defenses were "always required for every situation." As far as I know from my 20 years of security practice, there is no "always" in defenses; each defense is contextual.

It's just not true that every nation-state cyber army is gunning for every connected person. There are distinctions, and applying these distinctions allows us to focus on the most likely attacks, at the most likely levels of sophistication, from actors who have readily observable levels of risk tolerance and who will expend varying levels of effort to achieve goals. The astute defender usually needn't pay attention to everything, all the time—which is in any case an impossible charge (see inset).

If I pull my five threat actor attributes together into a set of four attack pre-conditions, I come up with the following:

- There must be active, motivated threat agents who are interested in attacking systems of the sort under assessment.
- The attack methods required must lie within the technical capabilities of the attacker and be well enough understood by the attacker to be useful.
- The attack must not expose the attacker to negative consequences beyond the attacker's tolerance for exposure.
- The effort needed to complete the attack must be less than the expected rewards of success.

Still, and nonetheless, if successful compromise by an attacker has no impact or loss to the owner of the system—the organization whose goals the system is intended to further—or the system's users, then there can be no risk. Without impact, there can be no risk to an organization, even in the face of an easy-to-exploit condition.

In the foregoing discussion, three often overlooked attributes of an attack emerge:

- Impact
- Attacker value
- Required effort

> Except perhaps defenders whose adversaries include dedicated nation-state actors. For this select set, the defender must implement as much as possible, knowing that every defense will likely eventually fail against the onslaught of highly resourced and sophisticated adversaries. The concept in this case is to slow the attacker down sufficiently that there may be time to catch the attack as it unfolds. In addition, each defense should add detail to the emerging picture of the attack, even as it may fail.

The first two, impact and attacker value, are not necessarily equivalent, although sometimes that which an attacker intends is, in fact, the impact to the victim: bank accounts drained, services disrupted. Sometimes, though, the relationship between the value of an exploit and the attacker's ultimate goal is more tenuous.

Consider the formation of the Mirai camera botnet[*] that was used to disrupt Internet communications through a DNS service distributed denial of service (DDOS) attack. Compromise of each Mirai camera quite likely was not even noticed by the camera's owner. The camera appeared to be functioning in whatever capacity for which it was installed.

Although the controller of the botnet (the "attacker") could capture images from cameras and may very well have, there is no indication that owners of the cameras were particularly inconvenienced, even during the DDOS attack.

The victim of the attack seems to have been a company called DYN, whose DNS services were disrupted. Alongside DYN were some users of a few major Internet services in select regions. Very likely, some of those who couldn't access FaceBook® during the attack owned one or more of the cameras causing the attack.

Still, the loss of trust in DYN's services and lost advertising revenues to Facebook are the organizational costs, while inconvenience from prevention of use of services would be another impact. These are quite disconnected from compromise of tens of thousands of Mirai's underlying Linux® operating system—which was the attacker value: controlling thousands of Internet-connected Linux devices.

To focus on either impact or attacker value in isolation without considering the other attributes paints an incomplete picture. We must understand whether an attack scenario will help advance the attacker's goals. And, we also must consider whether attacker success will affect something that system stakeholders care about protecting.

The third item above, "required effort," can often help us to understand the attacker's work/reward ratio. How much is a successful attack going to deliver for the effort?

For exploits that require a great deal of setup and perhaps are only a stepping stone, the reward has to justify the entire set of actions. Plus, if any of the preconditions are generally unknown to attackers, they will need time to discover these for themselves (unless all the necessary steps and preconditions get published in a research paper).

In the Mirai camera case, the effort was next to nothing: the default password was well known. The password was used via a well documented protocol (SSH) to access the camera at high privilege. Setting up the botnet was only a matter of discovering eligible targets [At which, it must be said, attackers, professional bug hunters, penetration testers, and security researchers are all very good. These all use an intersecting and constantly improving suite of tools, tools which are readily available, often open source].

In contrast, the WiFi authentication attacks named "KRACK Attacks" (Key Reinstallation Attacks) discovered by Mathy Vanhoef, published in October of 2017,[†] require fairly deep understanding of the intricacies of WiFi's WPA2 key interchanges. As I wrote in my blog just after publication of the new technique:

"However key reinstallation depends on either working with the inherent timing of a Wi-Fi during a discreet, somewhat rare (in computer terms) exchange or the technique depends upon

---

[*]   Fruhlinger, 2018.
[†]   Vanhoef, 2017.

the attacker forcing the vulnerable exchange through some method (see below for examples). Both of these scenarios take a bit of attacker effort, perhaps more effort than using any one of the existing methods for attacking users over Wi-Fi?"[*]

Whenever a new attack's value overlays existing, well-known, perhaps already weaponized efforts, then the attack's effort versus gain equation becomes important. Is the new attack method easier or harder? Is it more easily coded into a repeatable, automated form ("weaponized")? Is it harder or easier to detect? Does the new method extend in some way the reach of the attacker?

Attacker effort to pull off a successful KRACK seems to have been greater than the use of any number of other, readily available methods. So far (up to this writing), KRACK doesn't seem to have received much threat actor usage, as interesting as it may be from a computer science and security perspective. Of course, such research can lead to much tighter security implementations, which is precisely what has happened in this case; my thanks to Mr. Vanhoef for excellent research.

The foregoing examples, I hope, help to clarify dimensions that can be used to understand attackers and how they work, as well as to analyze and qualify issues as they arrive—these activities, I believe lie within the expertise that security architects must master.

As we consider different threat agents, their typical methods, and most importantly the goals of their attacks, I hope that you'll see that some attacks are irrelevant against some systems: these attacks are simply not worth consideration. The idea is to filter out the noise such that the truly relevant, the importantly dangerous, get more attention than anything else.

An astute reader might question why I have proposed yet another threat system?

The answer is simple: extant methods such as the Diamond Method,[†] MITRE's CRITS,[‡] and the UCO ontology,[§] to name a few, are focused on the problem of analyzing artifacts of an attack or an attack campaign.

These existing approaches are useful, certainly; I encourage readers to follow the references. There's a great deal to be learned from the study that's been put into helping analysts figure out what threat actors are doing and why. An attack might be a singleton, perhaps highly targeted, or it might be one part of a campaign against numerous targets. When reacting to a potential attack, and for researchers who are trying to attribute attacks to particular actors, graphing malware samples, targets, period of attack, originations, etc. (please see any of the references, above) will be critical.

But for security architecture, it is sufficient, I believe, to know that such attacks occur and to generalize about what different classes of attackers seek. That is the knowledge set that is wielded to assess the *potential* for successful compromise:

- What does the attacker ultimately want to achieve?
- What are the attacker's methods, both known and probable?
- How are the attacker's methods applied to vulnerabilities, both known and potential?

---

[*] http://brookschoenfield.com/?tag=kracks-attacks
[†] http://www.activeresponse.org/wp-content/uploads/2013/07/diamond.pdf
[‡] https://crits.github.io
[§] https://github.com/ucoProject/UCO

- How will a successful attack affect assets, users, owners, and ultimately the organization that must be protected?
- What steps can be taken to thwart attack? That is, what are the best defensive measures against likely attacks?

These are the questions that need to be answered by security architects. We have to be conversant with those attacks that will be levied against systems under analysis, and the sorts of defenses that have been effective against such attacks. This is a set of knowledge that overlaps something like MItre's CRITS, but which must do two different things:

1. Attacks must be grouped into methods that obtain attacker intermediate or ultimate goals and their targets.
2. The security architect makes an educated guess, as highly informed a guess as possible, about what might happen; security architecture is meant to be proactive—before attack, not during or after.

There is guesswork involved—hopefully before entering the real world of probing for cyber weakness—that is, before attackers begin to probe the system under analysis. Plus, threat modeling will be improved markedly through a feedback loop between the informed guesses used during the threat modeling analysis and validation (or not) of the guesses by penetration testing (see inset).

Threat modeling and penetration testing might be considered bookend techniques for a robust and mature software security practice. Threat modeling (really, any and all architecture analysis for security, whatever it may be called, started at an early stage of structural conception) is an up-front analysis meant to strongly influence the structure (architecture) and design of systems as they are being built and implemented. Penetration testing "proves" the security posture that was intended to be built.

Can you perhaps see how these two activities would influence each other? Penetration testers, at the very least, must understand the visible and accessible architecture of a system in order to probe its defenses and identify its weaknesses. If weaknesses are found, then the threat model must be updated to account for any missing defenses that then can be added.

> These two processes—threat modeling and penetration testing—are too often conducted by separate entities who are not working in concert. It was Eoin Carroll, in his capacity as a Senior Security Architect at McAfee, who helped me to understand the importance of tying these activities tightly together. Threat models can and should be proved through testing of many sorts. Please see Chapter 9 in *Core Software Security* for more about the use of various software security testing techniques.

Penetration testers act as a proxy for real-world adversaries. Hopefully, before the system is exposed to adversaries, penetration testers can find any holes in the required defenses so that those holes can be plugged enough to sufficiently resist attacks by those who intend to damage the system and/or its owners.

Threat modelers—that is, security architects—must understand attackers, their techniques, and their goals (both short-term and ultimate). These so-called "guesses" must be made sufficiently accurately such that defenses will be built as the system is being built. This early analysis is an attempt to avoid so-called "bolt-on" additions of security defenses after implementation, or worse, after go-live, or worse still, after compromise. "Built-in" is much cheaper than bolt-on. Built-in will presumably fit the overall plan of the system (its architecture).

Hence, the foregoing is the purpose of my high-level tables; they provide a quick reference frame for making stronger guesses.

Table 1.1 Summarized Threat Attributes

Threat Agent	Goals	Risk Tolerance	Work Factor	Methods
Cyber criminals	Financial	Low	Low to medium	Known proven
Industrial spies	Information and disruption	Low	High to extreme	Sophisticated and unique
Hacktivists	Information, disruption, and media attention	Medium to high	Low to medium	System administration errors and social engineering

Table 1.1, copied from *Securing Systems*, and its completion in Table 1.2 are meant to assist in the previously described process of analytical educated guessing (see inset). Security architecture should be applied before the system is completely implemented, if possible, while there is still room for change (to account for new defenses). Thus, the analyst is, in my humble opinion, greatly aided by bearing in mind just who will attack, why, and what techniques they are likely to employ in their efforts. Since these are (highly) educated *guesses*, it is, again, in my humble experience, not necessary to fully understand each attacker's strengths and weaknesses in detail; a stereotypic picture of *types* of attackers is generally all that is required, such as in the tables presented herein.

Penetration testing against a complete or nearly complete system can then test the security architect's guesses, as my friend and colleague Eoin Carroll likes to say. Eoin has shown me that there's a natural feedback loop between a security architect's threat model and a subsequent penetration test. The penetration test can prove that the threat model has been thorough enough. Or, if it has not, whatever penetrations (that is, successful attack tests) have occurred must improve the threat model.

> In Securing Systems, I dive deeply into the threat modeling process, hopefully putting flesh onto the bare bones laid out in this book. Readers are encouraged to peruse any of the six full system analyses contained in that work for more information.

In *Securing Systems,* I examined in some depth three types or classes of threat agents:

1. Cyber criminals
2. Industrial spies
3. Hacktivists

I did not complete the matrix, because *Securing Systems* was meant to be as much a series of exercises in threat modeling analysis as a definitive work on security architecture knowledge and patterns. I left the remainder of the matrix as an exercise for the reader.

Table 1.2 High-Level Threat Agent Attribute Matrix

Threat Agent	Goals	Technical Ability	Risk Tolerance	Work Factor	Activity Level
Cybercrime	Monetary	Low (known proven)	Low to medium	Low	Very high, continual
Industrial espionage	Information	Medium to medium-high	Low	Medium	Low. For enterprises, medium
Nation-states	Information disruption	Very high	Very low	Very high	Medium but constant
Law enforcement/government compliance	Compliance information	Medium	None—they are the law	Medium	Intermittent
Insider	Monetary	Varies	Low	None	Occasional
Insider	Revenge	Varies	Very high	None	Occasional
Usage abuse[a]	Unauthorized use	Low	Low	Low	Constant
Hacktivists	Media attention for cause	Low to medium	Used to be high, now much lower	Medium	Intermittent
Hackers	Status	Often very low	Low	Low	Low
Security Researcher	Career enhancement	High	None	High	Medium

[a] I'm indebted to my students who added this important adversary, users who seek to obtain more services than those for which they've contracted. Users are not in the same technical category as cyber criminals, though their acts may be criminal, depending upon the jurisdiction. They aren't generally making a living through their attempts to enhance their services. They often simply feel entitled to "more." Consider abusers seeking more content streaming than that for which they've paid.

As I began to incorporate some of the new material that I developed from Securing Systems into my classes {see inset next page], I brought the exercise of building a threat agent matrix as a part of the coursework. Very quickly, class participants requested a completed matrix.

In my classes, I hand out the matrix after each team has completed their very own threat agent attribute table for themselves, and after each team has presented their matrix to the other teams. The exercise seems to be quite powerful, in that it gets everyone in the class thinking about who

Damilare Fagbemi, Senior Security Architect at Intel, Inc., helped refine the third version of the threat modeling class that I continue to give. Damilare delivers a similar class for Intel. We regularly discuss our various teaching discoveries and challenges. Damilare's continuing support has been critical to whatever success my threat modeling classes achieve. His contributions remain vital, not just to our classes, but to the industry as a whole.

their adversaries are and what are their typical attributes. The very act of considering these problems sets up participants with the correct mindset to play adversary to systems under consideration.

Because the exercise has proven so effective, I'm quite hesitant to put a completed threat agent matrix into a published work. The matrix has to be a "living" document; the cyber adversary threat landscape is dynamic and constantly changing. Classes of actors and their typical attributes are going to change over time. In no way should Table 1.2 be considered canonical.

Plus, your experience with your adversaries may be different than mine. Please take Table 1.2 as a suggestion on how this problem might be approached, an attempt to build a high-level picture of types of threat actors, what each type's stereotypical goals are, and something about their capabilities and tolerances. Please do not take my threat agent matrix as gospel. Instead, treat the matrix as a pointer, as an exercise in assigning some order for a dynamic and somewhat opaque problem space. Make your own table; decide upon attributes that bring order to your threat landscape.

1.2 Useful Exploits Don't Die

In fact, it may be said that, "Old exploits don't die, they just fade away," with ever diminishing use. Unfortunately, as a defender, one can never toss an aging and seemingly forgotten exploit technique into the dustbin of history. Attackers will use anything at hand—old, new, whatever. Just because many target systems have been upgraded to plug a vulnerability doesn't imply that there aren't existing systems that are still vulnerable. For many attacker goals, a step forward may be achieved via a single, vulnerable system.

Importantly, not much seems to completely disappear from the Internet. Old machines, running long unsupported, end-of-life software get sold, donated, or given away. These systems still remain connected *somewhere*, and thus remain potential victims of exploits supposedly long past. The grim reality is that these systems and their pirated knockoffs make up some part of the complete Internet demographic, often being used in poorer areas and/or by less knowledgeable people.

It may be impossible for users' systems at the bottom of this chain of reuse to fix the existing vulnerabilities on their systems since much or even all of the software on the systems may be past support—long past. That is, the makers of the software no longer fix issues, even newly discovered issues. The owners of the systems are often just out of luck.

The nasty truth of this situation is that there always remains a vulnerable population against whom old exploits may successfully be employed. So, why should the builders of exploit kits ("EK" in security parlance) remove old exploits? There's no compelling reason to.

Thus, EK are *additive*. New exploits are added, but old ones are not removed. EK are the workhorses of attackers; some EK are maintained by the developers of the adversarial world. [Some EK are maintained by security researchers for the benefit of researchers and penetration testers. That does not prevent these EK from also being used by adversaries.] The developers may not use their kits against victims; their business model is as a support to actual attackers. Attackers well supplied with already programmed—that is, pre-canned, also called "weaponized"—exploit code are then freed up to concentrate on their attack campaigns rather than mucking about identifying code to exercise particular vulnerabilities.

Attackers work within their own rich ecosystem of researchers, developers, service offerings, consultants, etc., which mirrors the legal software business ecosystem. It's a strange and complex digital world that we live in.

1.3 Everything Can Become a Target

> My assertion lies at the heart of modern cryptography. Cryptographic strength is measured in "work-years" to decrypt without the keying materials. The assumption being that there is no encryption that cannot be undone, given sufficient time and resources.

I've been declaring for years that, "whatever can be engineered by humans can be reverse engineered by humans." That is, in this context, whatever protections we build can ultimately, with enough resources, time, and effort, be undone (see inset). This is an essential piece of the probability puzzle when calculating or rating computer security risk. The fact that the attackers can learn, grow, and mature, and that they will rapidly shift tactics, indicates a level of heuristics to the defense of systems: expect the attacks to change, perhaps dramatically.

A (hopefully) informative example of the above truism might be taken from a pair of processor (CPU) issues named Spectre[*] and Meltdown.[†]

As Adam Shostack, author of *Threat Modeling: Designing for Security*,[‡] so succinctly put it: "The back and forth of design and critique is not only a critical part of how an individual design gets better, but fields in which such criticism is the norm advance faster."

The Spectre/Meltdown issues are the result of just such a design critique process as Shostack describes in the pithy quote given above (see inset).

Let's look at some of the headlines from before the official issue announcement by the researchers:

The Register: Kernel-memory-leaking Intel processor design flaw forces Linux, Windows redesign.[§]

Wired Magazine: A Critical Intel Flaw Breaks Basic Security for Most Computers."[¶]

> In my humble experience, Adam is particularly good at expressing complex processes briefly and clearly—one of his many gifts as a technologist and leader in the security architecture space.

There were dozens of these headlines (many merely repeating the first few, especially, *The Register's*), all declaiming a "flaw" in CPUs. I want to draw the reader's attention to the word "flaw." We shall dig into the applicability of that designation to these particular issues in order to highlight a constructive dialog that should occur around designs as our understanding of the design's security posture matures over time. *The Register* reporting was based largely upon speculation that had been occurring among the open source community supporting the Linux Kernel following a couple of changes that had been made to kernel code. It was clear that something was amiss, likely in relation to something in CPUs; concerned observers were guessing what the motivation for those code changes might be.

---

[*] Kocher, P., Genkin, D., Gruss, D. et al., 2018.
[†] Lipp, Schwarz, Gruss et al., 2018.
[‡] Shostack, 2014
[§] Leyden and Williams, 2018.
[¶] Greenberg, 2018.

It may help to step back just a moment from Spectre/Meltdown details to see how a report of issues is typically (though far from always) handled. One approach is known as "responsible disclosure." But not all researchers believe in responsible disclosure (more on that below). The supposedly "responsible" process involves embargoing (preventing from inadvertent revelation) the existence of the issues and their technical details until a fix can be readied by those responsible to produce fixes. That is, issues are to be kept secret until users can be protected.

If the facts of the issues' existence—or worse, the technical details—are made known ahead of the availability of a fix, then attackers have a terrible advantage. Attacks can proceed without even the hope of a direct defense. Hence, the "responsible" in "responsible disclosure": don't give attackers any help.

How anyone could argue with the logic of responsible disclosure is beyond me, frankly, though I've listened to arguments against it. These make no sense to me, except from what appears to be a self-righteous and/or completely disconnected perspective. "Do no harm" is one of my main aspirational dictums in life. However, there are those who believe otherwise, who believe in immediate, "zero day" disclosure, users' protections be damned.

There appears to me to be some sense that so-called "full disclosure" is the only weapon researchers have to somehow force software makers to deliver fixes. Having lived on the other side of that argument, I can assure my readers (at least) that any honest software maker (I wouldn't work with dishonesty) often has many business drivers with which to contend. Plus, not every fix is a few lines of code. If a major product needs to be redesigned, there isn't any way to deliver a "fix" immediately. Spectre and Meltdown actually fit into this case: they are artifacts of design decisions not easily remedied with a few lines of code.

There is so much arrogance on each side of this debate that I cannot see a reasonable solution emerging any time soon. A few researchers routinely disparage developers as incompetents whose software shouldn't be made available—even comparing developers to dogs (yes, that has happened at major security conferences). Some on the other side routinely disparage legitimate and highly valuable research as the product of a few "yahoos" who lack a moral compass or are even "criminals." There seems no likely meeting of minds between these poles.

I've set out the context in which researchers and designers exist in order to frame the important dialog between security research aimed at discovering new attack techniques and the designers of the systems and protocols upon which that research is carried out. As Adam noted so wryly, achieving solid designs, even great ones, and most importantly, resilient designs in the face of omnipresent attack requires a dialog, an interchange of constructive critique. That is how Spectre and Meltdown were discovered and presented.

Neither of this collection of (at the time of announcement) new techniques involved exercising a flaw—that is, a design error; in other words, the headlines quoted just above were erroneous and rather misleading [although salacious headlines apparently increase readership and thus advertising revenue. Hence, the misleading but emotion-plucking headlines].

Speculative execution and the use of kernel mapped user memory pages by operating systems were intentional design choices that had been working as designed for more than 10 years. Taken together, at least some of the increases in CPU performance over that period can directly be tied to these design choices.

Furthermore, and quite importantly to this discussion, these design choices were made within the context of a rather different threat landscape. That is, consider my matrices above.

Some of the actors didn't really exist, or at least, were not nearly as active and certainly not as technically sophisticated circa 2005 as they are at the time of this writing (2019).

If I recall correctly (and I should be able to remember, since I was the technical lead for Cisco's web infrastructure and application security team at that time), in 2005, network attacks were being eclipsed by application-focused attack methods, especially web attack methods.

Today, web attacks are very "ho, hum," very run of the ordinary, garden variety. But in 2005, when the first speculative execution pipelines were being put into CPUs, web applications were targets of choice at the cutting edge of digital security. Endpoint worms and gaining entrance through poor network ingress controls had been security's focus up until the web application attack boom (if I may title it so?). The web application was fast displacing these concerns as attackers shifted to targets that were always available via the Internet.

Indeed, as we learned at the time, attacks hidden within web application messages might get shuttled through applications to richer internal and backend systems, as web front ends were being attached to existing backend resources. It took a few successful compromises to understand that a web application that passes data through defenses to other systems has to act as the "firewall"—the message protection layer for those secondary and tertiary systems laying behind web layers, perhaps deep within the supposedly protected layers of an organization's network.

In other words, the threat landscape changed dramatically over the years since the initial design of speculative execution CPUs, as it must continue to evolve. Alongside the changes in types of attackers as well as their targets, attacker and researcher sophistication has grown, as has the available toolset for examining digital assets—that is, systems, software, hardware; 2018 is a different security world than 2005. I see no end to this curve of technical growth in my crystal ball.

The problem is, when threat modeling in 2005, one looked at the attacks of the past, those of moment, and tried to project from this knowledge to those of the foreseeable future. Ten or 12 years seems an awfully long horizon of prescience, especially when considering the rate at which technical change continues to take place.

Still, as new research begins to chew at the edges of design, I believe that the wise and diligent practitioner revisits existing threat models in light of developments. If I were to fault the CPU and operating system makers whose products are subject to Spectre or Meltdown, it would be for a failure to anticipate where research might lead as research has unfolded. CPU threat modelers could have taken into account advances in research indicating unexpected uses of cache memory that contains remnants of a speculative execution branch. Such examination of the unfolding train of research might very well have led those responsible for updating CPU threat models to a potential for something like Spectre and Meltdown.

Was there such research? Indeed, there was, with publications starting three years previous pointing perhaps somewhat indirectly toward the new techniques. Spectre and Meltdown are not standalone discoveries but stand on a body of CPU research that had been ongoing and published regularly for several years.

As I wrote for McAfee's Security Matters blog in January of 2018, "Meltdown and Spectre are new techniques that build upon previous work, such as 'KASLR' and other papers that discuss practical side-channel attacks. The current disclosures build upon such side-channels attacks through the innovative use of speculative execution . . . An earlier example of side-channel based upon memory caches was posted to Github in 2016 by one of the Spectre/

Meltdown researchers, Daniel Gruss."[*] Reading these earlier papers, it appears to me that some of the parent techniques that would be used for the Spectre and Meltdown breakthroughs could have been read (should have been read?) by CPU security architects in order to re-evaluate the CPU's threat model. That previously published research was most certainly available.

Of course, hindsight is always 20/20; I had the Spectre and Meltdown papers in hand as I reviewed previous research. Going the other way might be more difficult.

Spectre and Meltdown did not just spring miraculously from the head of Zeus, as it were. They are the results of a fairly long and concerted effort to discover problems with, and thus, hopefully, improve, the designs of modern processors. Indeed, the researchers engaged in responsible disclosure, not wishing to publish until fixes could be made available.

To complete our story, the driver that tipped the researchers to an early, zero-day disclosure (that is, disclosure without available mitigations or repairs) were the numerous speculative (if you'll forgive the pun) journalism (see headlines quoted above) that gained traction based upon misleading, at best, or simply wrong conclusions. Claiming a major design "flaw" in millions of processors is certainly a reader-catching headline. But, unfortunately, these claims were vastly off the mark, because no flaw existed in the CPU or operating system designs.

While it may be more "interesting" to imagine a multi-year conspiracy to cover up known design issues by evil CPU makers, no such cover up and conspiracy appears to have taken place.

Rather, in the spirit of responsible disclosure, the researchers were waiting for mitigations to be made available to customers; CPU manufacturers and operating system coders were heads down at work figuring out what appropriate mitigations might be, and just how to implement these with the least amount of disruption (see inset). None of these parties was publicly discussing just why changes were being made, especially to the open source Linux kernel.

Which is precisely what one would expect: embargo the technical details to foil attackers and to protect users. There is actually nothing unusual about such a process unfolding; it's all very normal

> As a part of my role at the time, I was privy to the embargoed details of Spectre and Meltdown before the researchers' disclosure. Hence, I was aware of how engaged at least one CPU manufacturer was in developing fixes for the issues.

and typical, and unfortunately for news media, quite banal. [Disclosure: I've been involved in numerous embargoed issues over the years.]

What we see through the foregoing example about Spectre and Meltdown is precisely the sort of rich dialog that should occur between designers and critics (researchers, in this case).

Designs are built against the backdrop and within the context of their security "moment." Our designs cannot improve without collective critique among the designers; that such dialog remains internal to an organization, or at least a development team, is essential. I have spoken about this process repeatedly at conferences: "It takes a village to threat model."

But, there's another level, if you will, that can be achieved for greater constructive critique. Once a design is made available to independent critics—that is, security researchers—research discoveries can and, I believe, should become part of an ongoing re-evaluation of the threat model—that is, the security of the design. In this way, we can, as an industry, reach for the constructive critique called for by Adam Shostack.

---

[*] Gruss, Maurice, Fogh et al. 2016.

1.4 Warlords and Pirates

"A former FBI official says the sprawling Russian black-market forum for illegal hacking and fraud services known as Infraud Organization—its motto was "In Fraud We Trust"—was operated like a 'dark-web cousin of major commercial marketplace sites.' The official said it shows one thing: that we're clearly not just fighting solo hackers at this point."[*]

Cybercrime, as I have been saying for some time, is a business. Although there are single practitioners, lone wolves, much of the activity is a part of larger crime organizations' business model.

No matter how comfortable any organization is with its current security posture, everyone should remember that sophisticated adversaries will be studying current practices for weaknesses, continually poking at these on a regular basis. In other words, attackers are intelligent and adaptive.

The wise security practitioner will also keep abreast of the development of analysis tools. In my first response to a security incident (I think it was circa 1992 or 1993), there were virtually no tools that might be applied beyond those used to develop software, source and assembly debuggers, binary file editors, etc. I ended up removing a worm by manually rewriting a Macintosh executable's process jump table (the offsets in the binary file at which various functions happened to be stored after the linking process). Luckily, by that time, I possessed enough computer science understanding to figure out how the worm was propagating and how to stop the propagation.

Today's toolset makes my 1993 collection look like paleolithic stone tools by comparison. One can stop a binary for which one has no source code upon any logic condition. Tools will attempt to decompile the code back to a reasonable approximation of the original source code. One can inject code into the binary and run scripts based upon data conditions, poke and prod the code and data nearly as one wishes. It's a completely different ballgame, affording attackers and researchers far more access, far more information than we dared to dream might be possible in the foreseeable future back in 1993.

We felt lucky enough when we could get source debugging to help us figure out coding problems. Today, that's almost a given, even if the decompilation is merely an approximation. The available tools are rich in functionality and deep in analysis in the hands of a skilled technician. To paraphrase myself, "Any software that can be engineered by humans can be reversed by humans." Those of us on the defensive side must understand the level of adversary sophistication brought against our defenses.

Given a rich set of available resources, it should be no surprise that some humans would wish to take advantage of others. Humans have been taking advantage of other humans ever since the first band of humans figured out that stealing from their neighbors, and quite possibly, getting those neighbors to do much of the dirty work of life (we call it "slavery" today) was easier than eking out a living through some labor-intensive combination of hunting, gathering, horticulture, animal stewardship—whatever the local mix might be. I'll opine that thieving is as much a human activity as is toil; humans seem to me to be quite good at inventing a rationale as to why theft has moral validity: "We're civilized, they aren't," "We're civilizing them," "We're smarter," "We're 'humans', they aren't"—pick your favorite justification; they've all been tried. Cybercrime seems to be yet another in the long series of opportunistic, if highly amoral (to my sense), manner of getting.

---

[*] Vaas, 2018.

To me, cybercrime seems precisely analogous to piracy. Or rather, cybercrime may very well be the 21st century's version of piracy. Cybercrime attacks have the same opportunistic, hit-and-run quality. The Internet is a common resource, big enough to offer a similar type of anonymity as was once provided by the oceans. There are safe-haven localities that are loath to prosecute cyber criminal activity, just as there once existed pirate cities, ports, enclaves, and islands where stolen goods could be traded and some much-needed rest and relaxation could be had for sea-tired crews.

Analogously, pirates also formed teams, partnerships, even navies under the command of a single leader. We have exactly that scenario today: major criminal networks retain cybercrime divisions. These criminal enterprises can garner significant revenue; it's big (criminal) business.[*][†]

But cybercrime activity is not limited solely to criminal networks. Or rather, the distinction between crime for purely business gain and that for national interest is fuzzy at best for some countries and some gangs.

"The North Korean government uses a shadowy network of cyberactors to conduct financial crimes on behalf of Kim Jong Un's regime that have attempted to steal over $1.1 billion in 'particularly aggressive' attacks on global banks."[†]

North Korea may be at the far side of a continuum between purely state-sponsored crime and purely business driven. Still, other countries have made use of purely criminal enterprises, quasi-governmental groups, and so forth; the picture is indeed fuzzy (see inset). If the attacking organization is large enough, I think of these as governed by a "warlord"—that is, by a person or persons who maintain a private, non-governmental army which is used for the enrichment of the warlord and her/his/their retainers.

> The current picture is again analogous to the famous pirates of the Barbary Coast during the 17th–19th centuries. Governments along the North African Mediterranean coast offered shelter to pirates or even allowed their own navies to pirate so long as the tax on pirated booty was properly paid.

The upshot for those of us not aligned with a warlord or pirate navy, not conducting governmental or quasi-governmental cyber operations, is that we're the collateral damage of a very confusing mix of governments and gangs sometimes operating independently and sometimes coordinating. Ugh. It's not pretty.

Most importantly, these actors have at their disposal:

- Weaponized attack code
- Exploit kits (EK)
- A rich and robust vulnerability and exploit development tool set
- A burgeoning knowledgebase on cyber attack techniques
- A flourishing marketplace in exploits and cyber attack services

Which all comes together to make a defender's life "interesting," at best. Welcome to my world, and the world of what Gary Berman (entrepreneur and comic book author) calls, *The Cyber Heroes,* those who've dedicated themselves to protecting "us" from becoming further collateral damage in an ongoing cyber war (even if not all involved are state actors).

---

[*] Ismail, 2015.
[†] FBI, 2019.
[‡] Cohen, Marquardt, and Crawford, 2018.

1.5 What Is the Scope of a Security Architect?

Security architecture—that is, the application of information security to systems—may be called *the art of securing systems*. As we will see in Chapter 2,* security architecture applies a particular set of knowledge to systems—relevant attacks and the defenses that will mitigate or, hopefully, prevent those attacks that seem relevant from succeeding.

1.5.1 Are There Really Two Distinct Roles?

In *Securing Systems,* I made a distinction between the practice of security architecture as applied to systems that aren't to be a part of an organization's protections and to those that are intended to form a defense. In practice, this distinction exists, and practitioners sometimes, perhaps often, specialize in one side of the art or the other. That is, security architects might be specialists in building an organization's defenses and reactive structures, the organization's security *architecture*. Alternatively, an architect might specialize in analyzing systems to identify security needs, security *requirements* that should be built in order to protect the system and its organization's goals for that system.

For instance, The Open Group proposed a number of security reference architectures (see inset) that directly address an organization's need for sound advice on how to build a set of defenses that rest on strong and battle-tested security principles.

As far as I know, The Open Group's only offering in the system analysis arena is Factor Analysis of Information Risk (FAIR): a risk standard that can be applied to systems, and really, any digital security problem.

Risk Must Be Fundamental

Surely, every system analysis for security, threat model, should be based upon a solid risk methodology such as FAIR, which is my personal favorite as well as the theoretical basis for Just Good Enough Risk Rating (JGERR),[†] authored by myself and Vinay Bansal (Distinguished Engineer at Cisco Systems, Inc.). JGERR may be thought of as a quick-and-dirty child of FAIR meant for the dozens of quick risk ratings that usually come up during threat modeling.

Whatever approach a security architect chooses to base risk ratings upon, it must have a firm theoretic basis. Too often, risk is measured by the discomfort of the analyst, which leads to mushy, inconsistent

> The last time I checked the progress of The Open Group's reference architectures for security, these had been integrated into a set of enterprise reference architectures. I believe that this is an important step, reflecting how the enterprise security architect should approach the problem of a security architecture: as a key component of the enterprise's architecture—"enterprise" in this use should be taken as equal to "organization of sufficient size to warrant an organization architecture," which is a much broader categorization than the commonly used definition of "enterprise."

---

[*] Chapter 3 will provide an analysis of attacks and defenses for a well-known vulnerability, Heartbleed to put the technical flesh on the bones of what is presented in Chapter 2.

[†] JGERR is described in some depth in *Securing Systems,* Chapter 4.

risk ratings, which then may propagate into poor organization risk metrics, usually inflating the metrics, leading to a sense of an increased, perhaps unreal amount of risk being carried.

Teams subject to poor risk rating methods may "shop" for the best rating, because they don't trust the higher, perhaps inflated ratings. Or, as Jack Jones (author of FAIR) once told me, executives may feel inclined to accept nearly every risk in the absence of solid and consistent risk assessment.

Readers can probably draw the line from poor risk rating to organizational distrust of security architecture, maybe even all of the security function? Certainly, organizational friction lies down that slippery slope. As you may see, choice of risk rating methodology is a critical component for any mature and robust security practice; The Open Group is to be applauded for standardizing FAIR and making it available to organizations.

Still, risk assessment is only one portion of the security architecture of systems large and small, of system assessment for security. Since The Open Group hasn't had much help in this area, the vacuum has been filled by materials from the Open Web Application Security Project (OWASP),* SAFECode,† and similar organizations. Of course, a few practitioners have tried to set down their thoughts, methods, and experiences for threat modeling in a few books, including yours truly (please see bibliography).

I've personally lived both of these roles in my career; the distinction exists, but I wonder if this distinction is more an artifact of organization structures rather than a real divergence in practice.

Analyzing a discreet system or set of systems performing a particular function indeed requires a different focus from thinking through the structure of an organization's entire security implementation. Still, in both instances, one must consider the sorts of attacks most likely to occur and how these will be prevented, or if successful, dealt with. The art which ties both these strands together is the art which we have proposed here to lie at the heart of security architecture: attacks and their defenses.

It seems to me that the different specialties in security architecture appear to be more a difference in kind, in degree, in scope, rather than some fundamental split in practice. Both analyses must base themselves firmly upon solid risk methodology. Both must understand the desired risk posture of the organization as well has have a reasonable feel for the amount of risk the organization is willing to carry ("risk tolerance").

Again: Attacks and Defenses

For system assessment, one must consider attacks relevant to that system *in the context of the security architecture,* if any, that may surround that system. To build a security architecture for an organization, the security architect must consider the attacks to which *any and all* systems of the organization may be subject. This organization analysis should be more holistic to the threat landscape in which the organization exists.

On the other hand, every system analysis must be holistic to that system. The details of existing network protections, incident response capabilities, access controls, etc. will be taken into account in both analyses, what I called "Mitigations" in the "ATASM" mnemonic (Architecture,

---

* OWASP.org
† The author is a co-author of SAFECode's Threat Modeling Guide

Threats, Attack Surface, Mitigations): the existing protections. Such protections would be a part of the organization's security architecture. I hope that you see that these two seemingly distinct practices are really views of the same coin from its different faces.

The analysis that leads one to the contextually relevant attacks, let's call that "threat modeling" for the sake of discussion, is best done as an early part of any development process, as well as being an ongoing conversation as architectures, designs, and implementations evolve. Certainly, there is very little that an architectural risk assessment of a sys-

> I do not mean to imply that the risk assessment portion of a threat model of a production system that has no further intended changes is useless. Risk assessment can help an organization build a picture of risk "debt"—the risks that have already been taken and are carried forward. At the very least, building this risk knowledge may help make better decisions about what further risk to add to existing risks carried forward.

tem can do if the system cannot be changed (see inset). Consequently, threat modeling is an activity that starts early in the development cycle.

Patterns, Standards, and Context

The art of architecture involves the skill of recognizing and then applying abstract patterns while, at the same time, understanding any local details that will be ignored through the strict and inflexible application of patterns. Any unique local circumstances are also important and will have to be attended to properly. It is not that locally specific details should be completely ignored; rather, in the interest of achieving an "architectural" view, these implementation details are overlooked until a broader view can be established. That broader view is the architecture.

There is a dance between adhering to standards and fostering innovation. New technologies come along that disrupt standards. These innovations may provide significant benefit if adopted. Usually, there are early adopters who help prove the usefulness and benefits (or not) of new technologies. The successes of the early adopters help to drive adoption through an organization.

"Computer security exists as an attribute, an emerging property (or not!) of systems that exist within an extremely rapidly changing context, that is, digital technology. It is simply too difficult to anticipate all circumstances, external and internal, in a policy at this time. Rather, policy becomes the bedrock to which many systems can mostly conform. The standards that set out how the policy will be enacted create an easy path, a reasonably secure path that can be followed. At the same time, policy and standards help to define areas and situations that will require creativity—those systems, connections, technologies that are necessary, but which cannot conform: the exceptions to standards. Sometimes, these exceptions will reduce the security posture. Sometimes, exceptions will offer an opportunity to mature security in new ways or open opportunities to adopt new technologies." *Securing Systems,* p. 354

Imagine an organization that insists upon strict adherence to a standard of one application server per application. That was a very durable model in the mid-2000s. That model forced an operating system and application server sandbox around each application (or set of inter-operating "applications"). In the days before proven web application firewalls and in the context of poor understanding by developers of secure web coding techniques, strictly separating applications at a level below the application code made a lot of security sense. At the very least, a compromised application couldn't disrupt other applications; the sandbox prevented the attacker from breaching each application's sandbox boundaries.

One of the downsides engendered by an application server sandbox was that providing each single application with its own, individual application server required a rather large investment in virtual machines on top of significant physical server resources. That was *the* cutting-edge model at the time. There was no cloud into which to expand; clouds as we now know them didn't exist.*

If an organization insisted upon never allowing any new technologies beyond the model described above, that organization would have missed containerization completely. DevOps tooling tends to be built around containers and/or clouds (which also can offer highly containerized solutions). Consider just those two developments: They've greatly disrupted the architectures and methods by which we deploy web applications. The movement to serverless architectures is a currently (as of this writing) unfolding disruption.

Failure to account for experimentation with new and disruptive technologies is a massive error in the service of a surer security path. It is my strong experience and opinion that, alongside standards that make the "easy path the secure path,"† the mature—actually, the wise—organization provides for experimentation with new, potentially disruptive technologies and techniques.

However, the wise security architect will bear in mind that sometimes a developer does not follow the easy path to security but employs a new technology in a place where it is not needed or does not really fit. The developer insists upon the use of the inappropriate technology so that it may be included on her, his, their resume. This use case has nothing to do with the fitness of the technology or the "easy" path; the use is intended to enhance the programmer's career.

Identifying an inappropriate application of a technology can be tricky. One of the obvious giveaways is if the requested technology will have obvious negative effects. For instance, many years ago, when web services using SOAP (Simple Object Access Protocol [XML protocol]) were in vogue, I found a few teams using them when doing so might add significant performance degradation. SOAP calls must all occur in ASCII (American Standard Code for Information Interchange). Binary data must be converted to ASCII for transmission over SOAP and then converted back to binary after communication. That may make perfect sense for transactions that occur at human pace, but it's a huge performance hit for data exchanges meant to proceed as quickly as computers can process them.

ASCII conversion can cause data to balloon up to eight times larger. So, such a conversion should be thought through thoroughly. It's particularly troubling when both sides of the web service, client and server, are to be located on the same machine, when the SOAP server is implementing a simple, atomic Application Programming Interface (API). SOAP services should be transactional, not atomic, if possible.

These were all red flags to me that somehow the proposed design didn't make sense. After all, simply linking a library, either statically as a part of the executable or dynamically, would be orders of magnitude faster. Data could be exchanged with a library in its binary form without

---

* Or rather, clouds as we use them today were in consideration, a few were being designed.
† As Steve Acheson so sagely advised me many years ago.

It's one thing to blow the whistle on a situation that one believes might expose the organization to poor performance or higher costs. It's quite another when dealing with those who are solely working for personal benefit. That is, when one is working with those of low moral standard, who lack integrity, proceed with caution! Exposing people of this nature to management can be tricky; one may expect such individuals to protect themselves with every tool they can muster. An unmask must be thought through; who protects the person? Who are my allies and what is their relation, if any, to the project in question? I do try to prevent great harm from taking place. But I also try to remember that low-integrity people may move to something new soon enough to give me a greater hand to undo damage, or they may fail of their own accord. This situation hasn't arisen often in my 30+ years in high tech, but it has come up a few times, which has been a great teacher about organization politics.

any conversions. When reviewing a design that screams, "there is a simpler, more effective way that is well understood," the security architect may well have encountered one of these situations in which there is another reason (often that cannot be named safely) for making poor choices.

When my "Spidey sense" is screaming that something doesn't make sense, I've now learned to step back from security issues to question what the reason might be for doing something that obviously doesn't make design sense. Quite often, the designer has ulterior motives, like trying to squeeze in technologies that will bolster her or his resume.

What does one do in such a situation? I question directly the choice and my reasons why it appears to be odd or just plain wrong, why there appears to be an easier or more elegant solution. Sometimes, that's effective. But, in some organization cultures (highly empowered at the team level) there may be nothing one can do about it.

If reasoning with the team fails, one can always go up the team's management chain. Also, the executives who are sponsoring the development, or who are the customer, may wish to understand that I have serious concerns about the way the software is designed. I've won internal awards for exposing poor design choices (see inset).

As always, analysis and discernment are critical: I don't want to stop useful experimentation with new, promising technologies. At the same time, if something doesn't seem right, I believe it's my duty to question choices, even if I must step beyond the scope of security.

At the most essential, all security architecture activity can be reduced to analysis of attacks, rated by solid risk rating, leading to defenses, as we shall hopefully see in the next section and throughout this book in various ways.

1.6 Essential Technique

1.6.1 Threat Modeling: An Essential Craft

Attacks and their defenses are the value proposition that security architects bring to the design and implementation of software—that is, development, engineering, or research and development. Over the years, "threat modeling" has gone by various names:

- Architecture risk assessment (ARA)
- Architecture review or security architecture review

- Security architecture assessment
- Security engineering
- [Secure] design review
- Secure design checkpoint
- Security requirements

And quite possibly, a few other terms that are, by now, lost in the mists of time.

Although practitioners are certainly free to disagree with my collapsing all the above terms into one analysis that in their processes seem quite distinct, I came to realize how threat modeling analysis actually rather completely underlies what appear to be different analyses. Threat modeling is the method that practitioners must apply no matter at what point in development a security analysis is taking place, no matter whether completed or initial or inflight a project or effort may be.

For a couple of years, my duties as a Principal Engineer for software security at Intel® included sitting on Intel's software security review panel, SAFE (Security Architecture Forum). We reviewed projects from initial concept through the completion of the design. At Intel, there are several review stops for security; more or less the same body of people would engage across projects and at these different review points during development.

Of course, I was a full participant, attempting to apply my best understanding of security architecture to each project as it came before the SAFE board. At the same time, as I often do, I was a participant observer, considering what I heard during the interactions between development teams and board members, assessing the efficacy of our process (or not) as reviews proceeded. I found the experience of watching my peers—that is, other Principle Engineers—practice security architecture very enlightening—not only to refine my own craft, but also in stepping back from the content of the work to observe how we do what we do. The projects ranged across myriad and often vastly different architecture types, projects at every stage of development, using nearly every type of software development methodology (waterfall, Agile, Extreme, etc.) (see inset). SAFE would typically interact with two to four projects each week of the year. That's a lot of projects in any given month, quarter, or year to observe and from which to learn.

As I watched the SAFE review process unfold, it became crystal clear to me that no matter at what stage or in which review point we board members

> I encourage every serious practitioner to work at a really large development organization at least once in a career. First, one gets to rub shoulders with some of the very best in each discipline. Further, one learns how to meet the challenges of scale: huge projects combining the work of many sub-teams, application of security methods to vastly different development approaches, and, perhaps most importantly, finding the essences that lie beneath or at the heart of varied expressions of technique and process.

were with a project, in order to complete the review, we were all threat modeling in our heads, call the review what you will. This was quite a revelation.

What differed was the level at which the threat model analysis occurred.

For instance, during an official threat model review, we had to dig deep, to attempt to cover every credible attack via every reachable attack surface (exposure) and find reasonable, workable, implementable defenses that could be built by the team presenting their project.

However, if a project had just been initiated, the level of threat modeling was vastly different. All we needed was to think through a few gross possibilities in order to derive the very broad security requirements and to understand the risk posture that the effort would need in its usage and deployment context.

The architecture assessment phase in the Intel Secure Development Lifecycle (SDL) is intended to identify those efforts that will require deeper security analysis, while at the same time passing those efforts whose security architecture needs will likely be (comparatively) minor. The threat model analysis for this review needs only to determine the credibility of a significantly impactful successful attack. One credible attack that might cause Intel's or the product's stakeholders significant harm is all that was required to flag the project for further engagement. The analysis technique is threat modeling, nevertheless.

I don't mean overstate the importance of threat modeling, call it what you will. Rather, as I've written and as I hope that you see in succeeding chapters in this book, security architects must wield attacks and their defenses as a primary knowledge set that is applied to software systems. Threat modeling lies at the heart of the practice of security architecture.

But threat modeling is not the only skill that is applied. Security architects, as I have written, must first and foremost be architects.

1.6.2 Architecture Is Primary

"I would suggest that architecture is the total set of descriptive representations relevant for describing something, anything complex you want to create, which serves as the baseline for change if you ever want to change the thing you have created."[*]

I would go further than Zachman to state that understanding, ability to discuss, and potential change are the benefits derived from architecture.

To understand a thing, we must be able to describe it in simple enough terms to grasp it; to discuss it intelligently, we must be able to name its parts, explain their function and their interactions. That is what architecture affords us through the clever and judicious application of abstraction. I like to explain that architecture is a practice whose main tool is abstraction.

In order to reduce complexity sufficiently for comprehension, architects abstract structures for analysis while obscuring detail which may mask underlying structure or which is not relevant to structural comprehension. This is abstraction: drawing out some information in favor of other information that is unnecessary. Identifying and (conceptually) manipulating structures is the goal; abstraction is the technique of architecture.

Hence, security architects must be skilled in highlighting those structures that have security implications (typically, functions of a system, its software units of implementation, often called "components," and the communications between these structural elements). Like any architect, we may obscure or elide (leave out) extraneous detail that is unnecessary to understanding and analysis (the analysis is often threat modeling). By the application of judicious abstraction, security architects are no different than any other type or level of system, software, integration, or enterprise architect.

Because the nature of the analysis (attacks and defenses) is different, what structure is abstracted and what detail eliminated may differ, even radically, from that which is useful to

---

[*] Zachman, 2007.

architects charged with other aspects of a system's developing architecture. But the mental process is the same, even if the working diagram differs.

1.7 Aiming Design Toward Security

Although any particular branch of architectural analysis may be focused on different results, there is one aspect of the practice of architecture that must be precisely the same: We all have to have a firm and precisely communicable idea about what must be achieved by a system. In order to architect, we have to know what we are building, what goals we are trying to achieve.

1.7.1 What Is Secure Software?

In the practice of security architecture, we must then understand what software security looks like. What are the behaviors that secure systems must exhibit? How is a "secure system" defined?

Over the years that I've been practicing, as I open a discussion about security with development teams, I've noticed that quite often (not every time, but regularly), team members will immediately jump to one of four aspects of software security:

- Protection of data (most often via encryption techniques)
- Implementations errors (most often, coding securely)
- Authentication and/or authorization of users of the system
- Network-level protection mechanisms

This set of responses has been remarkably stable for the last nearly 20 years, which is interesting to ponder all by itself. Despite the dramatic shift in attacker capabilities and techniques over the last 20 years—a huge shift in attacker objectives—developers seem to be thinking about one of the above aspects of the security picture. I don't know why development has not kept pace with the expansion of adversarial thinking, but apparently it hasn't (though, of course, my evidence here is completely anecdotal and not at all scientifically validated).

Lately in my threat modeling classes (and sometimes other presentations), I've been polling my audiences about what jumps first to mind when I say, "software security." Not surprisingly, members of my audiences typically find themselves considering one of the above categories unless a participant has broader security exposure. My informal polls underline a need to establish a baseline definition of just what software security must include, the field's breadth, its scope.

To address the challenge that development teams often lack a sufficiently complete picture of what software security entails, as well as to provide a set of secure design goals, I came up with the following secure software principles. "Secure" software must:

- Be free from implementation errors that can be maliciously manipulated: ergo, vulnerabilities
- Have the security features that stakeholders require for intended use cases
- Be self-protective; resist the types of attacks that will likely be attempted against the software
- In the event of a failure, must "fail well"—that is, fail in such a manner as to minimize consequences of successful attack
- Install with sensible, "closed" defaults

The foregoing are the attributes that "secure software" displays, to one extent or another, as it runs. These principles are aspirational, in that no running system will exhibit these behaviors perfectly; these cannot be implemented to perfection. Indeed, so far as exploitable conditions are concerned, whether from implementation, from a failure to identify the correct security requirements, or a failure to design what will be implanted correctly, software, at its current state of the art, will contain errors—bugs, if you will. Some of those errors are likely to have unintended security consequences—that is, vulnerabilities allowing adversaries leverage or access of one kind or another. This truism is simply a fact of building software, like it or not.

Then there is the matter of security context and desired security defensive state: a system or organization's security posture. Not every system is expected to resist every attack, every adversary, every level of adversary sophistication and level of effort that can be expended (given the universe of various threat agents; please see my discussion of adversary types elsewhere in this book as well as in *Securing Systems*).

Hence, presence and robustness of the above secure software behaviors must vary, system to system, implementation to implementation.

Still, I expect software to account for the above behaviors, even if by consciously accepting the risks generated by a considered absence or weakness of one or more of the principles given above. My software principles are meant to drive secure design decisions, to be goals to reach for. None of these principles is built as stated. These principles don't tell you how to protect a credential that must be held by a system. Rather, from these principles, design choices can be evaluated. These are guideposts, not design standards.

1.7.2 Secure Design Primer

We know with fair certainty that credentials (secrets) that are placed in the binary executable of software are relatively easy to uncover, given today's reverse engineering tools. For commercial software whose distribution involves execution within third-party environments—say, commercial, off-the-shelf (COTS) software that is run by the purchaser, distributing a secret tucked away in the static data of an executable—has proven to be a very poor design choice.

Such packaged secrets are routinely discovered by both attackers and researchers. Once held by an attacker (whether through discovery or published research), the attacker then has the ability to wield the secret successfully against whatever challenge it was meant to protect. If there are 10,000 copies of that executable in use, attackers can undo at least some aspect of the security for all 10,000 of those installations. Unfortunately, this design mistake happens far too often, with the resulting consequences.

How do our secure software principles apply? If programmers have coded the credential into the binary with correct language semantics (easily coded—for most languages, this is just a declaration), then there is no "implementation error." This is a design error. It's a failure to have the security features that stakeholders expect—that is, credentials have sufficiently been protected.

Furthermore, attempting to "hide" a secret as static data in an executable isn't self-protective. Quite the reverse, given the binary exploration and execution analysis tools that exist today.

Often this design miss assumes that the credential is "safe enough," so the use of the credential (which is legal) and the actions taken after the challenge has been passed will not be monitored; there is no failure—the credential is working as expected, but in the hands of adversaries.

So the "fail well/fail closed" principle doesn't really apply. It would depend upon the installation and configuration sequences of the software as to whether the placement of the credential in the binary is a "sensible, closed default."

I hope that the preceding trivial example demonstrates how the software security principles are meant to provide appropriate targets for deriving a secure architecture. The design patterns that will achieve these results require quite a bit more detail, which then must be applied in context.

A high-level set of secure design patterns and their application can be found in IEEE Center For Secure Design's "Avoiding the Top 10 Software Security Design Flaws."[*] This booklet is free, under The Creative Commons license. (Disclosure: I'm one of the the co-authors.[†]) The design patterns discussed in the booklet are:

- Earn or give, but never assume, trust
- Use an authentication mechanism that cannot be bypassed or tampered with
- Authorize after you authenticate
- Strictly separate data and control instructions, and never process control instructions received from untrusted sources
- Define an approach that ensures all data are explicitly validated
- Use cryptography correctly
- Identify sensitive data and how they should be handled
- Always consider the users
- Understand how integrating external components changes your attack surface
- Be flexible when considering future changes to objects and actors

Each of the design patterns explained in the booklet is meant to fulfill one or more of the software security principles listed above. First, we define how we intend secure software to behave (secure software principles) and then set out the means through which those aims are to be achieved (secure design patterns). With software security principles and design patterns, we know what we are to build when we wish to build "secure software."

1.8 Summary

We've explored the societal context of an unfolding "Computer Age" and the effects on the people in what I call the "connected life." This context points to a need for a general improvement in computer security if we are not to fall prey to cyber pirates, warlords, and armies. In order to build sufficient security into software, there exists a specific job role: the security architect. This book attempts to address what security architecture practice is, what we do (essentially, threat modeling) and how we do it, and to offer a few tricks of the trade achieved through many mistakes and missteps, a great deal of help from brilliant practitioners, and a lot of diligent practice.

---

[*] IEEE, 2014.
[†] Iván Arce, Kathleen Clark-Fisher, Neil Daswani, Jim DelGrosso, Danny Dhillon, Christoph Kern, Tadayoshi Kohno, Carl Landwehr, Gary McGraw, Brook Schoenfield, Margo Seltzer, Diomidis Spinellis, Izar Tarandach, and Jacob West.

The following chapters examine more closely the art and some considerable computer science of attacks and defenses. As well, I will try to offer sufficient views of security architecture such that it may finally be more firmly defined. Once in command of what security architecture might actually be, the remainder of the book will concern itself with the practice thereof, from the perspective of the learner, the practitioner, and the strategist. I hope that these explanations will prove useful to your practice.

Chapter 2

What Is Security Architecture, and Why Should I Care?

2.1 Define Security Architecture

In *Securing Systems*, I defined security architecture as applied information security: "Security architecture applies the principles of security to system architectures" (p. 14).

Further: "There has been an emerging trend to codify the techniques and craft used by security professionals. These disciplines have been called 'security engineering,' 'security analysis,' 'security monitoring,' 'security response,' 'security forensics,' and most importantly for this work, 'security architecture.' It is security architecture with which we are primarily concerned. Security architecture is the discipline charged with integrating into computer systems the security features and controls that will provide the protection expected of the system when it is deployed for use." (p. 6)

That definition was intended solely to provide a basis for describing a particular practice within the wider set of practices commonly attributed to security architecture, Architecture Risk Assessment (ARA) and Threat Modeling. Threat modeling is indeed a core tool for security architects as well as being a key task within a Secure Development Lifecycle (SDL, or Secure Software Development Life Cycle, S-SDLC).[*]

---

[*] Schoenfield, 2014. pp. 255–324.

2.1.1 Software Security

An SDL is a holistic methodology for producing software that exhibits the following attributes[*]:

1. Be as free as humanly possible from errors that can be manipulated intentionally—for example, be free of vulnerabilities that can harm customers or our brand.
2. Have those security features that customers require for their intended use cases.
3. Be self-protective; resisting the types of attacks that will be promulgated against the software.
4. "Fail well" in the event of a failure. That is, fail in such a manner as to minimize consequences of successful attack.
5. Install with sensible, "closed" defaults.

> Of course, design issues can be vulnerabilities, too. Therefore, security architecture may actually deal with all five principles. If we assume that "free from vulnerabilities" is concerned primarily with implementation errors, then Principles 2–5 cover the areas that a practice of architecture focused on security will most likely address. In computers, demarcation between areas is fuzzy. There is no hard-and-fast separation of scope at this conceptual level.

Security architecture as defined in *Securing Systems* is the practice concerned with attributes 2–5, above (see inset). Usually, security architecture tasks are performed during the architecture and design portions of the SDL—that is, early in development, before coding or in the early stages of coding, before any integrations that may be required to put the system together, and well before the validation of the near complete implementation (see inset below). For iterative development life cycles, like Agile, architecture and design work may extend and run parallel with coding and even testing. Security architecture practices may also iterate as a part of the architecture and design work.

2.1.2 Security Architecture Practices

There are other aspects of security architecture. As I noted when defining security architecture as it applies to threat modeling, beyond the security aspects of a system architecture, architecture practices can (should!) be applied to the building of a security infrastructure or a set of security services.

A security infrastructure might include network boundaries and zones of relative trust. It would normally include the placement of firewalls, intrusion prevention systems (IPS), exfiltration eavesdrop-

> Of course, when developing software through any iterative methodology like SCRUM Agile, an architecture may change during the iterations. Architecture changes may take place through some or much of the iterations. Architecture changes, whether through iteration, feature request, or what-have-you, will normally trigger a re-evaluation of the security requirements of the system under development.

pers, technology watching for data loss events (DLP), anti-malware (AM) protections on end points, a security information event management system (SIEM) to collect and process the

---

[*] The secure software attributes' (more properly: design principles) wording has been updated somewhat from Schoenfield, B. (2014). Applying the SDL Framework to the Real World (Ch. 9). In *Core Software Security*, pp. 322.

information generated by these other devices, public key infrastructure (PKI) to provide keys for encryption services, etc.

Each security "tool" (so-called) is, in and of itself, a complex system. Each is often deployed, one at a time and perhaps ad hoc, and disconnected from other, disparate security tools. But security tools are collectively much more powerful and synergistic if deployed as an interconnecting and interacting architecture. It is designing the panoply of security tools as a single, cohesive, interlocking set of protections (which should usually overlap), as a defense-in-depth, as a set of security services that will support an enterprise architecture; that is one of the two main tasks for a security architect, each a focus of the set of practices commonly known as security architecture.

Indeed, a security architect can provide an enterprise architecture with a cohesive set of security capabilities. The capabilities thus specified support the mission of the enterprise and its various functions with sufficient protections and controls to bring the enterprise architecture to the organization's desired security posture. An enterprise security architecture must be a key supporting component of any comprehensive enterprise architecture.

In order to accomplish this task, the security architect must be conversant with enterprise architecture theory and practice, as well as the specific enterprise architecture with which to work. Alongside skill in understanding and manipulating enterprise architectures, a security architect charged with designing required security functions must also be familiar with a gamut of security technologies and methodologies. The security technology and methodologies will be combined into a cohesive enterprise security architecture.[*]

2.2 Relevant Knowledge Domains

Whether building a cohesive set of security functions or analyzing non-security systems to achieve a desired security posture, all successful practitioners within any of security architecture's domains must have a working knowledge of the sort of attacks that may potentially be leveled at the object of the analysis: enterprise, organization, systems, what-have-you. Understanding of relevant attacks is one of the key knowledge domains that security architects wield, no matter the object of security architecture.

In order to manipulate system structures (architecture) to build appropriate defense, the security architect must have sufficient understanding of the following:

- Attackers and their typical methods ("threat landscape"[†])
- The attacks themselves and what they achieve
- Chaining exploits to access particular system targets
- The system targets of attack (vulnerabilities) and attackers' ultimate attack goals
- The programming patterns, design patterns, and security features and controls that will interrupt or prevent attacks

---

[*] See The Open Group, 2011, for an example of enterprise security thinking.
[†] Sometimes referred to as the "threatscape."

Indeed, knowledge of a threat landscape and understanding of the exploitation of various types of conditions of the typical objects of attack by particular attack actors is required in order to build any kind of defense or to build a security architecture, a set of services, that will monitor for and then assist detection of ongoing attacks. The level of detail at which attacks must be understood varies depending upon the domain and the systems under analysis. In order to build an enterprise security architecture, general types of attack classes are required. In order to secure a kernel-level device driver, a great deal more specificity of particular, relevant attacks is required. Still, attacks and exploits are a common currency for security architects.

Without knowledge of attacks, there simply is no way to specify what must be done in order to respond, whether the security architect is focused on building systems and infrastructure that provide security services or is charged with assessing non-security systems to identify risk and provide security requirements for that system. Attacks are the mental currency that glues other, also required knowledge domains together into the whole known as security architecture. Knowing how an organization or system is likely to be attacked is the seed from which a security architect starts her, his, or their mental practice, no matter to which problems the practice is applied.

To provide an enterprise security architecture implies that a security architect must understand not only digital security, but also software, system, and enterprise architecture. This is no small undertaking; The Open Group has certified a few Enterprise Security Architects. Beyond the Open Groups certified Enterprise Security Architects, few people have held the title at organizations. Generally, in my experience, if this position is filled (usually by a very senior security architect), an organization's Enterprise Security Architect will work very closely with one or more of that organization's Enterprise Architects and will be a key contributor to the enterprise architecture. We will return to the connection between enterprise architecture and security architecture a little later.

Security architecture as it applies to non-security systems encompasses more than threat modeling. One may think of security architecture as the application of information security practices to digital systems (as I proposed in *Securing Systems*). It is more properly the intersection of a number of disciplines:

- Information security, and especially, the application of security controls
- A study of existing and potential threat actors ("threat agents")
- Digital attack types and exploits, which must include the nature of vulnerability and misuse
- Risk as it relates to software and digital systems
- Applied cryptography (at least at an architectural level)
- Software development practices
- Computer languages and their compilation and execution
- Software interactions with underlying hardware
- Software design
- Software and system architectures
- Communication and data exchange protocols
- Computer network structures and packet routing
- Data storage mechanisms and protocols
- Runtime and execution models and environments
- Operating systems

- Central processing unit (CPU) execution, and machine language execution in general
- Random access memory (RAM) usage and misusage

In fact, it may be said that security architecture may encompass most aspects of information security as well as a fair sampling from computer science.

The above may seem an imposing list. A typical security architect may specialize in several of the above areas of computer science but she, he, or they must be conversant in all the areas of information security listed above and will at least have a working knowledge of the other areas; the competent security architect will usually know when she/he/they are out of their depth and must seek the help of one or more experts.

For instance, in order to protect data in storage, one must have a working knowledge of how file systems work, where the file driver comes into play as a part of an operating system, and at least a glancing understanding of how the bits actually get written into storage.

Likewise, in order to protect a running application, one must have a working knowledge of the operating system under which the application will run, its services and security features, and its weaknesses, as well as the format of a loadable and executable file; how memory is accessed, allocated, and deallocated from the language in which the program was written; how the runtime stack works; what is the relationship between multiple programs running at the same time; even the details of concurrency, such as semaphores, inter-process communications, execution privileges, and runtime boundaries.

I hope that through these two simple examples, you will begin to grasp the complexity of the problem space. We haven't even touched on the subtleties of large-scale, multi-tenant cloud systems. If you're curious about the sorts of challenges in an analysis of such a system, please turn to the cloud example in *Securing Systems*, Chapter 11. Let it suffice for the moment to note that the list given above attempts to define the scope and domains that security architecture may need to put into play in order to accomplish the task of defining what security is required for a system or an organization. The work may proceed from high-level structural requirements down to the details of design and implementation (see inset).

> "Structure" and "architecture" are used nearly interchangeably in this work. I use both of these terms in the hope that readers new to architecture better understand the arena in which architecture provides a key tool of analysis.

Let me then broaden the definition given above drawn from *Securing Systems*: *Security architecture applies the principles of security to system architectures.*

If the art of ARA and threat modeling is applied information security, then security architecture is *the modeling of complex systems in order to divine their security properties and structures and then to specify these security properties and structures so that they may be implemented.*

This broader definition leaves the security architect free to be an architect, to model things in the abstract that will eventually become digital systems and software. Indeed, if architecture is a practice concerned with modeling complex things, then security architecture is the modeling of digital security.

The scope of "digital security" for our definition must include systems intended to deliver digital security as well as the digital security of any computer system or set of systems. We must further refine our working definition because we don't know what digital security consists of. Digital security is meant to encompass any possible exploitable weaknesses of a computer system and the potential defenses for those exploitable conditions. If you prefer, digital security will be the preservation of the classic security triad, Confidentiality, Integrity, and Availability (CIA).

Digital (or computer, if you will) weaknesses and their defenses are the basic language of information security. Security architecture deals with these in a structural manner rather than delving into each particular weakness's technical details.

Therein lies a defining difference between security *testing* and security *architecture.* In, say, penetration testing, the technical details of each vulnerability and its exploitation become very important; attempts to exploit vulnerabilities to demonstrate potential attack is the primary goal of a penetration tester. The penetration tester must be able to identify potential attack surfaces and then skillfully apply appropriate exploit techniques in order to test defenses (or the lack thereof).

Instead, at the structural level, for the purpose of modeling, types of weaknesses and their exploitation techniques can typically be grouped together into general classes. Again, the architect deals in structures and patterns and employs abstraction to identify, represent, and manipulate them. Exploitable conditions might be grouped into memory overrun attacks or browser scripting attacks. The details of each variant or sub-variant of attack groupings are not particularly useful when analyzing a system for potential attacks (threat modeling).

2.3 More About Architecture

Stepping back from the problems of security for a moment, it may be worth delving just a little into the practice of architecting software systems. The more complex a thing becomes, the more pieces it has, the more variables, the more it can be broken down from the whole into its parts ("parts" being undefined, or in fact, multiply defined, depending upon who is taking apart the whole and who needs to know precisely what). In fact, the moment something becomes too complex for a person to hold in her, his, or their mind, the thing under consideration will require the application of architecture to it.

Architecture is an abstraction of that which must be understood or modeled in any particular moment of understanding. "Understanding" in this context means any number of human processes for which architecture will be a tool: building something, planning something, maintaining something, changing something, and destroying or taking something apart.

Architecture is a tool for reducing the complexity and "noise" generated by a thing's details so that its structure may be understood, communicated, built, and changed. Architecture is the human mind's playground when designing, implementing, and changing complex things. From the point at which an architecture solidifies, it then is a plan for and map to the structure of a "thing."

Which brings us to the matter of abstraction and use. When drawing or painting, the artist does not see the object that is drawn during the drawing process. Instead, in order to get a representation of a three-dimensional object, one must perceive those shapes that occur as the eye reads light as light hits the object. One must focus on visible edges of the subject, contours of light and dark that come from shadow and superimposition, one object over another, foreground object to background object. That is, the lights and shadows must be captured accurately if one is to represent what one sees. Thus, one does not see a face, or a tree: one abstracts the shifts between light and dark, between shades of color. Often, these are seen as shapes. The artist records the shapes as seen, making sure that they are placed accurately and in size scale to each other. A representation thus emerges out of this process.[*]

Similarly, when modeling something complex, one must focus on parts of the whole, while ignoring, for the moment, other detail. This is the process of *abstraction*. Some details are represented while others are ignored and not represented. Abstraction is precisely what we do in architecture. We aggregate things based on some organizing principle—say, the concepts that make up a business, or those blocks of function that have some major input or output, or by technologies.

In fact, as I noted in *Securing Systems,* the practice of enterprise architecture offers us some standard views to help us understand computer systems (p. 58).

Of course, there's nothing real about a software system; it's all ones and zeros. Those pretty windows being shown on your computer display with their wonderful drop shadows are just a trick of the eye as groups of bits are moved around in the graphics memory that then get displayed as coloured shapes. The eye, being the wonderful instrument that it is, perceives these bits as three-dimensional objects, which we then manipulate with our pointing device. Our brain is fooled into a visual paradigm that allows us to work with our ones and zeros in some organizing manner. This visual *tromp l'oeil* is an abstraction with which our brains interact as somehow being real.

Luckily, there are levels of abstraction employed to generate useful digital system architecture views. In enterprise architecture there is a conceptual view, a functional and/or logical view, the technical view, and perhaps various physical views. Each of these views has something meaningful to offer the architect; none of these views has primacy. At a conceptual view, an architect can get a sense of all the domains that must interact successfully within a complex business. A conceptual view may provide a wonderful conduit for businesspeople to interact with architects about how they want to organize the major processes of the business. In fact, I've heard it said that an architecture is a conduit for communication. In my experience, this is one of the primary functions of architecture: to facilitate constructive interaction. Each of the other views similarly provides a necessary abstraction with which to work.

Architecture then becomes a tool for hiding details that obscure the overall structure. Further, architecture offers us a playground in which we may manipulate pieces of the structure with little physical penalty or cost. In a software system, structures might be the APIs, technologies, data and method objects, libraries, and other code bodies that will make up the system. It's a way of organizing what could be a mess of "spaghetti." And nearly every experienced software developer has had the pain of dealing with the messy spaghetti of code such that the system becomes unmaintainable—that is, not understandable and fragile when changed.

At a coarser grain of abstraction, the solutions architect will play with the component systems that eventually will be integrated into a larger and more complex system, which will deliver some important piece of the organization's digital presence and functioning.[†]

---

[*] Edwards, 1989.

[†] Of course, there are other dimensions through which a digital architect adds value. Please see Rosen, 2008, for more.

2.4 Architectures of Security

The above examples are exactly analogous to what a security architect must do. The security architect understands the flows, components, and data of an integrated solution in order to bring the solution to a known and (hopefully) provable security posture.[*]

The attack surfaces and controls to protect the attack services, the defense-in-depth, can be modeled through architecture, as described above. All the pieces or components of the digital defense of an organization can be modeled, just as the conceptual and logical architectures of an enterprise can be modeled. The security view is yet another view used to model the security infrastructure that will support the enterprise architecture. Just as the networking team will have to model the networks that will be used, so the security architect must model the security systems.

Of course, security architecture is concerned both with the security systems—a security infrastructure, if you will—while at the same time, security architecture also encompasses any digital system's security posture.

"System" might be enterprise level, solution level, or distinct software application. There exists a special domain of the security architect which lies beyond the modeling of security systems; that domain is the understanding of how to apply digital security to systems that are not designed for security purposes at all. Neither of these tasks is primary; they are each a part of the domain typically termed security architecture.

In smaller or flatter organizations, a security architect might have to do it all. In such a situation, there may not be architects who specialize in one or the other of these domains. Most security architects that I know have at least a working knowledge of both domains, even if they have specialized in one side or the other.

In order to craft a defense-in-depth for a system, one must understand many different types of attacks, network on up through message layers. In addition, one must understand the types of controls that one must apply for these various classes of attacks. Thus, seasoned security architects get pretty familiar with security infrastructures, even if they work largely on discrete software packages, or at the solution's level on complex integrations of systems.

Because security is the "cross functional domain," security architects typically have to move up and down the Open Systems Interconnection (OSI) model[†] with fluidity. Indeed, it's hard to be effective without understanding what firewalls and network segments do as security treatments, while at the same time understanding that many attack patterns flow right through these because the attacks are encapsulated within the legal message boundaries of the protocols.

One cannot secure a standard web application without an understanding of network attacks and protections, moving all the way up the OSI model to message-based and URL-based attacks and their mitigations in the application layer. Alongside these fundamental attack and defense mechanisms, it is likely one will need an understanding of authentication and authorization systems (access controls), perhaps shared storage problems, usually databases, web protocols, and scripting languages, which then bring into scope script interpreters and browser architectures. Web applications are an exceedingly well understood portion of the security architect's domain, which is why I often use them as an example. There are other types of system architectures that are not so well understood, not so readily documented as web applications have been.

---

[*] I defined these terms in *Securing Systems*. I will more fully explain them later in this work.

[†] Microsoft, 2014.

2.5 Architecture as a Part of Cyber Security

There are many excellent books that explain in great detail how CIA make up practical information security. "Protect, detect, and correct" is a short descriptor for how information security attempts to deliver CIA. CIA is abundantly described throughout books, articles, blogs, webcasts, and numerous other sources.[*]

> The Turing Halting Proof implies that we cannot prove that any computing system is error free. My conclusion is a small leap from the point of the proof itself. Still in practice, that is what Turing's proof indicates: There is no way to ensure system perfection (or any other state); the problem is undecidable. The fact that most computer languages are Turing Complete makes the problem of defense difficult, because in order to be useful, computer languages must express any particular problem with near infinite variety. (That's not the direct meaning of Turing Completeness in a language, but rather, Turing Complete languages provide near infinite expression, which then makes computer defense difficult.) (Maruoka, 2011; Fuller, 2008)

Essentially, there exist three domains through which CIA of systems can be achieved. CIA is the goal, though of course there is no perfection in security, and certainly not in computing altogether (sse inset). Computer security in general and security architecture specifically exist in an uncertain world full of ambiguity, ambivalence, and, typically, multiple conflicts of priority as practitioners are faced with limited resources (see inset below). Still, we are trying to protect information from disclosure and the information and the systems that handle it from unwanted change. Plus, we have to keep the systems up and running if we are to use them as intended: CIA.

In order to achieve CIA, we can build protections into systems and also surround them with protections. We try to have running systems report their security state such that if there is an incident, we can detect it as fast as possible (detection). Which naturally leads to correction: thwarting an attack and then bringing compromised systems back to the intended state: protect, detect, correct.

Security architecture is primarily concerned with protection and the mechanisms used to detect attacks. Generally, analysis for detection falls to a different branch on the tree of information security: incident response.

> Prioritizing has the potential to test every dimension of your capability: technical, communication, conflict management, influence, collaboration, even organization politics. It's not the for the faint of heart!

One may think that correction lies entirely within the sphere of incident response, but it does not. At the very least, backups, build systems, deployment methods all have a structural component. The structure must be thought through for security, like any other aspect which will affect a system. Thus, security architecture has a play within the correct sphere, as well. As I expressed throughout *Securing Systems*, every structure connected to and interacting with any system under analysis has the potential to change the system's security posture. Deployment systems are no different from other functions integrated into a complex system.

Often, as a security incident unfolds, there will be hand-offs, perhaps multiple hand-offs, between incident response and security architecture. The incident may highlight a weakness in architecture or design, which then must be reworked for more strength and resistance. In

---

[*] Tipton, 2000; Intel, 2015.

fact, Cisco® Systems' 2005 loss of its customer password file* did, in fact, engender a number of changes in architecture as well as security architecture practice. That is, incident response fosters security architecture changes. I was the Senior Security Architect technical lead for Cisco's web applications and infrastructure during the password incident and its several years of aftermath. Several programs still employed at Cisco (so my spies tell me) came directly out of the security architecture changes required by that single incident.

I don't think it makes sense for me to reiterate all the material that's available on CIA or protect, detect, correct. If you're unsure about standard information security practices, I suggest that the material in this book will make more sense if you are at least glancingly familiar with the theory and practice of information security.

Particularly, one must have a working knowledge of the sorts of technologies and activities that protect CIA. Familiarity with approaches such as protect, detect, and correct put meat on the bones of just how CIA can be maintained. As of this writing, there exists a wealth of material on these concepts that is available, both freely and commercially.

2.6 Security Architecture in Software Development

Likewise, there is a plethora of literature that thoroughly describes and explains basic computer science, computer memory usage by loadable programs, stacks and heaps, operating system and program loaders, boot sections and boot code, basic input/output system (BIOS) code, hard disk accesses, networking protocols and TCP/IP implementations. I see no reason to regurgitate that here. A security architect must have a grounding in the principles and practices of computer science as well as software development. Otherwise, the uninformed or ill-prepared architect will be a significant disadvantage both when analyzing systems and when prescribing treatments.

First, software engineers, in my experience, tend to be a suspicious lot. When people without understanding of and skill in software development make pronouncements, software developers will quite often dismiss whatever might be said out of hand. Developers require faith that the person speaking knows at least something about the development of software, computer languages, compilers and linkers, development environments, and most importantly, debugging software programs.

Development teams typically need to know that suggestions and requirements are made from some firm grounding in the rigors of developing software. A security architect doesn't necessarily have to be the most brilliant or skilled developer in the room by far. But the architect had better understand the technical underpinnings of developing software. At the design level, the computer science part of security architecture must include software design and software architectures.

Personally, as of this writing, I've held a security architect title for approximately 18 or 19 years. The last software project for which I was programming was early in my security architecture career.†

---

* Leyden, 2005.
† A PERL tool for identifying UNIX log entries with potential security implications that was originally created by Gil Daudestil.

Even though my C/C++ skills are woefully out of date, I can still read code when I have to. I may not know all the details of the most current Java API, but I know how Java works. I do understand what byte code is, and the virtual processor that lives inside the Java execution environment (JRE). I have debugged hundreds of thousands of lines of code down to the assembly, even machine instructions; I've called hardware directly, and written code for operating system drivers and kernels.

Though my skills may be out of date, I still have an understanding of what developers face when designing, writing, and testing code. This gives me sufficient credibility that cannot be bought—it can only be earned. When a security person wants to get into security architecture—especially software security architecture or application security—if they have no background in development, that's the first place I'm going to suggest that they start gaining some experience.

There are of course, far too many domains within computer science for any single person to master them all. Still, above I've listed those domains that are most important for security architecture.

Beyond writing and debugging code, for the security architect, a firm grasp of software architectures and software design is essential. Although it is true that designing large, integrated systems is somewhat different from building the architecture of a single application or process, still, I personally think that gaining skill for architecting complex integrations provides a firm start from software architecture and not the other way round. Once familiar with the concepts of objects, modularization, data hiding, API building, atomization, transactions, service level agreements (SLA), functional layering, and the like, the architectural patterns employed within solid software architectures can be applied to system architectures at just about any level.

Besides, as we've noted, architecture is at least partially about abstraction. And good software architecture is the practice of abstraction. The rigor of building a software architecture that can be ported relatively painlessly to differing operating systems because it is strongly layered to offer abstraction through hiding operating system services (see inset 1) provides a good basis for understanding how to abstract concepts, components, or logical functions at whatever level appropriate to solve the problems at hand.

Those without a strong background in software design will likely struggle (see inset 2) more than those who have had it, because analysis of architectures proceeds from the internal construction of a particular piece or component of software on up to complex, global cloud integrations.

Perhaps I'm simply biased, because that's how I learned. Still, of the hundreds of architects with whom I've worked, and the literally thousands whom

> 1. A system that could not easily be ported would directly embed calls to the operating system API wherever they were going to be called—native and local OS services get called directly from wherever and all over. There would be no bottleneck routines. OS API calls would not be hidden ("covered") behind generalized functions such that local services are abstracted into typical services that are provided by most OSs. A portable application abstractly calls generalized services such that calling functions within the application need not understand the underlying details of each particular OS. I have built just such systems; the learning was invaluable.
>
>
>
> 2. This is a generalization, of course. Any particular individual will be unique and thus may not "struggle" much even though that individual has little software development background.

I've trained, it is those who come from software development and have a working capability in software design who progress into security architecture the fastest.

That is not to say that every *software* architect is automatically a great *system* architect. System architects often have broad understanding of many domains, databases, shared storage, network boundaries and trust zones, hosting and system administration, large-scale networking, alongside some level of business acuity that allows a solutions architect to translate business need into functions, components, technologies. Still, I want to underline that the ability to manipulate the abstractions of architecture have been learned by those who can design scalable, performant, sustainable, maintainable software architectures.

2.7 Generally, Experience Is a Teacher

Of course, studying the theory and practice of software architecture and design, solutions architecture, or enterprise architecture will be valuable and contribute capabilities to one's security architecture bag of tricks. However, in my experience as a security architect, as a trainer of security architects, and a mentor to dozens, if not hundreds, of security architects, I can state that there is no substitute for direct experience. I'm attempting to explain here some of the key knowledge that successful security architects tend to have at their command. Every great security architect with whom I've worked has also been a competent software as well as system architect. The vast majority have written software and been through the gauntlet of inevitable serious issues once their software was deployed and used. That's an important data point to consider. All of these stellar practitioners had spent some considerable time writing and designing software and designing systems small and large.

The gating factor in becoming a security architect is generally not gaining sufficient security knowledge. Although information security is certainly a domain worthy of study and is as deep and broad as any, perhaps more so being the "cross domain" or "matrix domain," gathering the security specifics in a particular context generally doesn't take that long, even for someone fairly new.

The more difficult piece will be understanding the implications of various choices at various levels of abstraction of an architecture. Hence, in my humble experience, it's much easier to train a good solutions architect security than it is to train someone that has done a good deal of security but has no software architecture or system architecture experience.

I do not mean to disparage the skills of information security practitioners. However, the practice of testing software for vulnerabilities, or responding to incidents, or even building a vulnerability scanner are not the same as creating system structures that are resilient to change—that is, architecting complex systems. Even being a Chief Information Security Officer (CISO) does not make use of the same skills as manipulating processes and technologies at various levels of abstraction (though, of course, some security architects do become CISOs).

Manipulation of processes and technologies are the domain of the system or solutions architect. A security architect has to understand what this process is as well as be conversant in manipulating such things at various levels of abstraction. Otherwise, the security architect doesn't have a method for understanding how to build a defense-in-depth that will be in sync with the system under analysis. "In sync" here means a defense that utilizes the available security services, if any, and takes into account both the strengths and weaknesses of the structure of the system being analyzed. That is, in sync means not "ivory tower," not theoretical, but rather, grounded in current realities. And this is true whether the security architect is assessing systems that are not for security or building security infrastructures and systems. Both require a firm grasp of the practice of software and system architecture.

2.8 Introducing Attack Methods

Attack methods, which are also commonly known as *exploitation techniques,* are the place at which computer science meets security architecture. The effective security architects with whom I've worked seem to carry an almost encyclopedic catalog of attack types that they can quickly and appropriately apply to the systems they want to defend. When analyzing systems, even in the very early stages of conception, knowing the types of attacks that a system will endure, against which it must defend and perhaps recover, allows the architect to imagine what kinds of defenses will need to be built.

> Though I've used the words, "early" and "later," these should not be taken to indicate a preference for any particular SDLC methodology, Waterfall, Agile, what-have-you. Even highly iterative development still must identify what must be built before it is built, should map out structure that then is designed, all of which can be happening in parallel with other development tasks, iteratively.

Very early in a new development process, when the system may still be entirely conceptual, any broad-brush security feature requirements can be identified. Such requirements might, for instance, be authentication and authorization, or encryption in transit and for sensitive storage. As development progresses, the requirements, now including security requirements, will be fleshed out into specific architecture elements and then precise designs (see inset). As the development process unfolds, threat modeling—the process to identify specific attacks aimed at particular points in the system ("attack surfaces")—requires knowledge of both attack mechanisms as well as mechanisms to thwart the attacks (defenses or controls).

Each attack type is then mentally connected to particular groupings of threat actors and associated to types of attack surfaces. By maintaining a thorough and up-to-date knowledge of active threat actors, making use of particular exploitation techniques to be exercised on particular interfaces, a security architect can quickly, perhaps almost preternaturally, home in on the most important areas of concern that are ripe for protection during an analysis. To do this, the practitioner needs to know which threat actors are most active, why, and how the attackers might go after a system of the type under analysis.

But the foregoing does not, in fact, imply that each good security architect needs to carry around the equivalent of the Common Weakness Enumeration (CWE) catalog.* Most importantly, few mere mortals have that much brain space (though it would not surprise me if some brilliant practitioner had CWE nearly memorized [see inset on next page]). But also, a detailed understanding of each attack variation is simply unnecessary in order to practice. This

---

* MITRE, n.d.

> At the beginning of my career, I was introduced to an Apple engineer who had all the operation codes in Apple II and III monitors memorized. He felt that assembly language was "too high level." Humans are capable of amazing mental feats.

is where security architects and penetration testers completely part company.

In order to penetration test, one must understand the intimate relationship between attack detail and vulnerability. There is no getting around this necessity; it is precisely this set of knowledge through which a penetration test is performed. The tester has to uncover potential attack surfaces (same as security architecture's threat modeling process). But at this point, specific attacks are used in order to categorically prove specific weaknesses. Potential areas of weakness are discovered through threat modeling; specific weaknesses are proved in penetration testing.

In order to protect a system, one does not need in-depth knowledge of attack detail. Exploitation techniques can be grouped at a higher level; the details are insignificant when building defenses. Take the case of stack buffer overflow as an example: stack overflows have been well understood since at least the point at which I began the first software security role of my career within cyber security. In order to prove that a buffer overflow exists in an executing program's stack, a tester needs to line up precisely the instructions required for that CPU, at memory locations determined by the stack at that moment of execution, such that the return pointer will get overwritten, changing the course of execution to code of the attacker's choosing.

To prevent a stack buffer overflow, a security architect needs none of the foregoing detail, but instead will be concerned with whether tainted (attacker controlled) data will be processed by the function that contains the overflow opportunity. An architectural analysis will focus on the flow of data toward the overflow, the rewriting of the function in which the overflow may occur such that the function becomes self-protective, and perhaps methods for removing potential attacks within the data before it reaches any potential points of vulnerability. The security architect most certainly must have a solid grasp on how stack overflows work in general. (See inset.) But the specifics of each overflow are not relevant at all.

> I do encourage every security architect to play around with one or two examples of every attack that will be relevant to systems that will be analyzed. My time spent proving Cisco Infosec's first C language secure coding guide has been invaluable to me.

At Intel® Security in 2013, I had the privilege to assist Catherine Blackader Nelson when she developed a catalog of attacks, weaknesses, and their most common mitigations at the architectural level (rather than the often unconnected details of each). Unfortunately, that work is held by Intel, and I cannot reprint it here. It was seminal work that I have never seen anywhere else and is sorely needed. I hope that Catherine or someone else gives us all a much-needed catalog of attack types matched with vulnerability classes and appropriate treatments.

Still, Chapter 3: Attacks and Defenses, will dive into more depth on this important problem: the intersection between attack and weakness at an architectural level. It is the essential problem that a security architect must grasp. Security architecture is the point at which attackers and defenders meet; an attack surface is the battleground of cyber war in which exploit meets either undefended weakness ripe for exercise or sufficient defense to prevent exploitation. The intersection between exploit, point of attack, and weakness is the heart of building defenses. Without this knowledge, a security architect cannot practice. What I have tried to describe can be expressed as a kill chain, or what I term, "credible attack vector," as described in both Just Good Enough Risk Rating (JGERR) (see inset) and Chapter 4 of *Securing Systems*.

Chapter 5: Learning the Trade will offer some potential avenues for acquiring appropriate level attack scenario knowledge. I've been working through various exercises in my classes that participants seem to find useful. I've tried to make use of public references that are available to every practitioner. Please see that chapter for more clues on how to build a more extensive catalog of attack types.

> Just Good Enough Risk Rating was published by The Sans Institute as one of their first in their Smart Guide series. However, SANS terminated the Smart Guide project and removed all of the content. Interested readers can find the JGERR Smart Guide posted at my blog: http://brookschoenfield.com/?page_id=271. JGERR is thoroughly described in Chapter 4 of *Securing Systems*.

I unfortunately cannot reproduce Catherine's threat and treatments catalog, as it belongs exclusively to Intel; that work cannot be reproduced without express permission. Instead, I will lamely attempt to capture the essence of an architectural view of credible attack vectors and typical treatments. This book will not attempt to set out a complete catalog of exploitations and treatments in their appropriate context at an architectural level. That book is yet unwritten, though it should be. Instead, I'll focus on why we work at a more abstract level, what amount of detail and understanding will

> There are even certifications for penetration testing. I will note that reading the very first edition of Hacking Exposed allowed me to at least get started practicing security architecture. Without an understanding of attack technique, a practitioner will be lost (McClure, 1999).

suffice, and how one puts this information to use as a security architect. That explanation has also not yet been published, so far as I know, anywhere but in this work. For the testing minded, there are numerous works available providing detail on hacking techniques (see inset).

2.9 Speaking of Defense

Attacks by themselves are not the complete security architecture skill picture. A skilled security architect must also know how to prevent successful attacks. The other side of the attack coin is the face of defense. The complete security architecture cycle involves planning for attack and specifying those defenses that will either prevent particular attacks or, at the very least, make the prosecution of the attack sufficiently difficult as to either prevent success or at the very least, slow an attack down enough to catch the compromise before it has been completed.

It is industry wisdom that firewalls must be deployed at network ingress from the Internet. I suppose that a practitioner could just accept this "wisdom" at face value. But what attacks will a firewall prevent? Which will be slowed down? What type of attacks walk right through a firewall and must be prevented in some other fashion? A security architect specifying a firewall must know the answers to these questions. Because even so-called "next-generation" firewalls are not a panacea (despite what some firewall vendors may claim). Certain types of traffic can be prevented. But other types, including traffic that contains attack code, will be routed right through a firewall and onto internal networks, potentially to be seen by humans or automated processing.

It is the matrix of attacks against vulnerability classes paired to their particular defenses that a security architect wields, not only when analyzing networks, systems, or groups of systems, but also when building infrastructures. In fact, one usually doesn't simply build security infrastructure out of whole cloth. Rather, one analyzes an organization to determine its required risk posture. One analyzes existing infrastructure and systems in light of the organization's security posture. The to-be-built infrastructure then is a product of this analysis; the infrastructure is meant to provide sufficient defense and security services such that the organization can meet its required security posture while also growing, changing, and adding and removing systems.

There is an interplay between existing and potential attacks and the defense-in-depth. Few organizations can afford to defend against everything. Furthermore, no defense is flawless. Because particular attacks require particular treatments (whether a security control or some other methodology meant to prevent weakness), each defense-in-depth will include standard and accepted defenses, while at the same time being a unique collection or even having unique, one-off defenses and treatments.

In sum, we might say that security architecture is the practice of identifying potential attack methods and then specifying a defense-in-depth against those identified attacks.

2.10 More Precise Definition

How digital systems' structures respond to attacks is the practice of security architecture.

The "how" and the "respond" in the definition above encompass an entire set of defense controls and maneuvers: prevention, ignoring, resisting, slowing down, and failing well when under attack. The "defensive" part of security architecture is a combination of technologies and techniques for tossing away apparent attacks (obviously erroneous input), preventing access to attackers, mitigating attacks (e.g., input validation or parameterization), resistance by closing down a portion of a system that is under attack, and slowing the pace of an attack so that it can be discovered more easily. For example, a common technique for slowing attacks is to use an entirely different method of communication or protocol between each component or layer in an architecture as messages are forwarded onward through the system.

The "how" can even be validated, at least for known attack types. That's what vulnerability scanners, web vulnerability scanners, fuzz testing, and the panoply of tools wielded by penetration testers aim to assess: what a system under test will do when faced with an attack.

In simple terms, security architecture tries to build systems that respond well to (oftentimes, by ignoring) digital attacks. Penetration testing, and really, all forms of security testing, aim to prove the security architecture of a system.

The goal is to make attack response predictable as well as preventive or at least resistant.

Given the foregoing definition, we end up being close to the coarse-grained definition I gave in *Securing Systems*: "Security architecture is applied information security" and quoted at the beginning of this chapter. That is, security architecture is the application of the practices of information security to systems and organizations. Information security encompasses protecting, detecting, and reacting to cyber attack.

As we have seen, there are many aspects to the practice of security architecture. Of course, there's a great deal of basic computer science. As we noted above, one cannot understand many attack types without a working knowledge of computers and computer languages and the basic tools of producing software. Plus, security architecture is a branch of software and/or system architecture. Architecture is a manipulation of structure and detail through abstraction.

What makes security architecture a separate discipline or a subdiscipline of system architecture is the understanding of technical attacks and technical defenses. A security architect must have an ability to forecast the attacks that are coming her, his, or their way and also must know the correct treatments for classes of attacks. This is the knowledge domain that is the specialty of the security architect.

Attack categories and defense treatments are the currency of security architecture; a security architect must connect the dots from threat actors through each type of actor's techniques to network and system attack points, thinking through how each defense will stop or slow down the attack, and how attacks may be identified as they progress. To perform these analyses, a working knowledge of many domains within computer science as well as the semantics of attack techniques and attack identification must be pulled together into a logical whole: the security architecture.

Along the way, the analysis may also have to grasp socio-economic and political drivers in diverse cultures and countries in order to understand the motivations and goals of differing classes of attackers (threat agents/actors). Plus, the analysis will be flawed without an understanding of the organization's goals and risk tolerance and the place that each system that may be attacked will play to achieve organization goals. Along with the computer science, there's a dash of political science, a bit of sociology, and some psychology stirred up with a decent feel for risk assessment. It's a heady mix that will test the limits of most practitioners from time to time.

2.11 Summary

In the next chapter, we will examine how attack and defense helps to define a security architecture. We will take a complex example attack and system in order to learn through example.

After Chapter 3 on attacks for architecture analysis, the remainder of this book contains what I hope are useful techniques, tricks, pitfalls, and perhaps the occasional bit of wisdom that my colleagues have shared with me or that I may have gained through dint of the many mistakes that I've made. Many of these are extracted from my earlier works, the difference here being that you won't have to dig through long explanations about SDL (or S-SDLC) or threat modeling techniques to find the bits and pieces that I included therein.

Instead, I hope that by consolidating these tricks, by extricating them from other contexts, they will be far more accessible, and thus useful in their own right.

This work is concerned with many aspects of security architecture and its practice. Some of the tips and tricks herein do pertain primarily to system assessment. But others are more general in that they apply to the practice of security architecture—not just to that portion of security architecture that involves ARA and threat modeling—that is involved in the secure design of systems and the organizational context in which a maturing security architecture practice thrives.

Chapter 3

Architecture, Attacks, and Defenses

It's no secret that cyber security professionals are interested in all aspects of cyber attacks. In a very real way, understanding attacks underpins the practice of cyber security. What does not get discussed very much, if at all, is exactly what each specialty in the profession needs both to know about attacks and to learn from them.

3.1 Yes, Exploit Details, But

A quick survey of books, presentations, white papers, and even whole conference agendas will reveal a deep fascination with the technical details of exploiting vulnerabilities. The extant literature is so full of this information that it nearly drowns out other aspects of working with attacks, perhaps even drowns out the many other aspects of practicing cyber security. In fact, there is so much literature in every conceivable media about attack details, one might almost conclude that attack details make up the sum total of all of cyber security. They don't, by a very wide margin.

There are a couple of classes of cyber security professionals for whom the specific mechanisms of each exploitation are of great value:

- Penetration testers
- Implementers of technologies such as vulnerability scanners and of those protections that must prevent specific attacks—for instance, a so-called "application firewall" or "web application firewall"
- Security researchers who are trying to push the edges of cyber security knowledge

You may notice in the list above that security architects are not among those who must delve into the details of each exploitation? As in other roles within cyber security, security architects must understand attack mechanisms, because knowledge about exploitation techniques provides indispensable information to choose appropriate defenses.

But, importantly, security architects are not required to understand the details of each individual exploitation. Herein lies an important difference between the goals of the roles listed above and the goals of the security architect. A security architect must be intimately familiar with the general mechanism of attack for each *class* of attacks against which that security architect's scope will be required to defend.

3.2 Security Architects Must . . .

Let's unpack this subtle difference a little bit more. A competent security architect will understand the computer science behind the mechanism through which an attacker exploits each particular *type* of vulnerability. "Type" or "class" means the general mechanism by which a vulnerability may be exploited. Buffer overflows are exploited by a set of particular manipulations. The specifics of any particular buffer overflow aren't all that useful.

Nevertheless, it is critical to understand that an attacker can bury within a legally encapsulated message a precise series of central processing unit (CPU) instructions that will aim, through the overflow condition, to place the flow of code execution under the attacker's control. Furthermore, it is critical that a security architect understand that there are mechanisms for encoding, and thus hiding or obscuring, such a set of instructions from potential protective measures. The precise sequence of instructions for any particular overflow are not really relevant for the purposes of building an appropriate defense—for the purposes of crafting appropriate security requirements to prevent this type of attack from succeeding.

The exact sequence of assembly language instructions required for any particular exploitation as tied to a particular memory location or misuse in a particular program are not required in order to fix the error allowing the vulnerability or to prevent the vulnerability from being exercised. Or, in the language of Web attacks, the exact sequence of SQL commands and collection of characters required to exploit a particular database through a particular program input are rarely required of a security architect.

To understand SQL injections sufficiently, the security architect has to understand how SQL commands are entered into program input and then passed to a database where they will be executed. The defending architect must understand how difficult it is to try and search for every potential set of characters that might get interpreted as SQL, because of course, SQL is a Turing Complete language. Furthermore, that security architect must also understand that even with highly normalized data, the potential to prevent abnormal database responses in program code will be near impossible.

Typically, SQL injection is prevented through so-called "parameterization" of database inputs. That is, the application has the canonical form for each query it will make on the user's behalf programmed into it, or in its local configuration store. The application has no need for a user's specific SQL commands, while at the same disallowing any set of characters that looks like SQL. Instead, the application only uses the legal and allowed SQL queries that have been programmed into it. Whatever the defensive strategy employed against SQL injection, the details of a particular SQL injection are actually not particularly useful.

In my experience, in order to become familiar enough with attack types, most practitioners will have had to somehow become comfortable with the exact details of one or more examples of each type of exploitation. Working through a source work like one of the *Hacking Exposed** series will be invaluable. When I got hired at my second security job, I felt that I really didn't have a good understanding of the prevalent attack mechanisms at that time. So, on the way to and from work, I read the first edition of *Hacking Exposed*. The book provided a good grounding for what I was being asked to do at that time—a grounding into the attack patterns of the day.[†]

Slightly later, as Cisco® Infosec's first application security architect, I was given the assignment to generate Infosec's first set of secure coding guidelines in Perl and C/C++. I didn't write the C/C++ guides and I worked from earlier, existing Perl guides that had been generated outside of Infosec.[‡] Still, I got to "prove," that is, code and then test, each example of coding error in order to make sure that every example within the guidance was, in fact, correct.[§]

Having previously read *Hacking Exposed*[¶] cover to cover and then being given the time to test many examples of attacks gave me a basic understanding of precisely what mistakes allow exploitation and just how those vulnerabilities can be exercised. This training has proved invaluable and has allowed me to build my software security career on a firm grounding. (As I've noted previously, I'd had years of intense programming and design experience upon which to draw. Among my prior experiences had been identifying network attacks from network captures and cleaning up worms and viruses manually.)

Today, there are many books similar, competing, and complimentary to the *Hacking Exposed* series. I'd guess that reading any of the available hacking books—that is, those focused on attack types or penetration testing techniques—will offer similar instruction.

3.3 Understanding Categories of Attacks

What was remaining in my education was to up-level specific attack details into "classes" of attacks. Nobody told me that I would have to make this generalization. But, I wasn't effective without understanding that a buffer overflow is not the same as allowing an attacker to run a system call, which is not the same as an SQL injection, though all of these usually are exercised via injection of attacker controlled data and may, then, all be members of a class of attacks that are often known as "injection attacks," or attacks involving "tainted data"—data that has not yet been cleaned and validated programmatically, after reception (from whatever source). In other words, there are classes and super classes of attack types.

---

[*] McClure, 1999.

[†] That is, about 20 years ago.

[‡] Someone in engineering had provided a set of Perl secure coding guidance from which I worked. At that time, I was new to the Perl language.

[§] I also presented the guidelines numerous times for a few years.

[¶] I have no financial stake in the *Hacking Exposed* series of books. To sell copies of these is not my point. At the time, the first edition was revolutionary, as at that time no one had previously collected examples and explanations of most of the active attack types.

For some attacks, there are preconditions without which that particular class of attacks may be irrelevant. For instance, SQL injection cannot take place except in the presence of an SQL language processor somewhere in the chain of data flow. Furthermore, the attacker must have a mechanism and vector through which to get attacker-controlled data to that SQL processor.

Likewise, if memory is not being programmatically handled, buffer overflows are much less likely. The C languages allow direct manipulation of program memory. Overflows are always a concern. The Java language hides these details from applications (except for native calls), thus, overflows are not much of a concern when working within a well-behaved and fully patched Java runtime.

Both of the above examples are injections, to be sure. Exercise of vulnerable conditions will almost always involve tainted input data (i.e., attacker-controlled data passed through to the vulnerable condition). By understanding the *class* of attack as an architectural pattern rather than as a specific attack, one can actually quite quickly build a set of relevant attacks and discount others for any particular system under analysis. This is the art of security architecture. The technique being employed is one of the key analyses that make up threat modeling.

My book *Securing Systems* was my attempt to explain what threat modeling is and how one goes about doing it. Threat modeling is the main analysis technique by which attack types are considered against digital systems (though one can threat model nearly any system, architecture, set of processes, situation, or organization). Security architects, whether they think about threat modeling formally or not, whether they think in terms of architecture or not, must identify the set of attacks that have potential for harm in order to build an appropriate collection of defenses—that is, threat model.

Understanding the "architectural" aspects of the relevant attacks for any particular system or set of systems is the bridge between the required knowledge of who might attack, how prevalent those attacks may be within the relevant period under analysis, and what those attackers might be hoping to gain through the attacks. In other words, from the knowledge of the attack, one then can walk back through a tree or mind map to identify likely threat agents, threat agent activity level, the likely attacker's technical sophistication, attacker goals, and any other information that may come in handy (please see my discussion of threat agents in *Securing Systems,* Chapter 2, and continued in this work, Chapter 1, The Context of Security Architecture).

An understanding of each class of attack's technical mechanisms is critical in order to understand what I call "system objective." The system objective will be the technical steppingstone or pivot through which the attacker's ultimate goals are achieved. In the Chapter 5, Learning the Trade, there's more detail about methods for acquiring sufficient attack knowledge.

Except for security researchers whose goal is to prove a particular attack can be successful, attackers generally are after something tangible, such as stealing passwords, gaining access to accounts, exfiltrating information, using a computer for further attacks, sending spam, storing illegal digital content, and the like.

In order to take over a machine so that it can be used without the knowledge of its ordinary user or owner (for instance, as part of a botnet), an attacker will have to piece together one or more steppingstones, system objectives, such that the attacker will gain sufficient privileges on the host and its operating system in order to install command and control software that will persist across restarts (reboots). The goals are the attacker's "intentions" to be gained through prosecution of technical "mechanisms." (Please see Chapter 5: Learning the Trade, for a deeper explanation of these. Readers may also wish to play with MITRE's ATT&CK Navigator™ [referenced in Chapter 5], which visualizes many well-known attack trees.)

For instance, a vulnerability that allows "code of attacker's choosing" isn't actually sufficient until that exploitation can be coupled with an escalation of privileges in order take control of an operating system (and thus, the host). (In a scenario in which the attacker is starting at a high level of privilege, escalation is not needed.) In a situation in which the victim is not running at sufficient privileges to install high-privilege software, an attacker must not only execute code, but also find a way to increase privileges such that the attacker's command-and-control software can be installed and run. In this trivial example, an attacker might need to exploit as many as three or four system objectives in order to successfully gain persistent control of the machine:

- Find a way to deliver the attack code payload
- Get the payload to run on the victim's machine
- From the "code of the attacker's choosing" payload, exploit a second vulnerability that increases privilege level above that of the operating system's current user
- Establish communications with the attacker
- Potentially download additional code for permanence across restarts

3.4 Attack Knowledge for Defense

Understanding system objectives and chains of system objectives executed sequentially is key to building a robust set of defenses. Defenses are generally against one or more classes of attacks. There is no one to one (1:1) mapping of defense to attack (the relationship should be characterized as many-to-many, usually notated as "M:N"). All potential cases exist: single defense against single attack, single defense against several attacks, two or more defenses against a single attack, and many to many. Understanding and then preventing system objectives is the art of cyber security defense. (Of course, cyber security defense exists throughout the protect, detect, and react cycle. We are focusing solely on security architecture for identifying and designing defenses, whether these be security infrastructure or for particular systems.)

Obviously, if there is no vulnerability to be exploited, that is the cleanest, most intuitive defense. Without a weakness to exploit, there is no steppingstone to attacker goals. However, it must be remembered that not all failures are technical. Social engineering requires no technical weakness; a human is "engineered," tricked into allowing the attacker to achieve the attacker's goals. Because a person's trust can be abused, humans are the vulnerability that, sadly, "cannot be patched."

Much has been written about the prevention of vulnerability, including my own offering in *Core Software Security*; preventing weaknesses when developing software comprises the subject of Chapter 9: SDL in the Real World. Vulnerability prevention must be a key aspect of software security, and thus, of those security architects concerned with software security.

Of course, one aspect of architecture is planning for the unforeseen. Because software almost always contains undiscovered errors, one must plan for the "unknown, unknown." It is also useful to consider that any particular part of a defense will fail, because software errors sometimes cause failure even in security software.

Still, it remains that software has vulnerabilities, and will continue to have for the foreseeable future. The plain truth of it is, human endeavor is filled with errors, and software creation and implementation are a human endeavor. Whether the vulnerabilities are caused through poor design choices or through implementation, there will be errors even after the most robust secure development lifecycle (SDL, or secure software development life cycle, S-SDLC), with equally rigorous validation. "To err is human . . . ," as Alexander Pope so famously wrote.[*]

A security architect must assume that at least one vulnerability of the sort that commonly occur in any particular language, execution environment, and operating system will escape past testing. Each class of vulnerabilities can be exploited with one or more known sets of exploit techniques.

Although new attack techniques do arise and will have to be understood and then defended, variations on a known technique usually don't require new defense techniques. By understanding exploitation techniques and their system objectives, a defense can be built to stop or at least delay exploitation of potential weakness types that typically appear in particular systems and collections/integrations of systems (as in an enterprise's collection of systems). The mental trick is to assume that typical weaknesses known to have appeared in the past will appear in the future. That is, all software has bugs.

As I wrote above, each attack type and its system objective are the bridge between attack and defense. Without knowledge about attack types for particular deployments of systems, one is basically tilting at windmills or trying to defend against everything.

As of the writing of this book, there are attackers who are as sophisticated and dedicated as any collection of computer scientists that exist. Some of these attackers also have access to significant computer resources. Please consider those nation-states who have the computer capacity to build nuclear weapons (supercomputers). Consider a nuclear-capable state that also executes computer attacks against their foes. Most well-funded commercial organizations are not going to have the computer security resources to match such attackers, much less organizations with far less resources at their disposal.

If an organization needs to defend against well-funded nation-state attackers, a different strategy will have to be employed; the usual collection of computer defenses won't be sufficient (although that doesn't mean these can be skipped!). Alongside a strong cyber defensive position, such an organization must also monitor systems and defenses carefully, searching for the needle in the haystack, for the one in a million signal that indicates that a sophisticated attack is under way.

Should any sign appear from within monitored traffic, events, and alerts, the organization's incident response team will need to react rapidly and decisively. That is, the organization cannot rely solely on its "protect" dimension, but in addition, must be skilled at "detect" and then ready to "react" immediately.

Incident monitoring and response typically exists within a different security domain than security architecture (though there are no hard and fast rules; your organization may differ). Still, identifying that sufficient monitoring technology and process are in place is often one of the defenses that security architects may require; detect and react capabilities are especially critical against attackers whose technology and resources may exceed, or even far exceed, those of the organization being defended.

---

[*] Johnson, 1836.

Understanding the types of attacks that nation-states may employ, from common to one-of-a-kind, allows the security architect to consider all the defenses that may be required, from the usual, such as firewalls, network zones, access controls, input validation, etc., on to exfiltration and anomalous behavior monitoring, to even requiring a crack incidence response function.

If one knows that at least one nation's cyber attackers regularly intercept common carrier shipments of routing equipment to replace the vendor's BIOS or firmware code with the attacker's intelligence gathering code (a real example!), then one must prepare for equipment to arrive to customers already in the control of that nation's intelligence organization. Because that particular nation's intelligence agency is likely to have sufficient resources to hide its compromise of systems in transit, then the vendor being compromised could institute a validity check of router firmware at the final destination. Such an action might be one of the only methods available that could uncover such a clever compromise. In reading media reports of this particular compromise, no such BIOS validity check was put into place.[*]

The vendors being compromised apparently had no idea their shipments to foreign powers were delivered as tools of one nation's intelligence agency. The usual panoply of digital security methods and tools would have been near useless in the foregoing example. That's because the routers in question would not reveal the streams of data going to the intelligence. The spy agency activities were hidden, not found within the logs of data on the router.

One might take a guess that traffic from routers existing outside a compromised organization or government's firewall would be completely invisible. However, one might see odd, unexpected streams to unknown destinations from routers existing within the firewall perimeter. However, a clever intelligence agency is likely to understand the details of TCP/IP routing such that the destination can be hidden until the compromised traffic gets outside any firewall, intrusion or extrusion sensors, or other equipment. Plus, with terabytes or even petabytes of data going in all different directions, traffic monitors must be very careful about what is being actively watched. Mostly, security operations watch what's coming in plus selective outbound traffic. The nation-state might easily hide its intelligence gathering in plain sight. Typical methods aren't going to work without fairly specific understanding of what might take place—that is, attack methods.

I hope that the foregoing example, taken from the real world, helps to explain how an appropriate defense requires knowledge of the threat agent as well as the attack kill chain. An attacker with a completely unique and unexpected methodology has a big advantage, as we have seen in the nation-state intelligence gathering example given above. Nobody knew. So, nobody could defend appropriately.

3.5 Example: Heartbleed Analysis

Each part of the attack equation must be understood in order to build effective and appropriate defenses. Let's take apart the famous "Heartbleed" vulnerability from 2014. By using Heartbleed as an example, I want to show more precisely the sort of human and technical information that is required to structure (i.e., architect) and design systems for security. Along

---

[*] Eadicicco, 2014.

the way, I hope to show what sorts of knowledge are unnecessary, as well. With the following explanation, I hope that you, the reader, can get a better feel for the types of analyses that security architects provide, no matter to what the discipline is applied.

When confronted with a new attack, what does the security architect need to know?

The Heartbleed "bug" was announced April 7, 2014. Co-discovered by Neel Mehta of Google® and engineers at Codenomicon®, after announcement, there was a media frenzy, and affected websites' security and maintenance teams went into high gear in order to respond to headlines such as, "'Heartbleed' bug undoes Web encryption, reveals Yahoo passwords."* There was a great deal of hyperbole; there was an industry sense that Heartbleed was an Internet crisis that demanded response—immediate response. A few choice headlines and quotes follow:

"Scramble to fix huge 'heartbleed' security bug" —BBC News Technology, April 8, 2014

"The Heartbleed Hit List: The Passwords You Need to Change Right Now" —Mashable, April 8, 2014[†]

"Security researchers have uncovered a fatal flaw in a key safety feature for surfing the Web," —CNN.com, CNN.com, April 11, 2014: 5:46 PM ET [‡]

Note the word "fatal" in the last quote, implying that Internet cryptography had failed, perhaps completely.

"Heartbleed" (a term coined by Codenomicon to describe the issue) was an implementation error introduced into the OpenSSL set of cryptography software that is widely used by websites and within commercial and open source software and systems. One of its most useful functions [though the set of libraries and programs offers many cryptographic functions] is a reasonably dependable implementa-

> As of this writing, named, often even branded, vulnerabilities are a regular occurrence; security folk perhaps are inured to the practice. Heartbleed was the first vulnerability to be branded and essentially marketed, given a website and press releases.

tion of Transport Layer Security (TLS). Indeed, OpenSSL has at times been considered "the" reference implementation of TLS (although it has its quirks, as do other TLS implementations).

When a browser (client) opens a connection to a website (server), or really, any type of client-to-server TCP/IP connection, one or the other side can request that the communications proceed encrypted. If the encryption request is accepted, a TLS connection is instantiated.

There are several methods for encrypting communications, though by far the most common is TLS, which is relatively transparent to either party. The "HTTPS" URI designator in a browser's site URL makes a request to instantiate TLS protection. If a website provides TLS for a particular page (URL), then the TLS will start for the connection.

The connection is between exactly two parties; there are no multi-party TLS connections. The two parties do not have to have a true client/server relationship; they may exchange data equally once a connection has been created. Still, the terms *client* and *server* derive from the fact that in TCP/IP (and thus, TLS, which rides on top of TCP/IP [Actually, TLS is encapsulated

---

[*] Shankland, 2014.

[†] http://mashable.com/2014/04/09/heartbleed-bug-websites-affected/#cA_kSeXnGkqb

[‡] Jose Pagliery, "Heartbleed bug: What you need to know," http://money.cnn.com/2014/04/09/technology/security/heartbleed-bug/

within TCP messages, which are encapsulated within IP messages.]) one party (client) must make the first request to the other party (server or listener) to open the connection. HTTP, having a request/response semantic, always implies a client/server relationship.

"Transparent" in this context implies that an application requiring encryption (and authentication, as well) doesn't need to understand and then direct the details of setting up and maintaining the encrypted tunnel over the life of the communications; once instantiated, programming proceeds like other TCP/IP connection mechanisms (often referred to as a "socket"). A few programmatic calls will generally suffice. Furthermore, today's operating systems and cryptographic implementation packages take care of most of the details for the calling program without the caller needing to program those details (data and function "hiding").

Using a package such as OpenSSL allows programmers to concentrate on application functionality rather than being experts in TLS and cryptography in general. OpenSSL and equivalent packages take care of most of the specifics.

Once opened, TLS provides for a "keepalive heartbeat" message to be sent at periodic intervals to the other side of the connection, which must respond, thus allowing each side of the connection to verify that the connection is still functioning (still "alive").

> "HeartbeatRequest messages SHOULD only be sent after an idle period that is at least multiple round-trip times long. This idle period SHOULD be configurable up to a period of multiple minutes and down to a period of one second. A default value for the idle period SHOULD be configurable, but it SHOULD also be tunable on a per-peer basis."[*]

"Sending HeartbeatRequest messages allows the sender to make sure that it can reach the peer and the peer is alive."[*]

A computer programmer making use of ("calling," including the OpenSSL functionality within a piece of software) OpenSSL would specify that heartbeats take place or not and may configure the periodicity (though there is a default period [see inset]). But the calling program does not issue heartbeat messages. These are taken care of down within the bowels of OpenSSL.

Heartbeat messages do not occur rapidly; they are small and relatively infrequent, in "computer network" time. Commonly, a keep alive may be sent every several seconds (see inset) (1–60 seconds is typical). We shall use this common expectation about periodicity to our advantage later in the analysis.

> For readers who are not fairly familiar with computer time periods, a second is an eon to a computer—that is, quite a long time. A second is longer than most computer-to-computer exchanges of messages take.

Given the preceding TLS heartbeat facts, let's now proceed to understand what Heartbleed is, assess its risk, and then try to figure what an astute security architect might do in defense.

The most obvious defense will be to fix the error; these usually come as patches, upgraded software, a new revision of OpenSSL that then must be rolled into production services. [Often updating software in production can be difficult, a "non-trivial" task.] In practice, it often takes some length of time before there is a patch available. However, in this case, the Heartbleed announcement was coordinated with an upgrade (though the coders didn't get it completely "right," introducing a new security issue into the first patch, which then later necessitated a second patch before Heartbleed had been fixed).

---

[*] Seggelmann & Williams, 2012.

But these types of production services are notoriously difficult to perturb; it may take hours, days, weeks, even months to get the new software installed and running. Hence there may be a significant period of exposure. What are the correct steps to take, if any? Any decent security practitioner is going to ask her, him, or themself that question. Answering those questions involves, as I wrote above, understanding the attack, what it can impact, how serious the impact will be, and what may be done to prevent that impact. That is the art of security architecture, in my experience.

Before we proceed with the analysis, I want to give you an example of how security architect responded in the heat of the moment (not me). As we analyze, from time to time, consider his actions in order to place the analysis into context. After the analysis, we'll examine his actions in light of the analysis. See what you think. Did he "do the right thing"? Or was his a major goof up? Or somewhere in between?

Imagine a rather large organization with a significant web presence. That set of web functions takes sensitive data from its customers transmitted over the Internet; the organization has millions of customers. During the "high" season for that organization's function, the personal data from tens of millions of customers is regularly, sometimes repeatedly, exchanged over the Internet. Consider the Internet absolutely untrustworthy and dangerous (which it is).

> I can reveal neither the identity of the architect nor that of the organization. I ask for you the reader to trust me that this happened, that the architect related his response as I've given it, here. Even if the story were fictional, which it is not so far as I know, readers may still consider this example as hypothetically worthy of reflection.

The security architect with web responsibility for our example organization responded to Heartbleed, as he told me, within "10 minutes" of deliberation. He turned off TLS until he had a trustworthy, non-vulnerable version installed (see inset).

Let us proceed.

3.5.1 Heartbleed Technical Analysis

The Heartbleed error was an implementation error. This is perhaps the first important data point for analysis. If the error had been in the TLS protocol (and in fact, there had been a serious protocol error announced about six weeks before Heartbleed's announcement), then most if not all TLS implementations would be vulnerable.

Indeed, protocol errors tend to take a lot longer to fix. Why? Because the standards body responsible for the protocol has to meet and come to agreement about the error and its fix. They then have to draft a new specification, which then is approved. Then, protocol implementers will have to incorporate the new specification into their implementation. All in all, protocol changes can be a rather lengthy process (that is, months at best; often years).

Contrast the foregoing with an implementation error: One can figure out what's wrong with the code, rewrite the error to fix it, test it, and then release the fix. The error will most likely be confined to a single implementation, or at worst a subset of the implementations. (This can happen when there has been a broad misunderstanding by implementers of the official specification, or in cases in which something that hasn't yet been specified but is widely implemented is discovered to be vulnerable to exploitation for unintentional behavior [see inset on next page].)

> At a time in my career when I had been writing TCP/IP code, there was an unspecified part of the TCP protocol that many implementations coded in a unique and local manner. That lack of specification turned out to be an exploitable denial of service (DOS).

That is, Heartbleed was confined entirely to OpenSSL, and indeed particular versions, not every release that was in the field.

So what was it, really? Heartbleed was a buffer over read. An attacker can read whatever memory happens to lie just above the buffer allocated by OpenSSL for a TLS Heartbeat response packet.

"The problem here is that the OpenSSL heartbeat response code does not check to make sure that the payload length field in the heartbeat request message matches the actual length of the payload."[*]

This class of attacks can be put into the larger structural bucket, Elevation of Privileges. The attacker doesn't have permission to read memory beyond certain limits. In this case, an attacker should have no ability to see any memory beyond that allocated for minimal 19-byte TLS Heartbeat response. But, because of a failure to check the size of the request, the attacker was given the capability to read memory with addresses above the end of the limit given in the heartbeat specification.

In case the reader does not have a clear picture about these allocations and deallocations, let me digress a little. (Those readers who are familiar with program memory can skip to the next paragraph.) In OpenSSL, as in most dynamic programs, when building a particular structure, say a TLS heartbeat response, the first thing that the program does when it receives a valid TLS Heartbeat is to allocate just enough memory for the response packet. Then, the appropriate and valid data items are placed in the correct positions within the packet. It is then passed to a function that will send the packet over the network connection. Once given to that function (or the function completes, depending upon whether the function copies the packet or not), the packet—that is, the memory used to construct the packet—may be deallocated. In programming parlance, the memory is "freed"—returned to the memory pool from which it was allocated. That memory pool, for most operating systems and loadable program types, will be the running program's "heap."

The heap is just an area of readable and writable memory that can be allocated and deallocated in chunks of whatever size may be required. When a program is loaded, the operating system gives the program a heap. For some executable types, the heap is given by the executable; in other types, a virtual heap address space is given, though the actual memory may be much smaller. The heap can then grow to its maximum. The starting heap size and its maximum are operating system, language, runtime environment defined.

In the case of a TLS Heartbeat Reply, the size is expected to have a payload of at least 19 bytes. "The total length of a HeartbeatMessage MUST NOT exceed 2^14 or max_fragment_length when negotiated as defined in [RFC6066]."[†]

The maximum size of a TLS heartbeat is given in binary in the specification. In decimal, it is 16381. What should happen when the response packet is allocated for OpenSSL to allocate 3 bytes for the packet header plus whatever size is requested by the sender of the Heartbeat, so long as that size is less than or equal to 16381.

---

[*] Chandra, 2014.
[†] RFC 6520, 2012.

OpenSSL Heartbleed allowed an attacker to specify a size of up to 16 thousand (K) bytes (the size of the maximum packet, sent in a 2-byte integer [A signed, 2-byte integer is 32767, while unsigned maximum would be 65535. But only a 16383 maximum is allowed—that is, 2^{14}.]). In the OpenSSL code, OpenSSL aborted the process into which it is linked with an error if it received a Heartbeat with a request that was greater than 16383.

There existed a significant error in the code after the packet was allocated. Vulnerable OpenSSL filled in only the first 16 bytes of the packet—not even 'max_fragment_length', as specified in RFS 6520, quoted above. Rather, the size of the return is hardcoded as 16 bytes (18 total including the header). So, attackers can retrieve over 16 thousand bytes from within the program heap that had not been overwritten by the heartbeat response routine before being returned.

Apparently, even some of the published analyses of the error were incorrect. Consider the following statement:

"Then, OpenSSL will uncomplainingly copy 65535 bytes from your request packet, even though you didn't send across that many bytes:"*

You'll note the larger number given by Paul Dicklin in the quote, 65535. 65535 is the value of a 2-byte unsigned integer. While the length field is 2 bytes, the conclusion isn't true, because OpenSSL would abort the whole process when confronted with a request over 16383! [The offending OpenSSL code calls the C programming language macro "OPENSSL_assert," which covers the OpenSSLDie() function, which exits to the operative system.]

The point of the analysis above is that whatever data happened to occupy the memory above the 16 bytes filled in by OpenSSL would be returned to the attacker unchanged up to the maximum size allowed, or whatever value was sent with the Heartbeat request. "Unchanged memory" in the context of a Heartbleed response means that the response contains whatever bits and pieces of data that chunk of memory happened to contain from the previous purpose for which it had been used; for instance, it might contain part of a decrypted message stream or a decryption key which then would be returned to the attacker within the overly extended heartbeat response packet.

Despite some of the media declarations during the crisis, the Heartbleed error only affected the confidentiality of data, and only data that was in memory at the moment when the exploit was prosecuted. (We shall examine this in greater detail below.)

There was no possibility for the attacker to change data in memory. Nor was there any capability for the attacker to inject data or computer instructions via the Heartbleed mechanism. This last—an ability to inject code into a running program—is usually the most serious type of error. In the hands of a sophisticated attacker, allowing that attacker "code of the attacker's choosing" often implies a complete compromise, if not in the first code injection, then certainly as the attack proceeds step by step. Importantly, no such capability was given to attackers with Heartbleed.

Now, of course, if usernames and passwords happened to get returned, an attacker could then simply log into an account and gain access to whatever the password protected. Depending upon what goodies might have been "heartbled," the attacker's next step might be quite significant. This level of privilege escalation is not a foregone conclusion in this case.

---

* Ducklin, 2014.

In other words, expressing this in terms of the classic "CIA" (confidentiality, integrity, availability), Heartbleed directly affected confidentiality only. And, as we shall see, there were limits to the exposure, even at that.

In my blog post written during the crisis, "Heartbleed Exposure, What Is It Really?," I wrote:

". . . getting a random bit is different than requesting an arbitrary memory location at the discretion of the attacker. And that is a very important statement to hold in mind as we respond to this very serious situation."[*]

Indeed, the discoverer of HeartBleed, Neel Mehta, tweeted, "Heap allocation patterns make private key exposure unlikely."[†]

Whether or not Neel Mehta was indeed correct is a subject of some debate at this point. Still, early on, it seemed to Neel that while this bug was serious, it probably wouldn't bring down the Internet.

Once security researchers began to run tests, there were claims of finding sensitive items such as TLS session keys or user passwords. Other test runs were not so successful. Unfortunately, as of this writing, most of those test reports seem to have been removed from the Internet; I could no longer find their references as I prepared this book. Hopefully, through the below analysis, it will become clear why results varied considerably.

Why would Neel Mehta say what he said?

In order to understand, we have to understand how memory is organized in running programs, and more particularly in programs that use OpenSSL. It turns out that there's more than one answer to that question. A key concept to hold is that Heartbleed is a fishing expedition, not a precision read.

For the operating systems that are relevant to this discussion, a typical executable program has a memory area allocated to it called "the heap," as previously described above. As new chunks of memory are required, heap memory is allocated for each use, and then, if the application is reasonably well behaved, when whatever actions have been completed with that bit of memory, the program (the code) deallocates, frees the memory for future reuse. [At least, the memory should be released. "Use after free" is a programming error and can result in a vulnerability, as well.] As the program runs, over time, areas in the heap are used and then returned.

Since the size of each allocation varies tremendously from a couple of bytes to big chunks of memory sized up to the limit of the heap, the same memory is written into, overwritten, chunked up, put back together into a larger chunk, broken into smaller pieces, and so forth.

The longer a program runs (this is a function of time), the more bits and pieces of data will collect in the heap and then become fragmented over the length of the run. As I wrote in my April 17, 2014, blog post,[‡] "it's a jumble sale." Approximately 16 thousand bytes was the largest chunk a Heartbleed would return. The contents of that chunk will be a mishmash of all the data uses that just happened to be allocated from that particular space above (at progressively higher memory addresses) the running length of the program. The first 16 bytes would have

---

[*] Schoenfield 2017, April 17
[†] Mehta, 2014, April 8
[‡] http://brookschoenfield.com/?p=213

been "padded"—that is, filled in by OpenSSL when the Heartbeat Reply was constructed. The number of bytes read without permission is as many as $16383 - 16 = 16367$.

Data in the heap is not completely random. Running programs are not random executions, reads, and writes of memory. In fact, the whole point of coding is predictable behavior. So, patterns in the heap do emerge. But these patterns are highly dependent upon a particular operating system, a particular use of OpenSSL, a particular allocation of memory to the program, and so forth. Without careful and consistent observation over a fairly extensive running time, it would be fairly difficult to get much precision about what data might be at any particular memory address at any particular moment. Hence, requesting memory above a predictable location into the unpredictable area (that is, the area above the actual allocation for the Heartbeat response) is not a precision exploit. One retrieves what one retrieves.

Particularly, in the case of OpenSSL, where the attacker is interested in a particular stream of decrypted traffic, or, even better, a session's encryption key, there's no way to ensure that the data retrieved via Heartbleed will pertain to the target TLS session. The data returned could be anything, including bits and pieces from other parts of the program that has included the OpenSSL library. (See inset)

Of course, if an attacker can execute thousands, tens of thousands, millions of Heartbleeds, the attacker is quite likely to retrieve a pretty big sample of the program's heap, if not nearly the whole of the heap. In possession of just about all the data garbage left within freed portions of the heap, the attacker would have quite a large part of that program's running data.

> In the case of routers and other network equipment, almost all the functioning of the "program"—that is, the router—will be the traffic. But in the case of some more business or other non-traffic–related functionality, much memory will contain the business data rather than network exchanges. That could be a boon to the attacker, as other interesting items might be retrieved—say, database credentials, addresses of whatever systems to which the target happens to connect, etc. Or, returned data may consist of a mess of unrelated calculations.

A common use of OpenSSL on the Internet has the library conducting multiple sessions at the same time: perhaps hundreds, conceivably thousands. In my reading of the OpenSSL specification, there is no tie between a heap in a session: all sessions use the same heap unless the calling program, the program using OpenSSL, configures an option to allocate a separate heap per session. I have found only one potential example of this architecture. In general, multiple sessions are handled on the program's single, combined heap. One heap.

The exception to my statement about one heap is NGNX,* an open source, multi-threaded, event-driven web server. It's widely used to manage large numbers of concurrent web requests.

NGNX has a configurable capability to allocate pools of memory to each thread. When OpenSSL is used with NGNX and pools of memory, each connection gets its own "heap," or memory area, from which to allocate.† A Heartbleed error in the context of individual connection memory implies that the Heartbeat response will reveal only data related to that connection, as opposed to data from any connection and across multiple connections, which is what happens when there is only one heap in use across connections. As I've written, many uses of OpenSSL use a single heap across all sessions. (See inset on next page.)

---

* https://nginx.org/en/
† Please also see https://www.nginx.com/blog/nginx-and-the-heartbleed-vulnerability/

> There is also an OpenSSL configuration to allocate a pool of memory specifically for OPenSSL's private use during initialization. In that case, a Heartbleed response would return solely OpenSSL data.

The above implies that for most OpenSSL use cases, any particular over read (exercise of the Heartbleed error) is going to get data from any of the sessions that have existed since the program started and the heap was initialized at program startup, with the caveat that a previous session's data has not yet been overwritten by a subsequent usage. As I explained, above, the data from each session is held in the common pool: the heap.

In order to be useful to the attacker, the data might need to be carefully sorted into sessions (if enough session information is retrieved upon which to sort). Even more sophisticated parsing, winnowing, and analysis [parsing, sorting, winnowing, analyzing data is sometimes called "munging."] are very likely to be required in order to find useful patterns and to establish some useful level of coherency from any large collection of data via Heartbleed (see inset). It's a fishing expedition without a fish-finding device or a seasoned fishing guide.

Just like fishing: sometimes one finds and lures the fish, other times, not so lucky. [Astute readers might guess that I do sometimes fish.]

"'We were able to scrape a Yahoo username & password via the Heartbleed bug,' tweeted Ronald Prins of security firm Fox-IT, showing a censored

> I don't intend to imply that deriving coherency is impossible. It most certainly is possible. But an attacker would have to collect sufficient data for the patterns to emerge, for an analysis to be successful. Analyzing random bits of memory data tends to be a fairly complex and non-trivial problem in computer science.

example. Added developer Scott Galloway, 'Ok, ran my heartbleed script for 5 minutes, now have a list of 200 usernames and passwords for yahoo mail.'"*

So, however Yahoo had set up its TLS implementation using OpenSSL, it was apparently fairly easy to get useful data. Or, perhaps Ronald Prins from Fox-IT just got lucky. (See quote, above.)

OpenSSL has a number of buffer configuration settings beyond the simplistic analysis that I've given up to this point. A program can configure OpenSSL to build a private set of buffers. These would be drawn from the heap at initialization. The reserved buffers would then be used on a Last In First Out (LIFO) basis, thus bypassing the program's heap allocation and deallocation routines.

When OpenSSL uses its own pool of buffers, a Heartbleed is more likely to grab data relevant to TLS connections. This situation is more advantageous to an attacker interested in compromising TLS/SSL connections. Please see Ted Unangst's explanation for a more thorough analysis of private buffer pools.†

It should be noted that if a Heartbleed over read occurs on the highest addressed private buffer in the OpenSSL pool, the extra data will most likely get returned from the active heap, just as I've already explained.

Once again, NGINX can make use of alternate memory schemes. The wise defender would be careful to fully understand exactly which memory configuration options are in use before deciding what, if any, mitigations one might employ against an issue like Heartbleed.

---

* Shankland, 2014.
† http://www.tedunangst.com/flak/post/analysis-of-openssl-freelist-reuse

As I've written before, without knowing the details of operating system and runtime environment—in this case, the details of heap management and perhaps process or thread memory assignment—there is no way to accurately assess the risk of the issue.

Another key piece of information will be what data is being transmitted over the encrypted sessions. For instance, if after the TLS session is instantiated, a user name and password are sent over the TLS encrypted tunnel, then it is possible that the decrypted password will be sitting somewhere on the heap, which *might* then end up among the bytes not overwritten (the first 16) in a Heartbeat reply.

If there is no authentication or if authentication is provided by X.509 certificates, there will be no password. The certificates, or parts of them, might get returned. Even the encryption/decryption keys (session keys) are in memory somewhere. The session keys aren't usually in the pool of memory available for allocation, as they are in use for the duration of an active session, and thus, marked "in use"—that is, unavailable to be used for an allocation.

It should be noted that applications sometimes have bugs in the way that they allocate and then deallocate memory. A specific type of memory issue is a "use after free" bug. Plus, it is not unknown for a language's memory handling routines to have bugs as well. It is possible that a buggy application or language library, or operating system, might return memory marked "in use." No permutation of a memory bug is impossible.

Remember that the SSL heartbeat requests a particular size of return. Thus, the extra bytes returned are still returned from blocks marked "available" and should not return memory chunks marked "in use." The Heartbleed error did not allow reading of unavailable memory, only facilitating a read of memory that had been previously freed or never used. For a properly running program without a memory allocation/deallocation bug (see inset), only available memory could be retrieved via the Heartbleed error.

Once the session is ended, the keys will be released back to the heap's available pool. But since keys are not reused, but are generated anew for each session, the old, disused keys are not valid and should be of little attacker value. (This is perhaps why Neel Mehta thought that session keys were unlikely to get revealed.)

3.6 Analyze to Defend

"You have to get inside the attacker's head. What is the attacker going to get out of it?"[*]

As we begin to consider defenses, I'll point out something that is perhaps obvious: Any TLS Heartbeat request that requests an out-of-specification value greater than 16,383 bytes is not only outside the specification (quoted above) but is clearly invalid. In fact, such a request is a dead giveaway of something amiss.

We also know that values greater than 16,383 will cause OpenSSL to exit (kill the running program) with an error. So, requesting an illegal value won't cause a Heartbleed.

Requesting 16,381 bytes is legal. Vulnerable OpenSSL only fills in the first 16 bytes. This is a perfectly legal request that must pass any specification validity check. So, checking size isn't going to demonstrate a Heartbleed attack.

---

[*] Grobman, 2016.

In order to identify encrypted Heartbleed attempts, the TLS would have to be terminated and then passed along to the recipient program by the security software (intrusion prevention or detection software or device).

But there is another odd semantic that might be a giveaway for detection: TLS Heartbeats come at a fairly slow rate, in computer terms. A heartbeat each minute is fairly typical.

The simplest defensive response to prevent Heartbleed is to turn off TLS Heartbeat support. That might cause some of a website's longer running connections to have to be re-instantiated, which users might find somewhat annoying. Still, data would remain encrypted and thus protected. No Heartbleed may be exploited, as all TLS Heartbeat requests would be rejected.

And, indeed, many sites did exactly this; they turned off Heartbeats until the site's OpenSSL could be updated.

In situations in which deployment of OpenSSL configuration of the Heartbeat is under the control of those who deploy OpenSSL, it will be relatively straightforward to turn off TLS Heartbeat. Unfortunately, one typical TLS strategy is to deploy a separate TLS termination function, often on a piece of dedicated hardware such as a dedicated switch or plug-in to which TLS traffic is routed for TLS termination and then sent on to its destination decrypted. Another typical termination architecture will be in multifunction, often very large load balancer hardware.

When these architectural choices have been implemented, deployers may have little or no control over the configuration of OpenSSL, because OpenSSL may be packaged as part of the product. OpenSSL's configuration options may not be exposed to the hardware administrator. Perhaps many TLS configuration options, like Heartbeats, may not be exposed for customer use.

In fact, unless equipment owners have studied carefully the various software licenses that have been included, deployers or site owners may have no idea that OpenSSL is the TLS implementation within a product. In these cases, the Heartbeat may be turned on by default, or even be turned on exclusively, because it is quite common to use TLS Heartbeat to prevent inadvertent loss of idle connections over time.

In a case in which the state of the TLS Heartbeat function is not under the control of the deployer or system owner, as described above, turning off the Heartbeat function in response to Heartbleed may not be an option.

The only recourse may be to contact the manufacturer of the product about whether it uses OpenSSL, how OpenSSL is used, and whether the manufacturer is going to respond to Heartbleed, and how fast. That, unfortunately, is a pretty powerless situation.

It's not easy to change a large website's architecture; it certainly cannot be done quickly in response to a major security incident such as Heartbleed. The security team responsible for the website is then at the mercy of its product manufacturers. The only recourse is to hound the manufacturer for a solution.

". . . [T]he Internet layer does not guarantee that all packets will take the same route, and therefore there is no guarantee that they will arrive in the same sequence and time intervals as they were sent, or that they will arrive at all."[*]

If I were in such a situation (in my actual response to Heartbleed, I was not, although perhaps my IT security colleagues might have been), I might have been tempted to consider

---

[*] Doyle, 1998.

turning TLS off. Such a drastic decision would have to take into account the types of data that would be exposed to a hostile Internet and to Internet routes that cannot be guaranteed, who my customers are, the risk posture of my company/organization, etc.

Such decisions shouldn't be taken lightly, nor in the heat of the moment. It's always useful to remember that it takes attackers a little while to begin exploiting a brand-new issue, even when example exploitation code is freely available. That lag between announcement and malicious exploitation can be used to perform the kind of analysis that I've set out above.

One of the difficulties with identifying anomalous Heartbleed traffic patterns will be those connections that placed the TLS Heartbeat within the encrypted tunnel. As of this writing, there is no agreed-upon specification to proxy TLS traffic, say for security software that must examine the decrypted traffic before passing it on to its destination. In fact, a proxy is considered an insecure break of the basic principles of the TLS protocol.

If you have ever been trying to connect to a site that uses HTTPS, perhaps through a hotel or café network where you first respond to a landing page that requests agreement to conditions of use, you may have noticed your browser throwing up a warning that a site or certificate is invalid or the site may be insecure. That warning is a well-written TLS implementation's response to a mismatch between certificates from an expected site and the certificate that has been offered to your TLS client (for instance, your browser or mail client).

It is an error in TLS for the client to receive anything except a server certificate that matches the Internet protocol (IP) address of the server tied to that particular certificate. When the authentication certificate does not match in some way, or particular portions of the certificate attributes and form are invalid or don't apply to the server from which it is supposed to have come, a well-written TLS client will throw an error, as it must.

Perhaps you see the problem?

The TLS protocol is specifically written to prevent a man in the middle from inserting itself between a valid server and a valid client. Hence, there is no supported manner, or even an elegant hack, to proxy a TLS connection. Basically, the server-side TLS termination has to be legal, and in general, that's how security products that perform some function on TLS encrypted traffic work. For more information, please see Olaf Bonordon's work with IEEE's Industry Connections Group (ICSG) on TLS traffic inspection for security.[*]

My point from the preceding explanation is that if OpenSSL is configured to place the TLS Heartbeat within the encrypted tunnel, it will be very difficult to identify Heartbeats occurring in some improper fashion: too fast, requesting overrun buffers, at some unexpected frequency or rate, identifying returned buffers that have excess data. All those definitive signatures of Heartbleed exploitation will take place within the encrypted tunnel such that security software cannot decrypt the traffic. An intrusion detection system (IDS) that has not terminated the TLS traffic I order to decrypt it will have no ability to identify signs of malicious traffic.

If traffic is confined to those architectures for which TLS has been terminated by a security function, then that function will also have the ability to identify Heartbleed traffic patterns.

Obviously, in the first day or two after the announcement of Heartbleed, few if any security products had had time to build identification such as I've listed above into their products. Further, as has been explained, many deployment architectures, especially those in which the

---

[*] Bonardon, 2018.

IDS is given a "tap" of promiscuous traffic out of the line of routing (to the side of the actual traffic exchange), then that IDS will be next to useless to identify a Heartbleed attack.

Let's recap the main points of the preceding analysis:

- Heartbleed does not give an attacker the ability to execute code of the attacker's choosing.
- The data returned through exploitation is not precisely random, but it is not ordered, either.
- The data returned cannot be chosen by the attacker.
- Depending upon memory configuration, exposed data could be across many TLS connections or be tied exclusively to a single connection.
- In the case of data from many connections, an attacker must analyze the data in order to tie particular data to particular connection and may have to reorder data to make it useful.
- Data might be very near to random bits and pieces with no respect to protocol or message.
- The issue is tied directly to TLS Heartbeat function: when TLS Heartbeat is turned off, then no Heartbleed exploitation is possible.
- Except for very slow exploitation, the exploitation of Heartbleed tends to generate anomalous traffic patterns.
- Different memory architectures and different OpenSSL connection use patterns generate very different Heartbleed data returns.

In essence, an attacker either has to get lucky or possess significant details about a particular architecture and that architecture's use of OpenSSL in order to understand and analyze the data returned through a Heartbleed.

Revisiting the security architect story that introduced the analysis, do you believe his defense was the best defensive move possible (made after 10 minutes of deliberation)?

3.7 Turn Off TLS?

Was that security architect correct to remove TLS encryption protections for all of his customers' sensitive data as it crossed a hostile and dangerous Internet during his organization's busiest period? Or, was his choice a gross error? Do you think that 10 minutes is sufficient time to carefully analyze, as we have done, to understand reasonably well just what exploitation of Heartbleed might potentially impact?

Without knowing my own architecture, what can be exploited, the impacts to my organization, the control I have over the equipment and its configuration, I would be shooting in the dark. It took, if I recall correctly, about four to five hours to complete my initial investigation of Heartbleed in order to understand it well enough to make informed decisions. The practice of security architecture depends upon attack and defense analysis similar to the preceding Heartbleed example.

The discipline of security architecture involves bringing together knowledge about how threat agents go about the business of malicious attacks and for what purposes, the computer science of attack types, mitigations, and defenses that will specifically prevent or stymie exploitation of particular attack types, impact analysis, which then must feed into some sort of reasonably rigorous risk analysis methodology.

We have already examined in a previous chapter the knowledge domains that will allow a person to bring together an analysis similar to the foregoing Heartbleed analysis provided in this chapter. Given the requisite background knowledge, I have here listed the key domains of knowledge that a security architect brings to bear in order to assess and to respond appropriately to an attack. I used the famous Heartbleed attack as an example analysis so that readers can understand a security architecture analysis. If you're not familiar with Heartbleed, much has been written about it; it should be fairly easy to gather sufficient knowledge to follow my analysis, above. And of course, the reader is free to check my work. It's always possible that I've misunderstood something, or simply made a mistake in explaining the details. Any such mistakes are obviously mine alone.

Still, I hope that the foregoing helps readers understand just how the form and impact of attacks are the currency of a security architect's practice. You will perhaps notice that there are key technical details:

- The semantics of the TLS Heartbeat
- The precise type of issue that will be exploited (in this case, buffer overrun)
- Patterns in program memory allocation pools (heaps) and memory allocation and deallocation patterns
- The semantics of TLS client/server authentication

In order to properly analyze this issue, we had to understand how the Heartbleed attack works within the TLS protocol and within the program that has included OpenSSL.

However, I hope you also see that I didn't have to write exploitation code, nor did I have to exploit Heartbleed for hours or days with my own Heartbleed code in order to complete this analysis. The details of the specific exploitation are not required and may even be unimportant.

Security architects operate at a somewhat higher level of understanding than, say, penetration testers. A security architect must piece together computer science understanding about operating systems and loadable programs against types of attacks like a buffer overrun.

Peppered into each analysis will be required understanding of (or investigation and research into) the relevant protocols and message exchanges. Further, a working knowledge of how IDS and TLS proxies function, as well as some working knowledge of typical website architecture patterns, were brought to the analysis. The purposes of defensive technologies and how these are placed within an architecture allow appropriate defenses or mitigations to be deployed. All of this comes together in the analysis, generally, before action is taken.

3.8 Security Architecture Analyses

I hope through my little ruminations on Heartbleed, you, my reader, now have a better understanding of what security architecture is and the sorts of analyses that a security architect might provide. Through the rest of this book, I hope to offer the security architect useful tidbits I have either been taught, picked up, or learned through the schooling given by my mistakes and errors.

It is my sincere hope that my analysis of Heartbleed has provided a sufficient example such that what a security architect does and does not need to understand about an attack has been explained. As with other aspects of the architecture disciplines, we are interested in structural understanding; some details of the attack are important. But, typically, an architecturally focused analysis doesn't require the precise code for exploitation. In fact, often times, it is more useful to understand what kind of attack it is, what the attack achieves, and the context in which the attack will be prosecuted and defended.

We have to know what the attacker is going to get out of exploitation, what will be lost by defenders, and what defenses are appropriate. It is this last—appropriate defenses—where technical understanding of the attack comes into play. As I've written before, there is no one-to-one mapping between each technical defense in any particular type of exploit. It is potentially a many-to-many relationship.

Precision when building defenses is one of my goals, and I believe this is so for the vast majority of security architects. Why? Because were always working with limited resources, and no defense is perfect. We need to build "just good enough." We can never build "perfectly fortified." Through understanding attacks, we can be more specific when building an appropriate defense in depth.

I'll note that I learned a great deal from studying the very first Heartbleed example code that was publicly posted. The code had been posted in the afternoon of April 7, 2014 (six hours after we'd started our response). But at the time that first bit of example exploit code did not give me all the information that I required for an in-depth analysis.

I spent several days gathering every test result, both internal and externally published, that I could lay my hands on. It was important to understand the predictability or randomness of results of exploitation.

At the same time, I read the RFC specification for TLS heartbeat, so that my analysis was grounded in what was supposed to have been taking place versus what Heartbleed forced OpenSSL into doing. My blog post to explain the risks (included in its entirety as Appendix A) was published internally at the end of the week. Later, our Public Relations department asked me to re-publish externally, which I did to my personal blog on April 17. In other words, I spent hours over several days researching Heartbleed so that I could offer as realistic an assessment of the risks as I could manage, as well as decide what defensive measures might be best put into place. Maybe I'm just slow?

As I noted above, the foregoing technical analysis of Heartbleed to discover the appropriate set of responses (defenses) are an example of threat modeling: what can the attacker do and how do we prevent those attacks. No matter what else we may call it, the most common term used today for this process is threat modeling.

In practice, when practitioners are performing an Architectural Risk Analysis (ARA) or an initial or final Security Review (SR) in their heads, the reviewers will be threat modeling as a part of the analysis:

- Who's going to attack this system?
- To achieve what purposes?
- With what techniques?
- Through what vectors?
- Exercising what potential conditions?
- Causing what harm?

3.8.1 Some Cheap Risk Concepts

I summarize the terms in this way (as I wrote in Chapter 4 of *Securing Systems* and the Just Good Enough Risk Rating [JGERR] Smart Guide[*]):

Threat Agent uses *Exploit* through *Exposure* of *Vulnerability* causing *Impact*

Expressed in this way, in order for there to be a successful attack, the following terms each must be true:

- Threat Agent
- Exploit
- Exposure
- Vulnerability

The exercise of the attack vector, also called a "Kill Chain," which I term—when all conditions exist—a Credible Attack Vector (CAV), must also have an impact—that is, cause some sort of harm.

Given a Credible Attack Vector, it's likelihood scales arithmetically, the magnitude of the harm to give a risk rating:

CAV * Impact = Risk Rating

Which is how JGERR works.

3.8.2 JGERR Risk Rating

JGERR style risk rating for threat models was covered in *Securing Systems,* Chapter 4. It's important to note that JGERR has generated thousands of risk ratings at multiple organizations by the time of this writing (see inset). The accumulated body of ratings demonstrates the usefulness of not only the method, but its results. You may consider JGERR to be "field tested."

JGERR is based on Factor Analysis of Information Risk (FAIR).[†] Although JGERR is highly simplified from FAIR. JGERR is not intended to replace risk calculation methods such as FAIR, but rather to make up for the shortcomings of CVSS (Common Vulnerability Scoring System[‡]) and DREAD (Damage, Reproducibility, Exploitability, Affected users, Discoverability[§]), which are often employed to substitute for risk. Please see Appendix C, Amending CVSS and DREAD, for a proposal to increase the effectiveness of CVSS and DREAD through assessing "attacker value."

> I do not mean to imply that JGERR is the One True risk rating system. Although I have ample proof that it works and some certainty that JGERR is based on sound principles (FAIR), there exist other systems equally workable. When I arrived at my current employer, I was delighted to see that they had been rating risk in a manner similar to JGERR for years. It doesn't matter how you divide up the terms that will make up a likelihood of exploitation, as long as the important factors are covered (listed in the above). Likelihood has many components. It is important to understand what these are and to factor them into your rating calculation. Don't ever average your rating components, whatever factors you use.

---

[*] http://brookschoenfield.com/?page_id=271
[†] https://blog.opengroup.org/2017/01/24/what-is-open-fair/
[‡] https://www.first.org/cvss/
[§] https://resources.infosecinstitute.com/qualitative-risk-analysis-dread-model/#gref)

3.8.3 At Base: Threat Model

Whatever risk calculation or rating system one may employ, a successful attack consists of a set of conditions which all must be met in order to be successful. Call these a kill chain or CAV—the name doesn't matter; how one divides the conditions is less important than the understanding that a set of conditions must all be met or an attack cannot proceed.

When threat modeling, one must build the set of CAVs for that system. Any attack which cannot meet all the conditions in the CAV (or kill chain, if you prefer) can be discounted completely, or at least, its immediate importance reduced. Any attacks that do meet all the conditions must be prioritized; the defenses for these will thus be the most important to implement the soonest. That is the art of threat modeling in a nutshell.

When I was a Principal Engineer at Intel®, Inc., I was a member of Intel's software "SAFE" (Security Architecture Forum) review panel. Intel's Secure Development Lifecycle (SDL) has a number of panel review checkpoints to ensure that designs are secure—that sufficient "security" will be built into software.

No matter which SAFE review activity we happened to be engaged in, I found myself threat modeling the software under review. The depth of threat modeling required for the review would change depending upon the review and the amount of the design that had so far been completed or under-

> At Intel, one may think of Principal Engineer and other organizations' Distinguished Engineer as being essentially equivalent. A peer jury process is employed to grant or deny the title; a candidate must demonstrate that she/he/they already exhibit the required leadership behaviors in their work. Principal Engineer at Intel is not an honorific, but rather, a recognition and expectation of technical leadership.

stood. But the analysis was (is) the same: find the relevant, likely attacks, then think through the appropriate defenses. That is, I was threat modeling.

Interestingly, though I did not directly question my panel counterparts, from their questions, from the comments, it became clear to me that everyone else on the panel was also threat modeling. Hence, it became obvious that threat modeling is the analysis technique through which we practice security architecture. That is, we call applying attacks and building defenses "threat modeling."

Architecture, as I have written in *Securing Systems* and in this work, is the practice of organizing structures of complex systems (digital or otherwise). For security architecture, our "special sauce," as it were, is applying relevant attacks and appropriate defenses. The analysis technique is threat modeling. In the above examples, in essence, we have been threat modeling.

3.9 Threat Modeling Definition

The formal threat modeling definition I've been using is:
"Threat modeling is a technique to identify the attacks a system must resist and the defenses that will bring the system to a desired defensive state."

"System" in the above definition should be taken inclusively to mean any organization, architecture, system, set of processes, whether manual or digital.

My definition highlights a few key points. First, threat modeling is not a design or an architecture, it is an analysis technique. Next, its purpose is identifying attacks and defenses. Third, and this is key, the defenses bring the system to its "desired defensive state." That is, not to bring the system to an ivory tower security perfection (which, of course, doesn't actually exist in the real world, anyway).

In order to complete a threat model, one must first understand what defensive state a system's stakeholders expect the system to achieve. To put that in a different way, *a priori* to analyzing the attacks and specifying the defenses, the analyst must understand against what the system must defend and to what level—what is commonly termed its "security posture."

3.9.1 Alternate Definition

The Continuous Thread Modeling Initiative, coming out of the Autodesk®, Inc. security team, defines threat modeling as:

"A conceptual exercise that aims at understanding what characteristics of a system's design should be modified in order to minimize the security risk for the owners, users, and operators of the system."*

This definition focuses on the results of identifying the right set of defenses to "minimize the security risk." But at the definition's heart, there seems to be an equivalence set:

- "technique" = "conceptual exercise"
- "identify the attacks . . . and . . . defenses" = "characteristics of a system's design should be modified"
- "desired defensive state" = "minimize risk"

I hope that there's not a lot of disagreement about the essential characteristics of the threat modeling process. As explained above, it's a mental exercise (often aided by diagrams and lists), aimed at enumerating under/unmitigated security risks, which then help to identify a set of defenses, or "modifications to a system's design," that will bring the system to an acceptable level of security risk. The analysis usually involves considering various attack scenarios.

In *Securing Systems,* I proposed that the best way to understand a system's security posture is via a risk analysis, not just of a system, but of the organization fielding the system, expectations of the users of the system, and the owners of the system: the system's stakeholders. This was covered as "Strategy" within the "Three S's" in Chapter 2 of *Securing Systems.*

From the understanding of stakeholder risk tolerance, one may then derive the security posture of a system, its "desired defensive state"—that is, the appropriate defenses that will resist those attacks against which the system and its stakeholders will defend.

I hope that in this chapter, we've covered "attacks a system must resist" sufficiently through the explanation and analysis already given above.

3.9.2 When Is My Threat Model Done?

There remains one further aspect to threat modeling that we must cover that was not explicitly explained in *Securing Systems*: when is a threat model complete?

---

* Tarandach and Schoenfield, 2019

The answer to that question is "never," unfortunately. But, the model is "never complete" so long as changes are being made to the structures of a system. Still, there are points at which one may confidently say, "we've done enough at this point," what those who work in Agile software development term, "Definition of Done"—a threat modeling definition of done. I wrote the following post for IOActive's Blog. It will, I hope, explain the definition of done (DoD) for threat modeling.

"Threat modeling is a qualitative analysis through which architecture and design choices are made based upon attack and defense analysis. This is a creative process that must have boundaries surrounding that analysis if it is to arrive at a completion.

"The constraints within which attack enumeration must be made are as follows:

- The risk tolerance of the organization owning/fielding the system
- The risk tolerance of the system's users (if any)
- The capabilities, goals, expended effort, and risk tolerances of the enumerated set of threat agents who will wish to attack
- The trust/risk profiles of the system's components, including infrastructure(s) and external entities
- The runtime/execution environment(s)
- The existing defenses (including infrastructure defenses and services)
- The highest sensitivity of data flowing through and being processed
- The probability of a particular attack scenario being low enough to be discounted

"While somewhat creative, a threat model must be grounded in hard data. Obviously, those active attacks that can be exercised against the system under analysis will be applied.

"Furthermore, an analyst also applies relevant past exploit/vulnerability pairs even if such vulnerabilities have not yet been found in the system. It's important to understand that even the most rigorous testing, as Edsger Dijkstra so famously quipped, "proves the system has bugs, not that it doesn't." If there have existed exploitable vulnerabilities in any component within the system under analysis, even though fixed in the versions included, then the analysis must assume that at least some similar issues will likely be found in those components at some point in the future.

"An analyst may stop enumerating attacks when:

- The attack scenarios seem demonstrably more complex than other methods of compromise that are easier and more readily available.
- The required preconditions to an attack scenario lie well outside the range of normal or typical configuration and usage.
- Significant inside assistance (for externally-originated attacks) is required to proceed. (Insider threat is a special category that requires careful analysis across an organization. It rarely should be tackled one system analysis at a time. Separation of duties are often determined on a per-system, per-function, or per-privilege basis.)
- Where no exploit exists for a particular vulnerability, or the vulnerability is not exposed for remote exercise or research (it's important to periodically revisit the threat model in light of new developments).
- Attack scenarios start to border on the ridiculous, the strained, or the dubious, or depend upon computer technologies that have yet to be invented (i.e., "science fiction").

"An analyst may stop specifying defenses when:

- Each defense has some overlap of protection with at least one other defense
- Each significant attack vector is covered at least partially by more than a single defense (see inset)

"Although threat modeling has a significant qualitative aspect, there are definite signs when the analysis has reached its completion state, that is, a threat modeling definition of done (DoD)."*

> For more stringent security postures, each attack scenario must be mitigated. "Significant" is meant to mean those attack vectors whose successful exercise will cause significant harm. It also implies attack vectors that are considered "credible"—that is, there is sufficient evidence that the attack vector can be exercised by an active threat actor should a weakness that can be exploited be released or reach production.

While a threat model is never complete until a system stops changing, there are, to my mind, clear indications that a round of analysis can be considered complete enough to build the "desired defensive state" (as given in the formal threat model definition, above). Only when structure changes, when adding or changing:

- Components or functions
- Assets
- Use cases
- Lines of communication or data flows
- Trust boundaries or levels of trust/distrust
- Shifting the exposure of potentially vulnerable components

Some of my colleagues also prefer to revisit threat models at some periodic basis, say every six months or a year. Personally, I don't see the need for this if the above triggers haven't occurred within the time period. However, if in a given situation it isn't crystal clear that everyone understands the threat model review triggers, then perhaps a review of the model, when it hasn't already been revisited from one of the trigger changes, will provide an additional level of catch-all review.

"Review" of the threat model is used consciously by me. Once a threat model has been built, one needn't start from scratch. In practice, analyzing how a set of changes adds attacks or requires a different or changed set of defensives, in light of the changes being made to the system, is all that is usually required.

A threat model review might conclude that no additional security changes need be made. Or, new security requirements for the added or changed structures might be generated. The review process can be quite short; I've been in reviews that took less than half an hour, depending upon the availability of the required information and the complexity of the system under analysis.

3.10 Summary

I hope that in this chapter, you've seen that security architecture is the practice of applying relevant, likely attacks to systems. This application exercise is employed in order to generate the

---

* The post has not been published by IOActive at the time of this writing. It will be in the future. Please check https://ioactive.com/resources/blogs for publication. (See Appendix E for complete post.)

required set of defenses that will bring a system to a "desired defensive state." An understanding of attacks and defenses lies at the heart of the practice of security architecture.

However, security architecture is not generally concerned with the details of each exploitation technique. Rather, we are concerned with types of exploitations, with classes of attacks. In Chapter 5, Learning the Trade, we'll explore some publicly available resources to help both with what the attacks are, and with the problem of organizing these in some form so that they can be applied in a consistent and repeatable manner. For this chapter, I hope that it's sufficient to understand what the process is.

Architecture is about structure. Security architecture practices applying attacks and defenses to structures. This application is to determine what defenses will need to be employed to resist the attacks.

The primary technique of analysis employed to practice security architecture is threat modeling.

Chapter 4

Culture Hacking

"It's not policy, it's culture hacking."

Noopur Davis, to the author at McAfee Inc., 2014[*]

Fortunately or unfortunately, depending on the reader's viewpoint and preferences, a fair amount of practicing security architecture, or just plain architecture—or really, any technical leadership role—is about culture and people, not about purely technical matters. Complex projects typically employ multiple teams, each taking responsibility for some portion or functionality of the whole. Teams must interact both within the team and with any other teams; everyone involved must coordinate their efforts: schedules, outputs, and, most importantly, component parts' interoperation and integration of the software pieces that each sub-effort is building.

4.1 Team Tourism

An entire project will develop its own working style. Likewise, each team will begin to define its team boundaries, expectations, interaction styles—basically, a team subculture of its very own. Even use of language will take on some dialect; on tech teams, this is most noticeable by the way in which common acronyms and other technical terms become understood by every member of the team, though to an outsider, it may seem like "alphabet soup."

Due to the organic formation of group-think, of team work style, the ability of anyone who must influence the team's efforts from outside that team must involve some cultural awareness in order to have effect. As I wrote in *Securing Systems* (pp. 180–183):

---

[*] Davis, 2014. [Ms. Davis is Senior VP of Product Security at Comcast Inc.]

"The first act is to understand the architecture. Most likely, those presenting the architecture to you will be thinking about how the system works, what it's intended for, how it will be used correctly. This is very different from the way a security architect must approach architecture. Architects interested in implementing a system focus on 'use cases.' In a security assessment, the security architect focuses on 'misuse cases.' This distinction is quite important.

"Because we're examining the system for security vulnerabilities and weaknesses, there is a conflict of interest built in to the assessment. The people on the other side of the table are concerned with correctness, concerned with implementing the requirements and specifications that have been gathered and which are supposed to define the system, its boundaries, its goals, and intentions. The implementing team may have been living with this system for some time? They may even have developed their own language of acronyms and aliases that help them speak in shorthand. Implicit within the acronyms are the assumptions that they've already made. If the security assessor, the security architect has been a part of the team, this will not be a problem: everyone will be speaking the same language. That is, unfortunately, not the usual situation.

"On the other hand, quite often the security architect is working with a number of projects, maybe more than a few*? She or he will not have been a part of the forming of the team, will not be party to the assumptions embedded in the acronym-speak to which the team have become accustomed. It may seem to the team that the security architect has been injected into a smooth and running process. The team's collective understanding and the jargon that represents that understanding, the acronyms, system names, aliases, and such represent a cognitive, shared team reality. Meanwhile, the security architect assigned to a running project might feel like she's stumbling about in an unknown country, trying to make sense of a partially understood dialect?

"You, the security architect, must work within the parameters of the shared reality of which you may not be a part and into which you've been thrown. You might wish to step carefully across this boundary? At the very first meeting, there may be considerable tension in the room. Obviously, a warm and friendly demeanor won't hurt. But beyond that, it may be useful to ask folks to slow down and explain the jargon terms to which they've grown accustom.

"By understanding the team assumptions and by unpacking the team's unique brand of jargon and acronyms, you can begin to enter into their mindset; they may even start to see you as a part of their team (if you're lucky). And being a part of the implementing team is the powerful position, though this may seem counterintuitive. Workgroups tend to defend their boundaries. They spent a lot of time building relationships and trust. Those carefully crafted relationships and the trust that has been earned will often be defended against all comers, no matter how friendly are the intentions of the outsider. Nobody likes to have their 'good thing' perturbed.

"You may be entering a team 'space' where you have not been given the relationship and trust that the team have collectively developed? And in fact, depending upon what experiences team members may have had with security folk in the past, you could well

---

* At one time, I was assigned to review 130 projects simultaneously.

be at a deficit? You may feel that you have the expertise, that you've been nominated by your organization to represent security, that you're empowered to drive security into systems, and you represent the policy and standards to which systems and development teams must conform. While that may be true, a human working group develops boundaries. There is already a process in place with which team members are more or less comfortable. Basically, they have something ongoing into which you are being interposed. The sooner that the team perceive you as a fellow member and not an interruption, the sooner you will have constructive conversations about the security needs of the system. Outsiders may very well be resisted by those who feel that they must defend team boundaries. Insiders, members of the team, are the people who are most likely to receive the benefit of active listening and constructive dialogue. Try to make the assessment not about winning and losing but rather about a collaboration for the good of all."

How we, the security specialist, enter into a running, well-defined team "mind" matters! In fact, our interactions, the sensitivity with which we conduct our business—especially early on in an engagement—greatly influences not just success with that team, but our future ability to influence at all. Awareness of the pre-existing levels of team cohesion can, at the very least, allow one to be sensitive to being in someone else's "home," on the team's turf, as it were. I personally also attempt to establish some small bit of personal connection and understanding with a few of the individuals on the team to ease any tension and to place some working ground upon which we can build trust.

I try to be just a little bit vulnerable about myself. But, the other side of that openness is to avoid taking up too much of people's time and attention: A little is good, but it's very easy to cross over into too much. One or two humorous quips are fine; letting folks know that today has been going well or not and why can sometimes bridge into relationship quickly. But attempting to be the "class clown" is tiresome, as is endless descriptions of one's troubles.

Recipients may feel as though their attention is being abused or that they must take care of anyone who seems too demanding or veers off subject for extended periods of time. It's always a balancing act for me; I don't always get it right on either side—reserved or revealing. Hence, I always try to pay attention to how others are reacting, to their attention or lack thereof, to conversational engagement. If I've overdone it, I shut up for a while, to let others control the interaction unless I have something critically important that must be expressed immediately (say because I might fail to expose a potentially serious risk).

Asking questions nearly always establishes trust. But the questions must be accompanied by an authentic desire to hear and validate responses. People's manipulation detectors (often quite unconscious) are usually very keen; I find that engineers as a group are particularly sensitive to social manipulations. Authenticity matters, too. If I ask something, I require of myself to listen attentively and without judgment to the answers. That one practice, above all, builds deep and abiding trust.

4.1.1 Build and Maintain Trust

My friend Martin Nystrom (author and Director, Product Management Security at Cisco) demonstrated the power of seeking answers authentically when we were both on the same security architecture team. The tougher things got, the more emotionally laden the discussion became, Martin had a practice of stepping back to seek from others their opinions. In this way, he teased out disagreements that otherwise might have remained hidden, simmering behind the scenes to derail solutions.

If there's magic in the world, this one technique, entered into in the spirit of reaching for the best agreements and solutions, is it. Listen as much as speak, maybe more? Perhaps it's better to call it *practice* rather than *technique*? However you wish to name it, seeking others' knowledge and viewpoint establishes and then builds trust that can underpin the team's navigating difficult challenges, while at the same time building greater cohesion, rather than less. It's "culture hacking" at the interpersonal level at its best.

Importantly, different cultures and, within those, varying individuals have very different tolerances and boundary expectations. I don't need to win over everyone, though. If I can build a tipping point of trust and connection, then the most introverted, reserved, even suspicious person will at least interact, which, after all, is all that is required.

At an organizational level, we may have to shift perceptions and misconceptions about security in general or about security architecture in particular. Having recently been hired by a company to lead security architecture, I was told that a past administration had declared that "all changes must be threat modeled." Upon hearing this, I immediately knew that I'd have to dig myself out of this hole, since any reasonably competent engineer knows that every change made to any system does not have security implications. Some do, and many do not. Plus, the level of security importance also varies. Engineers know this implicitly. A mandate requiring any valueless effort will cause that mandate to fail.

Lots of changes have no security needs whatsoever (think of user interface colors or text placements). Some changes will follow previously established security requirements that don't require any additional consideration. Hence a command that "every change be threat modeled" is obviously erroneous. Whoever declared this probably lost credibility and influence with those to whom the command was aimed.

Apparently, upon hearing that "every change" had to be "threat modeled," a manager at that organization then asked if he and his staff might then learn the technique. He was told, "Sorry, that's only for the security architects." Upon hearing this, I knew that I and my security architecture program were in serious trouble with these folks. They'd long since decided that security architects don't know what they're talking about and won't help; that security architects prefer to keep control of activities that seemed to the developers to be irrelevant, at least some of the time.

My guess (though I didn't ask it then) was that most of the folks in that room did have some experience threat modeling and had been doing it, at least informally, for a while. Once trust had been reestablished, those very same developers told me about the analyses that they'd been doing to figure out what security controls to build—their skill levels ranged from experienced to beginners. Once freed from obviously silly mandates, folks were willing to learn more, to improve their practices.

Freeing developers from a nonsensical mandate that was presented with no support or training and as a closely held secret technique is an example of what Noopur terms, "culture hacking." Get rid of anything that is seen as an impediment. Recraft (and sometimes, rebrand) what must be done, so that its value will be readily apparent to those who must execute.

I proposed a manifest for a different approach to software security in 2013: "Developer-Centric Security." The manifest is presented in Appendix B, Developer-Centric Security, page 177.

The previous security architects in my story (above) failed to see their work as being at least partially about culture; they failed to find out just what developers already knew and perhaps were doing about security. Most importantly, they failed to enlist the help of the very people who would have to build security into the software.

Instead, that previous security team alienated developers. That is something I try very hard not to do (please see Appendix B).

How did I build trust? I listened, first and foremost. I acknowledged efforts that had been made in good faith (no matter the skill applied). I focused first on attacks to which I could offer convincing examples and which directly applied to the technologies being built. In this way, by tightly focusing on demonstrable problems, I gained the developers' trust that I wasn't making up attacks—but instead that I was applying valuable knowledge, that I was trying to address problems of obvious importance.

This is one of my "tricks of the trade": Don't sweat the small stuff, especially at first. Focus on changes that will offer obvious improvements to existing design work. I'm never afraid to say, "It seems like you've already covered the most important attacks," if I believe that this is indeed true. Validating developers' existing efforts for security delivers a huge boost for a program. When these folks start to feel recognized, included, valuable, they become one's allies in the work, both execution of software security, but also as culture change agents.

"We must make a lot of predictions to be able to show calibration."

Ryan McGeehan[*]

Another trick that I've seen build trust over time (again, this is culture hacking) is to make the low and medium risk issues visible, but not to make a big deal of them. I write short assessments of these minor issues for decision makers, as a "For Your Information" (FYI). I don't fight about getting minor issues fixed immediately; I just write an exception for it with a date for completion that makes sense, given the risk rating. Once there's a reasonable fix plan and decision makers accept the plan, I move on. As Ryan McGeehan puts it, this is a "calibration" that one's risk ratings can be trusted.[†]

Development teams appreciate fair risk rating and inclusion in scheduling and prioritization.

From experience, I will tell you, over time, if many issues are rated low or medium as one might intuitively expect, co-workers and decision makers build a great deal of trust that the person rating the issues is not attempting to inflate ratings in order to force action. Repeated reasonableness about the exigencies of resourcing and schedules demonstrates a willingness to understand development problems and to work with business necessities.

Then, when a really critical issue comes up, everyone knows that the person rating it (me, let's say) isn't inflating scores, isn't pushing just to win. People trust the fairness of the rating because assessments have been understandable in the past. Thus, the one time I really feel the

---

[*] McGeehan, 2019.
[†] McGeehan, ibid.

need to push garners a great deal more weight, a lot more influence, based on the trust already established about ratings.

4.1.2 Don't Squander Influence

People sometimes ask me how I gain so much influence. As Nooper says, "It's culture hacking."[*] I spend a lot of time building sufficient trust such that folks understand that I'm on their side. Plus, I don't waste my influence on matters of lesser consequence, so that if I must press hard, my partners know that it's for very good reason, which I make sure I can articulate clearly, in both technical and business terms.

As I wrote in *Securing Systems* (pp. 122–125):

"There is obviously a technical impact that occurs from the exercise of most vulnerabilities. In our XSS examples, the technical impact is the execution of a script of the attacker's choosing in the context of the target's browser. The technical impact from a heap overflow might be the execution of code of the attacker's choosing in the context of an application at whatever operating system privileges that application is running. These technical details are certainly important when building defenses against these attacks. Further, the technical impact helps coders understand where the bug is in the code, and technical details help to understand how to fix the issue. But the technical impact isn't typically important to organizational risk decision makers. For them, the impact must be spelled out in terms of the organization's objectives. We might term this 'business impact,' as opposed to 'technical impact.'

"Continuing with the two examples that we've been considering, let's examine a couple of business impacts. As was explained earlier, an XSS attack is usually an attack via a web site targeting the user of that web site. The goal of the attacker will be something of value that the user has: his identity information, her account details, the user's machine itself (as a part of a botnet, for instance). The attacker is attempting to cause the user to unwittingly allow the attacker to do something to the user or to the user's machine. There are too many possibilities to list here. For a security architect who is trying to assess the risk of an XSS to an organization, it is probably sufficient to understand that the user of the web site is being attacked (and possibly hurt) through a mechanism contained on the web site. The organization's web site is the vector of attack, linking attacker to target.

"From the web site owner's perspective, a web site becomes a tool in service to an attacker. The attacks are directed at the web site's users, that is, the organization's users. For example, consider an organization offering an open source project, providing a set of executable binaries for various operating systems (the 'application') and the source code to which developers may contribute. Most open source project sites also foster a sense of community, a web site for interaction between users and coders. So, there's usually some sort of messaging, discussion forums, and search function. All the above functions are offered besides static and dynamic web content about the project.

---

[*] Davis, 2014.

"Open source projects often don't have 'leaders' so much as leadership. But imagine, if you will, that those who take responsibility for the project's web site must consider XSS vulnerability, which I'm sure, many must. What is the business impact of letting attackers target the users of the project's web site?

"I would guess that such a site might be able to sustain an occasional user being targeted, since success of the attack is not guaranteed, given an up-to-date, security sandboxed browser. Further, if the site does not require the user to turn on site scripting in their browser, users are free to use the site in a more secure manner, less vulnerable to XSS.

"But if I were responsible for this site, I would not want to squander my user confidence upon XSS attacks from my web site. Put yourself, just for a moment, in the shoes of the people dedicating their time, usually volunteered, to the project. I can well imagine that it is precisely user confidence that will make my project a success. 'Success' in the open source world, I believe, is measured by user base, namely, the number of users who download and use the application. And success is also measured through the number of code contributions and contributors, and by the level of activity of code and design discussion. If users do not feel safe coming to the project's web site, none of the foregoing goals can be met.

"Hence, the business impact of an XSS to an open source project is loss of user and contributor confidence and trust. Further, if the web site is buggy, will users have confidence that the application works properly? Will they trust that the application does not open a vulnerability that allows an attack on the user's machine? I'm guessing that user confidence and user trust are paramount and must be safeguarded accordingly.

"Now, we can assess the risk of an XSS bug *within the context of the organization's goals.* And we can express the impact of a successful attack in terms that are applicable to a given open source project: 'business impact.'

"Let us now consider the heap overflow case above. Like XSS, an overflow allows the attacker to run code or direct an application's code to do something unintended (such as allowing the attacker to write to the password store, thus adding the attacker as a legitimate user on the system). Heap overflows occur most often in programs created with languages that require the programmer to directly handle memory. The word 'application' covers a vast array of software scenarios, from server-side, backend systems to individual programs on an endpoint, laptop, desktop, smart phone, what-have-you. Apple's iOS phone operating system, a derivative of the Mac OS X, is really a UNIX descendant, 'under the covers'; iOS applications are written in a derivative of the C programming language. Because the universe of applications written in memory handling languages is far too vast to reasonably consider, let us constrain our case down to an endpoint application that executes some functionality for a user, has a broad user base (in the hundreds of millions), and is produced by a company whose mission is to produce broadly accepted and purchased software products. Examples might be Microsoft or Adobe Systems. Each of these companies produces any number of discreet applications for the most popular platforms.

"A heap overflow that allows an attacker to misuse a widely distributed application to attack a user's machine, collect the user's data, and ultimately, to perhaps control a user's machine really is not much different, in a technical aspect, from XSS. The attacker misuses an application to target the user's endpoint (and, likely, the user's data). The difference is one of scale. Scripts usually run in the security sandboxed context of the user's browser. Applications run directly on the operating system at the privilege level of the logged-in user. For broadly distributed applications, privilege might be restricted (typically on enterprise-supplied computers). But most users run personally owned computers at "administrator" or some similar high level of privilege. If the attacker can execute her or his code at this level, she or he has the "run of the box," and can do with the computer whatever is desired. Users are thus at great risk if they use their computers for sensitive activities, such as finances and medical information. In addition, at this level of privilege, the computer might be used by the attacker to target other computers, to send spam (perhaps through the email accounts of the user?), or to store illegal digital materials.

"I believe that it isn't too much of a leap to imagine the business impact to an Independent Software Vendor (ISV) from a widely distributed heap overflow that allows execution of code of the attacker's choosing. Again, the ISV is staring at a loss of customer confidence, in the software, in the brand, in the company itself."

4.2 Threat Modeling: Just Do It

One of my big discoveries since writing *Securing Systems* has been the power of introducing threat modeling throughout a development practice at any organization. I like to say that, "If there's magic in software security, teaching everyone threat modeling is it." When my dear friend Eoin Carroll* told me about the effects of hanging a hard copy of a team's threat model up on the wall in each development team's Agile stand up (meeting) room, I just had to start experimenting with making threat models more widely available.

What Eoin observed was that as individuals and teams thought about how to implement new features (user stories), they would glance up at the threat model to consider whether or not the item would have security implications. In other words, making the threat model accessible changed the behavior of teams such that security had become an integral part of implementation thinking: These teams had developed a "culture of security" because the threat model was present to consider. That is, one simple change to the development process had fostered a turnaround in thinking about security. That is the essence of "culture hacking."

Before Eoin posted these threat models, a security practitioner had to be present in the room in order to get teams to consider security. With the threat model available, the teams started to take responsibility for security themselves; they felt empowered and motivated.

That doesn't mean that each team was now expert in security such that they no longer needed Eoin and his teammates. As I've outlined previously in this work, security architects are expected to bring a set of specialties to software development that others lack, to wit: relevant attacks and their defenses.

---

* Eoin Carroll is a Senior Security Researcher and was for many years a technical leader within our security architecture team.

Still, my own experience (and I haven't talked with Eoin about this) suggests that over time, security patterns repeat. Every new item to be built isn't wholly unique; requirements that were applied to previous implementations will be applied over and over again. As software security specialists and development teams build a working relationship, the same or very similar security requirements come up repeatedly. Smart teams (and which development teams are not "smart"? I haven't met many "dumb" ones) will apply the known patterns themselves.

In fact, when I was at Cisco®, my counterpart IT architects (with whom I'd worked for years) and I used to joke when in meetings about who would say what had become obvious and usual for us? I could speak to typical IT requirements just as they could articulate for me many usual security requirements. "Do you want to say it or should I?" was a common question at meetings with new application development teams.

There've been few places in my career where I've seen one small process change have this much effect—as in, making a project's or a product's threat model available to everyone involved in building it.

Before Eoin's revelation, like most security architects, I always had performed threat modeling with the subject matter experts of a team, usually the most senior architects. Most of the team were excluded; the threat modeling process was essentially opaque to everyone but the most senior developers. Most especially, auxiliary personnel such as project managers or product managers were excluded, not because they weren't important in the overall scheme of building software, but because threat modeling was seen as a highly technical activity that shouldn't waste the time of people not directly involved.

In fact, a past administration for one of the software security programs that I led had told development teams that threat modeling was only for "senior security architects" and that the results needed to be highly restricted (please read the story in the preceding section). I had to dig myself out of that misconception hole for the first six months of that job, because, once development teams felt excluded, they decided that threat modeling had nothing to do with what they did on a day-to-day basis and could be completely ignored. Not the ideal situation to produce well-designed, secure software.

4.2.1 "Trust Developers?"

I will admit to you, the reader, that it's true that the results of the threat model, the security requirements, especially those requirements not yet built or perhaps delayed for later implementation, may be quite sensitive. That's the reason that many security practices hold threat models close, treat them as highly sensitive, and thus not sharable to development teams. I'd be willing to bet that this is the argument put forth by that past administration on why they didn't want to share threat models or the process of deriving models.

Dr. James Ransome, Ponemon Fellow, author, and all-round great guy, and I have talked about this problem a great deal. He and I have worked together twice to build and then run software security programs.* The chink in the armor of protectionism around threat models is that the development team have and hold the code! Please consider this carefully: They don't need the threat model in order to destroy the software for which development teams are

---

* James would provide management leadership and I would provide technical leadership for the programs.

responsible. If the team were to go rogue, they could usually insert all manner of awful things into the code, like backdoors or malicious code.

There are checks against collusive teams doing bad things (please see some of my public talks on secure development or take a look at my chapter in *Core Software Security*). Still, even the best run governance process ultimately relies on people, some of whom may not have the organization's best interests at heart. As James likes to say, "If you can't trust developers with the code, who can you trust?" It's a truism.

The way that we have handled this problem is to remind developers of their awesome responsibility to the company, that their success is tied to keeping the company's intellectual property from leaking out, including any sensitive security situations. Repeat regularly, through different media and presentation channels, but don't be such a nag that the message becomes part of the background noise of the job.

Nothing's perfect; someone will post some code or a sensitive project name probably for no other reason than that person is inexperienced or wildly proud of what they're doing. Handling these mistakes is part of security's role.

4.2.2 Threat Model Training Is for Everyone

To my point, introduce threat modeling and a project's threat model to everyone. At the same time, remind them that the model and, especially, its unimplemented results are confidential and not to be shared with those who don't need to know—particularly, outside the organization. Attackers can have a field day with a threat model, so it needs to be protected from inadvertent release.

What we discovered running around our global development centers is that when you include everyone, you get better threat models. One reason for this should be obvious but is often missed: Threat models are best when done holistically. A single missed or passed-over detail might very well miss an important attack vector or important impacts.

Let me offer an example from real life. We were examining a gateway product. The team had already done a rather thorough threat model. All I had to do was to review the results. Because I included everyone at that review, one of the more junior members of the team mentioned that the underlying operating system that had been chosen for this gateway, which would be delivered along with the product, had its SSH server running. The SSH server came with a published, default password. This is the way that the operating system was configured by its vendor in order to make debugging during development easier.

Because the team was highly focused on the functionality of the product, they'd forgotten to think about the entire run time stack (which is a point I make repeatedly in *Securing Systems*: One must include the run time or risk leaving attack surfaces undefended). This gateway might have been shipped with exactly the problem that allowed the Mirai Botnet to be formed and which had resulted in the famous DYN attack. That is, cameras deployed all over the world had SSH running with a published default password. The rest is history.

If we hadn't had everyone in the room, it's quite likely that during the review we would have missed this key piece of information—this readily available attack point that needed to be defended. In my presentations I like to say, "A threat model is a crossroads of many different domains and a collection of subject matter experts. Absence of any one of these can mean that the threat model is incomplete." That gateway's threat model is a perfect example of exactly this point.

Just as important as the completeness of the threat model is the culture hack that inclusivity offers us. Here's where the "magic" comes in.

Based upon hundreds of threat model classes taught at sites spanning the globe, I have observed that, once participants play at mentally attacking a system and identifying defences against those attacks, they come away with an integral sense of why software security is so critical. Participants gain an appreciation of the importance of the entire Secure Development Lifecycle (SDL or S-SDLC) (however that SDL may be expressed within their organization). For most participants, the shift towards a culture of security is profound, as long as they've gotten the chance to participate in the threat modeling process. As I noted above, if there's any magic in software security, it is allowing everyone to participate in building threat models, in learning the process, and in making threat models accessible throughout the development process and to everyone involved, even nontechnical roles.

To add to my exhortation to include even non-technical roles, I spoke at an internal security architecture event for Daimler, AB. Carsten Scherr runs Daimler's security architecture program, and Luis Servin is one of the technical leaders. They invited the security architects from throughout their supply chain to attend. Brilliant!

Inviting the architects from throughout their supply chain aligns security architecture practice of the third parties on whose security Daimler's products must depend. The inclusion of these key people means that each of the companies that attended now understand what Daimler expects from products whose security posture must affect the overall posture of products as they go into service. As we have seen in examples in this book, a threat model must be taken holistically, without respect to whomever may be responsible for any particular portion of an integration.

Carsten and Luis have realized that they cannot bring Daimler's products to their "desired defensive state," cannot bring their highly integrated products to the required security posture without the full participation of each of the suppliers whose products' security postures are going to contribute or detract from the overall posture.

So why not include everyone who must be involved in any discussions on how things must be done? I've never seen any company take such holistic care for their supply chain before. To my mind, this sort of out-of-the-box, inclusive thinking is what we, the industry, need to climb out of the design problems that we apparently keep creating. Include *everyone*! Really!

Participatory threat modeling is culture hacking—hacking development culture toward a culture of security.

4.3 More Culture Hacks

There are other culture hacks that achieve a similar shift:

- Accessible security architects
- An open process that has been built in collaboration with those who must enact it (i.e., developers)

- Integrating secure development practices into the organic flow of development
- Building trust between functions, maintaining that trust over time and through conflicts

Basically, what I've outlined in the preceding bullets is the essence of what I've termed *Developer-Centric Security,* whose manifesto is given in Appendix B.

Although I try to practice developer-centric security throughout my programs, the one practice that hacks a development organization toward a culture of security the fastest and the easiest is unmasking and demystifying threat modeling. Among the many things that you may do, start there and keep it up. Let me know about your results.

4.3.1 Nimble Governance

Some readers may find themselves disturbed by the idea of allowing beginners to perform threat models. After all, the whole purpose of a threat model is to identify those defenses that more obvious approaches such as using the various vulnerability and code security scan tools cannot find.

I've already made the point that there are special skills that security architects bring to the work—often significant skills that take years to develop. And now I am asserting that even rank beginners ought to be allowed into the process.

Suggesting that beginners threat model may seem inconsistent on my part, but it's not, really.

First, one of the subject matter experts who should be included in a threat model process is an experienced security architect who is familiar with the types of technologies that will be used in the system under analysis. The security architect should also have a working knowledge of the sorts of attacks that have been successful against these technologies and what defenses are typically used to thwart or slow these attacks. That is the best programmatic approach I know of.

Unfortunately, there aren't enough skilled security architects available for every threat model, which is one reason I've written this book (and *Securing Systems* before it). Those of us with some skill have to learn how to share it and to teach others. Still, as of this writing, there is a severe shortage of people with sufficient skill, call them what you will.

In many organizations with which I've worked, or about which I know, the strategy then is to throw the skilled folk at so-called "critical" systems. *Critical* in this regard has no definitive industry meaning and is usually locally determined based on budget, revenue generation, data sensitivity, and a host of other factors. The point is, the skilled folk can't be everywhere, especially in really large engineering organizations in which there are many different development teams and many different project threads. Some criteria or other are used to find a line above which the project will get security architecture engagement and below which it will not.

Another strategy will be to highly over-resource the few skilled architects such that they drop into a project and make some security requirement pronouncements which, supposedly, must be adhered to, no matter what else changes during development. Unyielding requirements play havoc with iterative development methodologies that depend upon experiment, learn, then pivot based upon what's been learned. That, of course, causes no end of security/development friction.

The two strategies above are not mutually exclusive and, thus, can be used in conjunction. No matter what mix of critical and drop-in is used, there's a guarantee that some threat models will not get done or won't receive the attention that they deserve, which leads to missed security requirements.

If we allow neophytes to threat model, we are also guaranteed to miss security requirements. One way or another, requirements are going to be missed. For those efforts which do not receive a threat model or which receive only a cursory analysis, isn't it better if the neophytes at least try? Most likely, they will identify more security requirements than if they had ignored secure design altogether.

In fact, this gets to what I call the rule of "zero versus one." If a design has no attack and defense analysis, then zero security requirements will be identified, if you see what I mean. The outcome is going to be relatively insecure.

If we introduce threat modeling to development teams, then they will try. If they find a single additional requirement that brings the design one step closer to its intended security posture, isn't that a win over nothing?

The other side of this approach is that every time developers practice threat modeling, they are going to improve. Plus, they will be integrating security thinking into their standard practice, as a way of working, as a part of their skillset. Threat modeling becomes one of developers' "always do it" tools. They'll get better at identifying more requirements, and thus there will be continuous improvement in security posture over time.

I cannot see the downside here, not in the long term. The trick is to prevent really bad things from happening. That's where governance comes in as a safety net to prevent the truly catastrophic from going forward and where a program can most effectively deploy its most seasoned security architects as reviewers. Reviews take a lot less time than a threat model analysis. I covered this in *Securing Systems*, pp. 372–373:

"... peer review of assessments and threat models is essential. Responsibility can be overwhelming. By sharing that responsibility, architects can relieve some of the stress that responsibility may cause. Furthermore, the weighty decisions that must be made, the thoroughness that must be applied, the ease with which one can miss an attack surface or vulnerability are all mitigated by having several people look over the results of the assessment. It's just too easy to make a mistake, even for the most experienced architects. For the less experienced or junior practitioners, peer review can help fend off catastrophe.

"What does a peer review process look like? When does an assessment require peer review? Who should perform the peer review?

"For large, complex, and challenging systems, there's probably no substitute for a formal governance review. A common approach for this is to place senior and leader architects onto an architecture review board. The large or critical systems must pass through the review board and get approved before they can proceed. Sometimes, the review board will also have a checkpoint before deployment into production. This checkpoint helps to ensure that projects that haven't met their deliverables can't move to production to the harm of the organization. A senior security architect will be part of the formal review board and have a 'no' vote if there is a significant risk that hasn't been sufficiently mitigated.

"On the other hand, forcing every project, no matter how small, through a formal review board can quickly create a bottleneck to the velocity of project delivery. I've seen this happen too many times to count. The desire to have every project get checked by the most trusted and experienced architects is laudable and comes from the very best intentions. But unless an organization has an army of truly experienced architects to deploy, requiring every project to be reviewed by a small group of people who are generally over-extended already is going to bring project delivery to a near standstill.

"Instead, some other form of review that is more lightweight and nimble needs to be found. I've had success with the following approach.

"I may be criticized for being too trusting. Certainly, considering some organization's missions, my approach will be too lightweight. But in the high-tech organizations in which I've worked, we have established a process whereby if the architect is unsure about an assessment for any reason, she or he must find a senior architect (senior to that architect), and an architect who is not involved in the project, to provide the required peer review of the assessment or analysis.

"This process does presume that architects will seek peer review. Architects have to perceive peer review as valuable and not a hindrance. If the security architects understand the responsibility that they hold for the organization, my experience is that security architects generally like to receive some additional assurance on their assessments when they feel at all uneasy about what they've found.

"I've used this same process four times now, at four different organizations. Those organizations were relatively similar, I admit. Still, in my experience, this works pretty well and catches most mistakes before serious harm takes place. One has to build a culture of support and collaboration or this approach cannot work. It is lightweight and dexterous enough not to interfere overly much with project delivery. And this lightweight peer review process does assume a level of competence of the architect to understand what is in her or his proficiency and what does not. We also encourage architects to seek subject matter expertise as a regular course of their assessments. Nobody knows it all."

The essence of my lightweight governance approach is peer review by one reviewer with more experience and one independent reviewer. If these cannot agree, then escalate to the next level of experience or seniority.

The final say, of course, belongs to management. But I've only seen these reviews get to management twice in nearly 15 years over four different organizations. It doesn't come to that among people who trust each other and have trust built from working through difficult technical questions.

For the most senior folks, they must turn to their peers, if there are any, or the next level down in the seniority or skill hierarchy. No one is above peer review; no threat model completes without a review. At the time I wrote *Securing Systems,* peer reviews might have been skipped in situations in which the threat model owner felt that the analysis lay completely within her/his/their scope of practice and knowledge set. Further experience shows that this lightweight review process is highly effective and quite nimble. Today, every model goes through a review.

The advantage of the technical leader turning to the most skilled is that it establishes a culture of peer review. The senior person models what she/he/they expect from everyone else. Also, it's great training for one to become the next senior security architecture technical leader.

In other words, performing peer reviews is great training. Just as code reviews make a great coder, threat mode reviews make a great threat modeler.

4.3.2 Build Skills by Sharing

Analyzing problems outside of one's comfort areas expands one's practice. Exposure to new architecture problems helps a practitioner to see the patterns that underlie project detail and which recur regularly across apparently distinct projects.

This organic learning opportunity is a driving reason for my emphasis on finding someone who's independent of the project under review. The very fact that the reviewer is unfamiliar lends a fresh eye to catch things to which one has grown too accustomed to appreciate. But the other side of that coin is training. For the reviewer, examining architectures, technologies, and security problems outside one's customary scope is the single most skill-building activity that I've seen. It's an accelerator toward security architecture competency.

Using my governance approach thus frees scarce security architects to grapple with the most difficult and complex problems, rather than having to continually repeat the same old, tired requirements over and over to each team. At the same time, this process ensures that every threat model will receive at least some level of assurance that it's been done to the best of available abilities and at least some level of independent review. Plus, this approach builds skills at all levels for continuous improvement in an organic and natural manner.

Finally, it's wickedly fast: It takes little effort to gather two other people and go over an analysis, often taking just 15 to 30 minutes. And who doesn't have 30 minutes to give to improving the work and skill of teams? If a preferred reviewer is not available, one can choose alternates, so there's almost no delay; peer review by a senior and an independent is nimble; it can be done iteratively as a threat model changes because it's so lightweight. I've seen this work four times now at different organizations, across different portfolios, and with up to 5,000 developers; I'm pretty convinced that it'll work for most organizations, while at the same time empowering (and freeing) development teams to take responsibility for secure design.

> Admittedly, all my roles have been at high-tech firms. I believe most of my "tricks of the trade," including lightweight governance as proposed in this section, will work nearly everywhere. If it doesn't, tell me why.

4.3.3 What to Do About "It Depends"

If I'm to truly practice developer-centric security, then one of the points of the manifesto is to fit naturally into the development process as it is experienced by developers and driven by any organizing staff, commonly called "project managers." Being not the most organized person in the world, and often spread out over numerous projects all running concurrently, I have found project managers to be a great boon to my ability to be useful to developers. This is true both for the project managers who can tie me into the unfolding process at key moments, if I can articulate those key moments to them clearly enough. But also, my own project managers on the security side have helped me prioritize and ensure that background tasks actually get some time beneath the barrage of interjections, incidents, and other time requests. To all the wonderful project managers who helped me, I give you a hearty thank you!

The downside of managing time in the development process is that activities such as threat modeling can seem like a terribly open-ended activity. When does it start? How long will it take? When can we say we've done enough? Is it secure yet?

And unfortunately, as I noted in *Securing Systems,* the best answer is too often, "It depends."

Sadly, the dependencies are often not in control of the very person who's trying to manage time, resources, and budget: the project manager. Or really, anyone tasked with keeping a development project moving toward its goals, toward completion of whatever cycle of changes are bundled into this, the "project." The sense of open endedness, of opaque dependencies that haven't been articulated well, is often anathema to people who take pride in organizing things. Hence, there is a built-in friction between security architecture and its inquisitive activities and the need to deliver stuff on time and under budget.

So what to do in the face of this built-in conflict?

One of the ways that I've dealt with this problem, besides building relationship and trust between project management and security (the obvious soother), is to take the threat model, this open-ended analysis, and deliver it in discrete phases. As the first structures of new software are being thought through, if I can get engagement at that time (a different problem), I don't try to do a complete threat model. Instead, I try to ensure that the high-level security requirements have been recorded. If there is any structure to work with at that point, I note any defenses that are going to be obvious for the structure as it's known at that moment.

I check in as the structure—that is, the architecture—is taking shape to add to the threat model for what is known at each check-in. In this way, I'm ahead of the details of implementation, even though neither the architecture nor the threat model are actually complete.

Implementers can be working with the security requirements that are already known. This is particularly helpful when working with iterative methodologies. The very nature of iterative development means one doesn't have to know all the details up front, but rather enough to get started.

An iterative approach, of course, means that the security architect can't just drop in in one fell swoop, deliver all the security requirements, and check in again just before go-live. I haven't found that that approach works very well under any software development methodology, anyway. So I don't recommend it. However, it does mean that the security architect has to be facile about dropping into a project, analyzing what can be assessed, and then perhaps parachuting into some other, completely different project and doing precisely the same. One has to become adept at task switching, and not everyone is good at that. Frankly, I just try to keep good notes to remind myself about where I was the last time I was involved. Plus, here's where my friends, the project managers, can help.

If the project management function is fairly mature, the project managers will be talking with each other about their various resources and their challenges. They can organize security engagements, along with whatever other engagements need facilitation.

Things are more problematic where whatever project management function exists does so solely for the project to which it is assigned; there's little coordination between projects. In that situation, I have to rely on my good note taking and my ability to schedule between projects so that one project's engagement doesn't overlap too terribly with others'.

4.3.4 Is the Threat Model Finished?

Another problem with which the security architect will have to contend is when the threat model is completed enough.

I wrote the following for my employer, IOActive®'s, blog. I've gotten a lot of questions about when a threat model is complete. I hope to help people understand that it isn't actually an open-ended process that, like some types of security research, must find issues, no matter how potentially tortured the conditions of attack might be. You might consider the following as a "Definition of Done" for threat modeling.

"Threat modeling is a process used by development teams and security architects to identify probable attack scenarios, which in turn help to define the set of defenses that a system must have (its 'security requirements'). Threat modeling remains one of secure design's most important analytic tools.

"Threat modeling is a qualitative analysis through which architecture and design choices are made based upon attack and defense analysis. This is a creative process that must have boundaries surrounding the analysis if it is to arrive at a completion.

"The constraints within which attack enumeration must be made are as follows:

- The risk tolerance of the organization owning/fielding the system
- The risk tolerance of the system's users (if any)
- The capabilities, goals, expended effort, and risk tolerances of the enumerated set of threat agents who will wish to attack
- The trust/risk profiles of the system's components, including infrastructure(s) and external entities
- The runtime/execution environment(s)
- The existing defenses (including infrastructure defenses and services)
- The highest sensitivity of data flowing through and being processed
- The probability of a particular attack scenario being low enough to be discounted

"While somewhat creative, a threat model must be grounded in hard data. Obviously, those active attacks that can be exercised against the system under analysis will be applied.

"Furthermore, an analyst also applies relevant past exploit/vulnerability pairs, even if such vulnerabilities have not yet been found in the system. It's important to understand that even the most rigorous testing, as Edsger Dijkstra so famously quipped, "shows the presence, not the absence, of bugs."* If there have existed exploitable vulnerabilities in any component within the system under analysis, even though fixed in the versions included, then the analysis must assume that at least some similar issues will likely be found in those components at some point in the future.

"An analyst may stop enumerating attacks when:

- The attack scenarios seem demonstrably more complex than other methods of compromise that are easier and more readily available.
- The required preconditions lie well outside the range of normal or typical configuration and usage.
- Significant inside assistance (for externally originated attacks) is required to proceed. (Insider threat is a special category that requires careful analysis across an organization. It rarely should be tackled one system analysis at a time. Separation of duties is often determined on a per-system, per-function, or per-privilege basis.)

---

* NATO, 1969.

- Where no exploit exists for a particular vulnerability, or the vulnerability is not exposed for remote exercise or research (it's important to periodically revisit the threat model in light of new developments).
- Attack scenarios start to border on the ridiculous, the strained, or the dubious, or depend upon computer technologies that have yet to be invented (i.e., "science fiction").

"An analyst may stop specifying defenses when:

> For more stringent security postures, each attack scenario must be mitigated. "Significant" means those attack vectors whose successful exercise will cause significant harm. It also implies attack vectors that are considered "credible"—that is, there is sufficient evidence that the attack vector can be exercised by an active threat actor.

- Each defense has some overlap of protection with at least one other defense.
- Each significant attack vector is covered at least partially by more than a single defense (see inset).

"Although threat modeling has a significant qualitative aspect, there are definite signs when the analysis has reached its completion state, that is, a threat modeling definition of done (DoD)."*

In short, a threat model isn't about dreaming up every imaginable attack scenario, even those that have never existed, or involve flights of fancy and science fiction. One extrapolates from a set of attacks that have been successful against technologies to be used or built in the system under analysis. That is, if C and C++ language programs often have memory errors, a threat model may assume that eventually similar memory errors will crop up or be discovered in this system's code.

That's not a huge jump. And there's nothing science fiction about it. It's very hard to get all the exploitable memory conditions out of a C language program, even with the most diligent set of SDL activities and tests. This is demonstrably true; all one has to do is look at the occasional memory issues that still occasionally get discovered in any of the major software house's code and then must be patched. Most of these companies have had an SDL for quite some time and are typically quite mature about their security testing for such issues. Nevertheless, memory issues do leak into releases.

The same may be extrapolated for web programs. Under even the best circumstances, an occasional issue will leak out. Therefore, it's prudent to extrapolate from relevant successful web attack knowledge when threat modeling a web program. We can presume that the web program may have such issues, if not presently, then sometime in the future, and which then will require defenses.

That is, as I said above, the threat model analysis extrapolates from known successful attack types against the technologies and architecture under analysis.

We don't have to go digging around for unknown attack types. There are plenty to apply. I tend to like to stay at the attack scenario level. One doesn't really need a specific example except if an engineer believes that I'm making the whole thing up. It's handy to have relevant

---

* The post has not been published by IOActive at the time of this writing. It will be in the future. Please check https://ioactive.com/resources/blogs for publication. Expected future post in 2020.

examples of successful attacks. Better, if those attacks have been against the company or the technology at hand. However, a few choice examples help to put the flesh on the bones for engineers who might be suspicious that one is making this up out of whole cloth.

If you're following along here, you may see that having applied the set of known, successful attack scenarios and then coming up with a reasonable set of defenses that will at the very least slow down an attacker enough to be caught, if not make the attack scenario too expensive or too difficult to exercise, leads to the completion of the threat model.

Of course, if structure is changed, technologies are added or taken away, new lines of communication are built, more sensitive data processed, or new attacks using previously unknown methods are discovered, these events should trigger a reevaluation of the threat model in light of the changes. So in some sense, our prototypical project manager is correct in that the threat model really is never done. However, for any particular set of changes, I believe there is a very definite completion point that can be articulated at least reasonably well.

4.3.5 Create a Security Contract

In a well-run project, the facilitator (often a project manager) will do their utmost to make sure that time is managed carefully, just like any other limited resource available to the project. That's not a bad thing in and of itself. Nobody likes to have their time wasted; nobody wants to sit around in a meeting that has to do with subjects that don't concern them. Productive people usually have plenty to do and not enough time to do it.

However, too often the way that time is managed to maximize productivity and minimize waste can get in the way of the kind of information exchange and discussion that is required to handle tricky architecture subjects like security (or any of the other "*ilities" with which a complex project must contend).

In an effort to be efficient, quite often items such as data interchange, API details, class definitions, or libraries are presented in a way that makes discussion over security expectations get lost. For those of you who are survivors of inter-project, inter-component meeting discussions, let me run a scenario for you and see if it feels relatively familiar.

Imagine that you're in a meeting and it's time to implement the connection between two components, each of which has been under development by a different team. Each side needs to understand the interface and expectations and the assumptions are made by the other side. An architect has been asked to present the interface. She/he/they have put together some slides describing the details that have been developed and which will be expected in order to integrate. As is typical for engineers who are not used to presenting, the slides are basically the documentation for the API scrunched down into bullets (as many bullets as will fit on a slide). This isn't a presentation at a major conference, so no one's expecting an entertaining flow or any jokes. "Just the facts, ma'am."

Often the inexperienced presenter, perhaps an architect, goes through the slides, probably mostly reading them off in trying to explain what they mean. Quite often, the presenter will have forgotten that they're speaking to other people, and might start to speak almost to themselves, quietly. The people who need to know what these facts are have probably already read a couple of the slides and may have decided that they pretty much already "get" the requirements.

So the listeners start to read email, or start to code, or whatever other task is more interesting than listening to someone quietly read their own slides.

Exactly 20 minutes will have been allotted for the presentation, which the diligent facilitator will pay close attention to. When the presentation completes, much of it will not have been heard. Plus, because time is limited, the facilitator can check the box that everyone now has all the required knowledge.

Then the other side presents their interchange expectations and technical details in much the same way with much the same results. The first side, having read the slides before the meeting, also stopped paying attention after a few minutes and do something else that seems more useful and a whole lot more engaging.

Somewhere in these two presentations will have been some kind of expression of whatever security requirements and, more importantly, security expectations are held by each side. These details, critical to security, may well have been buried in with all the other requirements and are expressed in a way that they don't really tell the participants what the assumptions are. Once the 20 minutes are up, discussion stops, and the agenda moves on to other topics.

I have seen exactly this thing hundreds of times. Unfortunately, I have also seen the result: misunderstanding of the expectations which invalidate each side's threat model. I believe I outlined the case above of a gateway that passes messages from untrusted sources which have not been validated straight on through to a component behind it. In such a situation, the consumer of the messages must take care to validate whatever data are passed or there's an opportunity to pass exploits into the consuming component.

If both sides of our hypothetical gateway and consumer haven't actually discussed what I call "the security contract"—that is, that the gateway expects the consuming component to provide its own self protection—then we just have coded a potentially delightfully exploitable condition. We have failed to implement input validation in our communications.

Although I've never measured it precisely, a good number of the worst design issues with which I've been involved that have turned into security incidents or risk exceptions have occurred from precisely the scenario I've outlined above: both sides of a communication or an interchange haven't had sufficient time to really go over their security assumptions with each other. Though time has been managed efficiently, the process has not allowed for discovery, investigation, discussion, true security understanding.

Interestingly, if I can get the presenting architects to sit down casually and informally, very quickly these smart people figure out that they had different assumptions—"centimeters to inches." I don't think there's anything wrong with managing time carefully; like most other people, I hate having my time wasted. And, I'll admit to getting bored listening to the technical details of something that I think I already pretty much understand. I'm not trying to demonize anyone with my little disquisition here.

But it does seem to me that we must also leave time for unstructured discussion in order to avoid these situations from getting out of hand and turning into an incident. An adjunct to this discussion about security assumptions will be explicit documentation devoted to the security controls implemented as well as the assumptions made: a security contract.

1. Make our security assumptions and requirements for interchange a formal document, the security contract that we expect consumers and communicators to understand and

to adhere to. This should probably be a formal document that goes right along with the documentation of an API, a library, a class, or an object.

2. Schedule time after the presentations for some open-ended discussion between the presenters. Ensure that at least one of the topics that have been given time for discussion will be the security requirements of the interchange and the security expectations and assumptions of each component. This discussion is not completed until everyone involved walks away with a full understanding of the other side's security.

With these two culture hack additions, the necessary understanding for ensuring that component threat models are pieced together properly can take place. Sometimes there's no shortcut for open and honest dialogue. With all due respect to the wonderful project managers who helped me stay productive and on task, sometimes overly careful time management can be an impediment instead of a help. A little loose conversation can sometimes solve a multitude of problems.

If the sort of focused but less highly facilitated discussion isn't possible to arrange, or as a support of such a discussion, a component's "security contract" can be drafted. This document declares precisely what a component offers for protection, its security assumptions as to what sort of attacks it will or will not defend (this can be very general; it's not a restatement of the threat model, although the security contract relies on the threat model). The security contract must state what assumptions the components communications make about the other side.

Security contracts are very useful in situations in which the developers of a component will never meet or interact with their consumers. Consider a product that's a gateway. If the product is sold as a gateway, and there are going to be thousands of purchasers, there is no way that the developers are going to talk to each and every purchaser, to be involved in each and every installation.

In these less personal situations, a security contract for the component becomes critical. Those who will use the component (gateway) need to know what security they're getting, and what security they are not going to inherit by using the product. In these situations, I insist that teams create a short security document that describes what the component defends against, and what it expects from other parts of systems into which it will be integrated. Such a document—a security contract, if you will call it that—can avoid a lot of angry customers.

I still think that a holistic eye on whether all the components will interoperate together securely is actually the complete threat model. Threat modeling is always hampered when confined to narrow views. Its particular requirement is analyzing the whole, because the model cannot merely be the sum of its constituent parts.

4.3.6 Threat Models Are Not Additive!

With the above in mind, absolutely narrowing down the scope of complex projects to workable pieces makes sense. With a big proviso: Threat models are not additive! When the pieces come together, the whole is different from each piece by itself; the total threat model is not a simple sum of all the sub-models. That was a big mistake that a big company at which I used to work made regularly: everything was just an "ingredient"—if the ingredient has already had its threat model, just add the models together.

Let me reuse the example already given. A gateway product is "just passing messages through," so it doesn't examine the content being passed. That's fine. That gateway must protect itself from everything that it might receive except that which may lie within the message content.

Let's suppose that the receiving component perfoms some analytic data processing on the body of those messages that had been passed through the gateway cited above. The consumer's threat model is focused on second-layer threats, on insider and administrative protections, which makes sense when the consumer is taken in isolation.

If we simply put these two models together, then we have just missed an important vector of attack via the message traffic. Attacks destined for the processing engine (the consumer) have no mitigation between these two components; the gateway assumes that the processor is taking care of data cleansing, while the processor assumes that the gateway only passes valid messages. Perhaps you leapt ahead and identified the problem easily? Yet, I cannot count the number of times that I've seen precisely this mistake being made.

The gateway passes untrusted message traffic. Therefore, its security contract with message receivers is that the message content cannot be trusted. Both components must be analyzed together, holistically, as a single, integrated system. Otherwise, message receiver beware.

4.3.7 Audit and Security Are Not the Same Thing

The larger the organization, the more likely it is that one is going to run into pretty divergent perspectives. Sometimes, my security architect's perspective might run smack dab up against a conflicting, maybe even incompatible, view. This is perhaps one of the biggest challenges facing those of us who pursue organizational transformation—those of us who are culture hackers.

Let me give an example. One of my dear friends (who shall not be named to protect her privacy), a recognized expert in her field, comes out of a compliance background. We disagree greatly about the nature of compliance and security. She believes that achieving strong compliance delivers appropriate security. I do not find this to be true, because standards and regulations often make assumptions about the nature of the problem space, assumptions about whom the standard applies to, about how the target organizations are structured, about whom the standard addresses, and about solutions sets. Because of the amount of time it takes to create, draft, and ratify a standard (years), the threat landscape and solution sets may have moved significantly since the codification of the language in the standard: these are rarely up to date.

Imagine a standard that assumes that software security is about building applications. Already, organizations that create embedded software or clouds might readily believe that "application security" doesn't include the software that these other organizations are building. Further, imagine that the standard always addresses information technology (IT) whenever the implementing organization is named. Many organizations do not build product software in their IT function, but rather, in their research and development or engineering functions. May they then believe that the standard is not intended for their software?

I didn't make the above up. In fact, draft 1 of ISO 27034 had exactly the problems described in the preceding paragraph. These issues crept in despite the fact that ISO 27034 was intended to cover software security in general, not just IT software delivery, not confined to applications only. Oops? I think so.*

The truth is, writing general standards is hard. Assumptions that change the scope can creep in rather too easily. Standard drafters might assume that everyone already knows what "penetration testing" is, so there's no need to define it. That's what the first and second revisions of Payment Card Industry Data Security Standard (PCI) did. But, unfortunately, there is no standard definition of penetration testing, and PCI didn't point to a particular definition as the one to which the standard refers. In fact, companies pass PCI audits of their penetration testing requirement with a wide range of testing, all the way from periodic vulnerability scans, through application vulnerability testing, to manually driven attempts to break in (which is the common, industry accepted definition of "penetration testing"). The three test examples I just gave vary greatly in the results that they deliver.

To achieve compliance, the goal is to meet a specific set of predetermined requirements: what's been codified into the language of the standard or regulation. These could be for regulation such as GDPR† or HIPAA‡, or a standard such as ISO® 27001 or SOC 2®.

Unfortunately, some requirements of a standard might very well be irrelevant to the situation to be secured. In fact, this happens a lot. Or, as in GDPR, the requirement might be so vague as to be essentially meaningless. As an example, take Article 32, which purportedly describes what security measures are required:

"ARTICLE 32: Security of Personal Data - Security of Processing
"Article 32 of the GDPR, which requires 'controller and the processor shall implement appropriate technical and organizational measures to ensure a level of security appropriate to the risk'
   "(a) the pseudonymization and encryption of personal data;
   "(b) the ability to ensure the ongoing confidentiality, integrity, availability, and resilience of processing systems and services;
   "(c) the ability to restore the availability and access to personal data in a timely manner in the event of a physical or technical incident;
   "(d) a process for regularly testing, assessing and evaluating the effectiveness of technical and organizational measures for ensuring the security of the processing."§

If we take (c), anyone who's practiced any security knows that the point is CIA: Confidentiality, Integrity, and Availability. This statement is so general as to be essentially meaningless.

Like California's SB 1386, the encryption line doesn't set forth any of the implementation patterns for encryption to provide real protection. Would it be enough to implement transparent, hard disk encryption, where the keying material is available to the logged in user?

As I remember, one of the dodges that less than fully honest and forthright companies started to use in order to protect themselves from breach notification under SB 1386 was to use

---

* http://www.iso27001security.com/html/27034.html
† European Union Global Data Protection Regulation.
‡ Health Insurance Portability and Accountability Act.
§ Gen. Data Protection Regulation 2016/679, Article 32. European Union, http://www.privacy-regulation.eu/en/article-32-security-of-processing-GDPR.htm

transparent disk encryption. Any legal reader of the storage would get decrypted information: That's what "transparent" means. However, although this measure provides near zero runtime security benefit, it meets the legal definition of "data must be encrypted." We might start to see organizations try similar legal dodges in the GDPR space, as well. Line (a) doesn't tell us anything about the difficulties that must be met for robust, protective encryption. One could legally claim that simply having some sort of encryption meets the intent of the law. But is it security? No.

My friend insisted that being compliant automatically delivered appropriate security. I hope I've proved to you in the examples above that this is not at all true. Still, we had to not only work together, but to be effective together. Somehow, we had to find a way that our differences didn't hinder effectiveness.

How does one go about that?

I can't tell you that I have a never-fail secret to share to meet the challenge of wildly divergent perspectives such as compliance versus security. I struggle with this probably is much as any other person who routinely works with a wide range of smart and often rather opinionated people.

What I look for are places in which we are attempting to reach the same goal, only from varying routes. I listen carefully for areas of resonance, for areas of alignment. It may be when actually trying to get something done that a conflicting philosophy is irrelevant. It may be that it's merely a matter of semantics or articulation. I try really hard not to get too hung up about the way things are expressed so long as security requirements are met.

In the case of my friend, if she insisted upon expressing things with a line from some regulation or standard, so long as implementers understood the security needs to be met, what does it matter?

By being malleable around expression, I can focus on the objective. Only in a case in which there's a conflict in what must actually be accomplished do I want to enter into a need for conflict resolution, negotiation, and compromise. Often enough, all roads actually do lead to the Rome of appropriate security implementation. Or, if a regulatory requirement really is inappropriate, or worse, irrelevant, there is always the "out" of carefully documenting the insignificant likelihood and impact from failing to comply. Most of the standards and regulations allow for a statement of noncompliance given in business risk terms. Done well enough, risk assessments offered in place of compliance will usually pass audit.

There's also usually a possibility for "compensating controls." Compensating controls are alternative defenses that achieve a CIA protection similar to those that a standard requires. For instance, a compensating set of controls for encryption of data at rest would be something like the following set of controls:

- Highly restricted network segment.
- Access requires multi-factor authentication.
- Strict, need-to-know only restrictions for privileged access.
- When access has been granted it would only be allowed for a limited period.
- The grant occurring through a formalized process employing separation of duties between grantor and grantee.
- Any access to the storagte requires that all high privileged actions will be logged and then monitored by an independent group (not the grantee).

The above controls would compensate for encryption of data at rest. If properly documented, these are likely to pass an audit and to be defensible in court as "encryption of personal data" and an "ability to ensure the ongoing confidentiality, integrity", as GDPR requires.

4.4 From Program to Transformation

"[A] sense of participation in something new and interesting is infectious. Rather than trying to be personally charismatic (I'm not!), I make the program, the work, charismatic. People like to have a little fun, enjoy a little creativity at work. Security architecture is so complex, and there are so many variables to getting things done, it's a perfect test bed for innovation. As I've stressed above, mistakes are going to happen anyway. If I can keep disasters from happening, while at the same time, I'm willing to try different ways of achieving ends even if these have some risk of failing, this invitation to play attracts supporters and helps to build towards a tipping point to a successful, self-sustaining security architecture program." *Securing Systems,* p. 363.

There's something intrinsically attractive about an effort that appears to be making a difference, that's going somewhere, that's demonstrating significant progress. Although I must be an enthusiastic cheerleader, I find that it's critical to demonstrate the objectives that the program wishes to achieve early and often.

If there is a need to increase secure design practice, probably through active threat modeling, then I need to threat model in order to help teams identify their security requirements. Start with the work at hand and establish a zeal to immediately get some results on the board, as it were. Astute teams will see the value delivered and wish to also gain those advantages. Delivering actual work as soon as humanely possible also starts to attract those who are curious about techniques, who may wish to add these to their technical bag of tricks. I get out and deliver right away. Word gets around.

I also need to share the process of threat modeling; I need to teach it to anyone who wants to learn. I need to encourage people to try to threat model their projects. And then I need to be of help if they ask me to refine the threat model or to check their work. It's important to be encouraging; it's very important to make stuff happen so that it's obvious to anyone who cares to look that there is a program underway and it's starting to have some impact. There is both delivery and modeling the culture that we wish to birth.

4.4.1 Pro-Social Modeling

I hold myself to the standard of modeling the behavior that exemplifies the culture that I'm trying to create. Of course, I'm not always successful; I'm sometimes more inconsistent than I wish to be. Still, despite my failings, I do find that striving for the culture I want to move toward helps others intuitively grasp what were all reaching for.

- If I want people to listen, I must listen well.
- If I want authentic discussions, then I have to enter into discussions authentically.
- If I want people to be open to fresh ideas, I must embrace creative and innovative approaches.

- If we are to successfully negotiate conflict, I have to put aside my own fears, my own biases, and try to negotiate conflict acceptably to all sides.
- If I want it to be acceptable to make mistakes, then I must admit gracefully when I'm wrong.

Modeling behavior remains an important tool for creating the culture that you want to bring about.

"The basic idea underlying social learning accounts of prosocial behavior is that people teach others to behave in prosocial ways by . . . modeling prosocial forms of conduct."[*]

Of course, I cannot claim to model every behavior that a team needs in order to become effective, certainly not anywhere near 100%. It turns out that modeling failure is as important as modeling the change that is sought—both are needed for effective culture hacking. That's because we are obviously all humans with limitations and challenges, just as much as we may be effective and incisive.

When someone with authority, someone in any leadership position, whether perceived or organizationally empowered, shows a willingness to admit mistakes, acknowledge failure to enact their own aspirations, and does so authentically, this is a powerful act. Doing so makes it safe for others to admit error, to focus on problems and solutions, rather than hiding or worse, so-called "blame-storming"—finding as much fault as possible, accusing and defending. Acknowledging misjudgment is a powerful hack, just as much as it's authentic leadership and plain old good manners. It's another type of "pro-social modeling."

4.4.2 Leaders Must Get Challenged

Sometimes when undertaking complex analyses, it's hard to know that one has missed something important, misunderstood some technical aspect, or gone down a fruitless path. As I wrote above, peer review is an essential governance technique for everyone, including the most experienced personnel. It can be a challenge to find someone who has the skill and insight to review a technical leader's work. Perhaps the following example, taken from *Securing Systems* (p. 365), will illustrate this particular culture hack.

"If I'm starting from scratch, I have to find that first person. This is harder if the work is already piling up, the architectures are complex, and the velocity is rapid. I've had two situations exactly like this. My first team member will be key to an ability to add lots of different skills sets, experience, and approaches. That first person's temperament and communication skills are as important as the candidate's technical skill.

"One of the first additions to the team must foster a spirit of lively interchange directed towards synthetic and creative solutions. This interchange must demonstrate that disagreement does not mean a loss of relationship, but rather a strengthening of trust. If the two of us can set an example of motivation, engagement, and an ability to work through conflict, this will create an environment conducive to diversity. Although it's great to get a first or second addition who is your equal, as long as these people are open to learning, and to being personally empowered, I believe that the right template will be set.

---

[*] Zeigler, Welling, and Shakelford, 2015.

"At one job, I had to build a team from absolute zero; I was the only member of the team, though the work was enough for five to eight architects. My first hire did not fit the above profile; that person deferred to my experience far too often to foster an engaged and empowered atmosphere. We then brought in a very junior person to train, which made matters worse.

"Understanding this unfolding dynamic, and how it would stunt the growth of the group, I begged my management for a senior person. I then talked a friend of mine, Ove Hansen, who is a very experienced security architect into joining the team. I knew Ove could find the holes in my logic and that Ove wouldn't hesitate to challenge my ideas (though professionally and politely, of course). Within about six weeks of bringing Ove onto the team, the dynamic of the group shifted to lively discussions and synthetic solution sets. The team needed an example; they needed a sign that disagreement with me was not only tolerated but would be encouraged."

I hope that you can see how important it is to carefully consider central team composition. In my experience, the dynamics and composition of the central team (if there is one) greatly influence how everyone associated and working with security architecture will behave. Not only do individuals model pro-social behaviors, but also any established body of security architects who model behaviors for those who may represent security architecture from within development teams, as well. It will be the working relationships of the most experienced security architects that establish the norms for everyone.

But a central team isn't sufficient for hacking one's way toward a developer-centric culture of security. Different levels of an organization are called upon for the various angles of the shift.

"For a practice such as the security architecture . . . , support and, ultimately, buy-in will need to come from the organizational decision makers, the grassroots, and across your network. That is, building a network of support, even when it's relatively few in number—upwards, across, and downwards—will greatly accelerate adoption and follow through for your security assessment program. Even with relatively few numbers of supporters, the organization will achieve that 'tipping point' that spells success for the entire program. Communications are important. Repeated communication will likely be a necessity." *Securing Systems,* p. 362.

4.4.3 Hack All Levels

Executives of course are important; without executive buy-in and support even the best intentioned and run effort will fail: Eventually, there will be resistance somewhere in the organization. Designing then building security costs money, time, resources, focus, effort. Somewhere along the way, some teams will meet resource challenges, trade-offs between security work and some, usually many, other competing requirements. While elsewhere in this work, *Core Software Security,* and *Securing Systems,* I've presented various ways to deal with those challenges, nevertheless, it is inevitable that there will be resistance to security—perhaps, downright rebellion. This must be expected.

When it is not obvious what should be done, when agreement cannot be reached as to whether to put off a security requirement against something more pressing, the usual approach will be to escalate. Those escalations sometimes end up in front of executives, and that is the point at which one finds out whether the executives are only giving lip service to security or if they will stand up for it.

This is not to say that supportive executives will decide in favor of security every time. I've never seen that. Sometimes, there are very good business reasons to put off security. That is always an executive prerogative.

However, if said executive always decides against security, then one knows where one really stands—nowhere, to be exact. A supportive executive will consider, will hear all sides, will take all the risk factors into account. Sometimes, it will be a matter of when to complete required security, not whether to do it at all. Sometimes, the executive will decide to prioritize security against other risk factors. That is as it should be. I don't expect to win—winning is not the attitude to cultivate for these escalations. Security risk needs to be fully acknowledged and validated. That's all I'm looking for in these situations. That's enough; I consider that executive support. When security is consistently undermined or disregarded, that is a clear lack of support. Without that support, much of an organization will follow suit. It may be time to look for a different organization.

Executive support is more than communicating how important security is to an organization. It's also standing up for security, making time for the hard decisions, making those hard decisions based upon the best information that can be had at that moment.

I learned fairly early on after assuming a technical leadership security role that mid-management were going to make or break my efforts. Typically, minor, low, even medium risks will be decided by mid-management—in most organizations, the directors or equivalents. If the risk is not catastrophic to the entire organization or is confined to a particular set of functions or teams, mid-management will often handle the issue.

Plus, directors often set priorities for their groups. If a director wishes to undermine security initiatives, at least for their teams, they can do it. In large, complex organizations, mid-management may have wide degrees of influence. Knowing whether they support, don't care, or are actively resisting is crucial, which is why one of the first things I do at a new organization is to have a chat with each of the relevant directors. Plus, I observe what they do as security requirements and security tasks are introduced.

Critical questioning is fine; that equals engagement. Engagement is a sign of support, although it might not feel that way when one is subject to a sharp director interrogation. As long as the enquiry seems to be about making the work better, about making security work with all the other factors that go into producing good software, that rings as support to me.

Again, just like executives, if, when push comes to shove, teams are consistently allowed to put security tasks off, to deprioritize security requirements, then that's either passive aggression or active resistance. I want to identify resisters. I can't meet their issues without actively uncovering them.

So that's one of my hacks: Find out what the issues are, perhaps what is being protected, and then I can start to craft solutions that don't ruin what's already been built. A great deal of the time, in functional organizations, resistance is about protecting one or more "things" that are working well.

One cannot always predict what one might threaten when one begins a program of culture change. Resistance is an invitation to investigate, to learn. Mid-management has the power to change, but also to resist. It is in this layer that I have often uncovered processes or methods that I must take into account in order to be successful.

For years, security architecture had been trying to improve the way that Transport Layer Security (TLS) certificate private keys had been stored. At that organization, it wasn't terrible, but it wasn't great either. Private keys were stored using operating system user privileges on the machines where the certificates were validated. Those hosts' accesses were quite restricted. Still, an attacker gaining those privileges would then have access to an important corporate messaging conduit. We wanted the private keys to be stored elsewhere and then retrieved strictly for validation, then removed.

Years went by; we (security) could never figure out why we couldn't get any traction; there were a million excuses. One day, I got to talking to the senior IT architect who was in charge of the whole system and the process. It turned out that junior engineers were tasked with creating the certificates; they had to have access rights to the system on which the certificates would be created. It was convenient and efficient to have the private keys local to the certificate validation. There were no funds for a solution like a hardware security module (HSM) purpose built for these sorts of operations.

Once I fully understood the need for junior engineers who probably didn't fully understand either the system on which the certificates would be used or the details of X509 certificates in general, I had the reasons for the protective, balky behavior.

Frankly, I don't remember the particulars that we worked out. But I made sure that the junior people would continue to function efficiently. Those separate certificate servers were running inside of six weeks (which was really fast, in those days, this being long before readily available cloud services).

No matter what the solution actually encompassed, one of the key requirements was not to break something that IT needed to keep working properly. That hadn't been apparent until I took the time to investigate the whole problem, not just the security needs. A solution that included both security and IT then became acceptable to all involved and went forward quickly and easily. This was a powerful lesson to me in looking beyond resistance to what needed to be accomplished in order to be successful for all involved.

Occasionally, in large organizations, one will meet someone who is playing for themself alone. That is an entirely different problem than resistance that has credible reasons. Each of us must work with those of low integrity as best we can. I have my approaches, but these might not work for others. I'm not a psychologist; I don't have pat answers for these sticky situations. Luckily, in my career, these horrible situations have been few and far between. Generally, I can assume that resistance is based upon organizational needs, not personal power dynamics.

In any event, mid-management, especially in large organizations, is a key player in actually getting security done. These important players must not be ignored.

Finally, I accept assistance or support from everyone and anyone at any level. Sometimes management and, especially, executives don't have a full understanding of what my friend Dr. James Ransome calls, "ground truth"—that is, what is actually going on in development teams. To move a software organization toward a culture of security, ground truth is critical. Without it, I guarantee that executive pronouncements, mid-management directives, strategy statements, Security Development Life cycle (SDL) documents, policies, standards, processes, and methods will flounder.

One of the most important things that I can do is to talk to developers and observe how they are actually developing software, because if the SDL directly contradicts or interferes with the development process, it cannot work. Smart developers will find a way around anything that slows them down or that they perceive as lacking value.

On the other hand, if something—anything—seems to help build better software, gets more bugs out quicker, the vast majority of developers with whom I've worked will embrace that task, that tool, that activity rapidly and with little resistance. It often comes down to perceived utility.

In my threat modeling classes, when I have a mix of developers and security practitioners, I often play a little game. I ask the developers how they feel when security requirements are included early in the development process. To a person (so far) the developers in my classes uniformly claim that they love getting as many requirements, security and otherwise, as early in the process as possible so that they know what they are to build.

Then I ask the developers how they feel when they get their security requirements after most of whatever they're building is completed. "Bleh!" They hate it! Rework! Schedules not met. Time wasted building the wrong stuff. "Yech! Security interjections are terrible."

I then ask the security folks how they feel when they're invited to participate in shaping requirements early. Again, uniformly, security folk love that. How about two days before go-live or production deployment? "Yech!" What can be accomplished so late in the game? Nearly nothing of any real importance.

I can then point out that the people in the class have the power to end this problem, right there, right then. Developers, when you have a new effort, invite security in. Security, when you're called in late, point out to developers how dysfunctional that is, how security cannot be architected after everything is complete.

In other words, security has to fit into the development process. But that fit cannot be accomplished by one expertise or the other; it must be accomplished by working together. This is why security must interact with grassroots developers directly. We must understand the entire project or effort process. Whatever security tasks (the SDL, essentially) need to be accomplished must fit within the processes and methods that will be used to build the software.

4.4.4 Coding Is Fraught with Error

One of the challenges that I've seen over and over again is the demand that people "code securely." Training programs are instituted. Coders take the courses, but mistakes keep occurring. Secure code analysis tools are purchased and integrated into build systems, but preventable vulnerabilities still leak out into releases. Why?

My first realization, thinking back to my own coding, is that coding mistakes happen. Period. The truism that coding mistakes will occur must be the ground upon which every part of solutions must stand.

There are two situations that increase the likelihood of coding errors, security and otherwise:

1. When coding something new, innovative, or creative
2. When coding really boring, rote, run-of-the-mill aspects

Obviously, whenever we try something new, we are bound to make errors. This is expected when learning to play a musical instrument. Why do we expect a different result when coding innovative algorithms?

Sometimes, when I'm in front of developers, I ask them if they've ever finished a piece of code that they felt was implemented very well. Then, when a bug has appeared in the field, perhaps six months after release, have they taken a look at the code, only to realize that it's very wrong? I get a lot of chuckles and knowing nods from my question. It's certainly happened to me. Many programmers have experienced something similar, because it's easy to miss some detail of logic or side-effect. It's possible to pass even rigorous testing regimes and still have coded a nasty bug. Many of us who've written significant amounts of code have dealt with these issues and many more: The library our code depends upon doesn't behave the way that we thought it did, or the way that the documentation claims.

Many years ago, I had to write an infra-red (IR) driver for one of the Consumer versions of Windows® (before Windows migrated to the NT device driver model). IR is incredibly time sensitive. I chased inconsistent behavior for months before I realized that the time function in that version of Windows was unreliable. Sometimes my code got called in the correct periodicity, but a lot of the time, it did not. When I changed the code to rely on a hardware clock, it finally worked as expected.

This is just one example of how, given complex systems, depending upon huge volumes of code, all prone to errors, can appear to be written correctly, but still misbehave. Software bugs are legion. I think that it's fairly safe to assume that any reasonably complex piece of code will have a few errors in it. Some of the unintended behavior will likely have security implications. Furthermore, the newer the code, the more likely it is that the code will have mistakes in it, some of which will be vulnerabilities.

The other situation that can foster errors is boredom. When coding commercially, there are generally standards about how the code is to be written, where the comments go, etc. One very typical task will be to "cover" a library (say open source software) that implements needed functionality. *Cover* in this context means to build functions calling the library to implement the needed functionality. There are a host of code structure reasons for doing it this way, rather than calling the code directly. For one thing, if the library needs to be swapped for a another, only the covering routines need changing, not all the places in the code where the functionality will be used.

However, setting up a bunch of covering routines to an organization's standards is not the most interesting task. It's a job that needs doing, and it needs to be done well. However, it doesn't take a computer scientist to write a bunch of cover routines. Hence, this task can be quite boring: setting up the standard class or method or function headers multiple times. It's mostly boilerplate. Boring work leads to mistakes, just as innovative work can.

4.4.5 Effective Secure Coding Training

Whatever the reasons, software mistakes happen, and happen regularly and repeatedly. What can be done about it?

Obviously, we can train people to generate more secure code in the first place. But do those five-day, secure coding classes really improve things? Maybe. Chris Romeo, CEO of Security

Journey, and I have talked quite a bit about what might constitute highly effective training. There are two problem areas:

1. People need to practice what they learn in order to integrate the knowledge into their coding.
2. Different programming languages and systems have fairly different security requirements.

It's more cost effective for trainers to deliver several days of training in a block rather than on demand. So instructor-led trainings have tended to be multi-day affairs. But that makes it hard for coders to integrate each technique into the code that they write. Class exercises are all well and good, but they might not match closely enough to what participants are actually writing.

Plus, each training has to be general enough to cover a range of situations and programming languages. That means that some of the work for some attendees will very likely be irrelevant.

Chris and I have discussed very short webinars, 15–30 minutes, focusing on a single area of secure coding, in a particular language, for a particular set of coding problems. Then, let the learners go off and apply what they've learned to their code, try to recognize the approach or lack thereof when reviewing others' code. The focus should be on practical application until the learners have integrated the knowledge into their skills. That is how most people learn: Do a single new thing until it's understood and integrated. Apply what has been learned until it becomes a part of what one does.

> I once attended a master class in jazz improvisation from Kenny Werner. In response to a question about how to practice, Kenny cited learning studies that demonstrate that people quickly become overwhelmed when they try to learn more than one thing at a time. This results in slow or even no progress. Practice a single thing until it can be done well, then apply it until it becomes part of one's repertoire. In coding, as in jazz improvisation, it's the same.

I've spoken to a few training companies about such an approach. We'll see if this works better than the five-day cram.

Still, people will forget, will mis-apply, just plain make errors. As I wrote, above, that's a given.

4.4.6 Make Validation Easy

That's where tools such as static analysis come in. Just like a compiler checks to see if the code is syntactically correct, so static analysis can check to see if there are potential security errors in the code. That should be a big help. Where does this go wrong?

One of the problems is that many (most) static analysis tools, and especially the commercial ones, are sold through broad coverage of types and variations of possible errors. But, lots of the checks aren't all that reliable. Although some types of errors might be found with very high confidence (say, 80% or 90%), many of the checks have a much lower confidence level. The tools then rely on a human to figure out whether or not there really is an error.

Plus, these tools benefit from a lot of configuration and tuning. They often need to be told about some of the details of the code and its standard libraries. Mostly, one cannot just add the tool to the build chain and expect reasonable results.

When I got to one organization, one team had a backlog of 72,000 static analysis findings. Another team there had 46,000. I'll bet astute readers can guess what those teams did with all those errors? Absolutely nothing. There were too many findings to begin to deal with any of the results; it would take years of work to winnow through that many findings, at the expense of actually generating any code.

The tool had not been tuned to the code base. It was not configured correctly. The two teams I mention simply turned on "all checks" and then, when there were too many findings with which to deal, they perceived the static analysis tool as useless. Security demanded that they add the tool. But its results were too noisy to be useful.

There is a solution to this problem, and this is precisely what we did at that organization. We configured that rather complex commercial tool to render only high confidence results. Most of these tools can be configured to deliver everything. But they can also be configured to analyze only for findings of high confidence. Once the two teams began to get valuable results, they became our model for all the other teams. Within a year, all the teams were finding great value in their static analysis because they focused on high confidence results first. Teams were free to experiment with confidence settings beyond the basics. Each team reached its own tolerance for tool noise. Security issues decreased significantly.

The other approach that I think helps is giving programmers as much security checking, as early in their coding process as possible. Nearly all the commercial static analysis tools as of this writing have a desktop version or option that allows coders to check their work as they code. This is very powerful because of a typical cultural expectation.

Generally, diligent programmers expect errors in their code as they're working on it. Any tool that can find errors (without generating too many incorrect findings and not requiring too much configuration and tuning) will usually be appreciated and integrated.

But there's a mental shift that happens when a programmer believes that the code is stable and correct. Code that has been released to the next stage of the development process (which varies depending upon the development methodology) can be a bit "out of sight, out of mind." Often, the programmer has moved on to other problems. There can be a bit of "prove to me that there's an error" once code has left the programmer's purview and moved on.

Hence, testing that occurs after a programmer commits code as "correct" may be a little too distant from the coding process. Whereas, tools that can integrate into the coding process, that find errors during coding, generally receive greater programmer attention. Hence, I like to get at least some security checking onto the coders' desks, into their integrated development environment (IDE), early in the coding process. Even if the checks are less rigorous than those that can be placed within a later build process, still, early identification of security mistakes is more organic than massive sets of findings later on.

Get secure coding analysis tools into the coding cycles. Then, perform a more thorough check during build. From experience, that seems to work the best. However it's done, these complex tools need to be properly configured and tuned to the code base that they will analyze. Otherwise, one is likely to end up with a lot of low confidence findings that hide errors that really should be fixed—that is, so-called "noisy" findings (72,000 potential errors!).

Fitting analysis tools into the development process so that they deliver recognizable coding value is a powerful security culture hack, because coders start integrating security checks into their work as a matter of course. Plus, it's a powerful training tool, since after making the same mistake a few times, most programmers will learn to think about that problem as they code and stop making it repeatedly.

In my experience, training and code checking tools go hand in hand, supporting each other. When they work together, it's yet another culture hack. It's a hack that happens at the grass-roots, where actual development takes place.

After a while, some of the more skilled programmers will want to increase their security skills. Out of these will come the next generation of security engineers, architects, and even teachers. Once a program has matured to the point at which it becomes self-sustaining and regularly spawns new generations of architects and teachers, that's a sign, to me, that culture has been transformed into a culture of security.

4.5 Summary

When threat modeling becomes a normal part of software design, when secure code analysis, both automated and manual, have become the expected norm, when testing regimes include vulnerability analysis and abuse cases, these are the signs that a development culture has shifted to include security as one of the things that needs to be implemented.

That doesn't mean that every security problem has been solved. There will always be a mix of varying skill levels from beginner to expert. Vulnerabilities will be missed by even the most rigorous testing regimes. Sometimes, security will have to take a back seat to other business necessities. New teams will be so busy ramping up that they will forget to enact security or will simply be too inexperienced to do it well enough.

Still, after many of the hacks that I've suggested in this chapter have been implemented and have become part of development's "wood work"—part of the fabric, as it were—there usually is a safety net for catching these exceptions, rather than security being the exception. I've been a part of such transformations a few times. It is from those experiences that the hacks in this

Table 4.1 Summation of Actions Described in This Chapter[a]

Do	Don't
Integrate into the shared viewpoint and jargon of development teams. Become a part of the team, engage, understand challenges.	Drop security requirments onto developers, then disappear.
Listen to understand. Ask questions to get at roots of conflict.	Dominate and insist upon "security's way or the highway."
Build support to a tipping point.	Try to win every conflict.
Give visibility to low and medium risks in a brief and easy-to-consume manner.	Waste influence on minor issues.
Jettison unworkable processes.	Continue because, "we've always done it this way."
Start with attack scenarios for which there are convincing, ready examples.	Begin by enforcing security requirements without first explaining each requirement's supporting attack scenarios.

continues on next page

Table 4.1 Summation of Actions Described in This Chapter (cont.)

Do	Don't
Introduce threat modeling to everyone who has any role whatsoever in developing software: imagining, defining, generating, validating, deploying, managing, coordinating, or supporting.	Restrict threat modeling to security practitioners only, or just to the technical leaders and security people.
Review threat model after structural or security changes.	Mandate "threat model every change."
Trust developers.	Treat developers like wayward children.
Engage throughout the cycles of development iteration.	Don't interject point-in-time requirements and then expect that these cannot be changed in subsequent iterations.
Let developers find as many security requirements as they can.	Assume that only the security expert will provide a threat model.
Expose learners to problems outside of their usual scope.	Isolate practitioners to their well-known problems.
Include one senior and one independent reviewer for a nimble governance process.	Drive all changes through formal review boards that then become a bottleneck.
Iterate the threat model alongside increasing specificity of requirements, structure, and design.	Avoid point-in-time, all-at-once threat models performed after the architecture has been completed.
Stop threat modeling when attack scenarios and defenses move to the tortured and fantastical.	Insist upon ivory tower, textbook sets of defenses.
Generate explicit "security contracts" for each component that will interact with other components. The contract must describe mitigations, assumptions, and any unhandled threats, especially those that may be vectored through to partner components.	Rely on API presentations as completed threat models. Threat models are not additive, they must be considered holistically.
Audit for compliance, not for security posture.	Base security posture on successful compliance audits.
Model security and interaction behaviors.	Claim behavioral perfection.
Reward team empowerment.	Expect smart people to agree and conform.
Build support at all levels; accept all offers of assistance.	Expect executive mandate to build a culture of security.
Account and mitigate for implementation errors.	Expect perfect coding.
Make implementation validation easy, accessible, and integrated into natural developer flows.	Rely on a single validation form, type, tool, and single point in the development process.

[a] Table 4.1 is supplied in the hope that its summary statements provide a quick reference to the tips and tricks that I've outlined in this chapter.

---

chapter have been drawn. These things work; at least, they've worked for me—most of them more than once. I hope that they help you with your secure culture transformations, too.

4.5.1 We All Can Use Some Feedback

There remains one more hack to note:

"In my communication plan, I include obtaining peer and grassroots evaluation and feedback. I don't necessarily take every bit of feedback exactly as it is expressed. But even wild accusations and projections often have a kernel or grain of truth hiding within them. In this way, I can tailor the program to the organization's needs more precisely." *Security Systems,* p. 362.

Although I've got a few tricks up my sleeve by now, these must always be tempered by the situation on the ground. Smart people prefer to have some control over things that affect their lives at work. Sometimes, the details matter quite a bit. So, each time I've attempted one of these transformations, I've tried to work with local needs, to work in local requirements, to build upon any successes I can find. Feedback and participation are key to success: I try to remain open to new ideas, new approaches, to give some sense of participation in shaping transformations to those with whom I'm working.

By working iteratively, we can try things, even things that I think, in the moment, might not work well. After all, we can always change it! We might learn something. We might find a new hack that's more effective. Why not? It's not as if all security problems have been solved. There's plenty of culture hacking work yet to do.

Chapter 5

Learning the Trade

As I've written previously, the tried and true training method for security architects has been to "shadow"—that is, follow—a seasoned security architect as she/he/they go about their daily tasks. That method does work for some, but the method has a couple of drawbacks.

What if you've just been appointed or hired as the only security architect for an organization? There will be no one to shadow. I've been asked for pointers multiple times by people in precisely this position.

What if you dislike the person to whom you've been assigned, or their style is radically different from yours? A person must have extraordinary confidence and sense of self to transcend feelings of alienation, feelings of antipathy, such that, despite these barriers, one still has a learning experience. Many people (even talented ones) will simply give up or close down, thus negating potential for growth.

Consider that there are many different ways to present material for learning. The presentations may or may not correspond to learning styles, which may or may not be based in sound research.[*] Nevertheless, "There may be evidence that indicates that there are some ways to teach some subjects that are just better than others."[†]

Although shadowing might be one avenue of learning, I believe that we must develop others alongside this timeworn method if we are to train the hundreds, nay, thousands of security architects required to fill existing and future demands (see inset).

In this chapter, I hope to share a few tools, a few tricks for accelerating the security architecture learning process.

> "Employment of information security analysts is projected to grow 28 percent from 2016 to 2026, much faster than the average for all occupations. Demand for information security analysts is expected to be very high, as these analysts will be needed to create innovative solutions to prevent hackers from stealing critical information or causing problems for computer networks." (Bureau of Labor Statistics, n.d.)

---

[*] Please see https://cft.vanderbilt.edu/guides-sub-pages/learning-styles-preferences/
[†] Cerbin, 2011

5.1 Attack Knowledge

One of the hardest areas in security architecture to acquire is a set of attacks and those typical attack scenarios that will apply to the architectures at hand. By now, in this book, I hope that you've seen, maybe even become convinced, that without knowledge of attacks, and knowledge at an applicable level, one cannot practice security architecture. Attack knowledge—relevant attack knowledge, at the right level of depth (attack types, not exploit details)—lies at the heart of the "art." To facilitate this learning, I've been experimenting with a few resources, which I will outline in this section.

Two of my colleagues, Christiaan Beek and Ismael Valenzuela, have contributed ATT&CK "templates"—that is, details of attacks. Each of them helped me understand how ATT&CK works, what it's useful for.

The MITRE® Corporation has sponsored a collection of adversarial attributes called ATT&CK™,* which groups the steps and techniques of known, multi-step attacks, such as various Advanced Persistent Threat (APT) and ransomware campaigns. One can go to the ATT&CK Navigator† and select one or several known campaigns, and the Navigator will highlight—that is, show in visual form—the various techniques that were known to have been employed by that campaign.

ATT&CK, like most of the tools, analysis systems, and ontologies that I've seen, is focused on the problem of attack analysis intended for use by incident responders—the analysis that must be done when presented with one or more indicators of compromise (IoC). Based upon my classes, I now believe that ATT&CK can prove useful for security architecture practitioners to familiarize themselves with the tools, tactics, and procedures (TTP) that make up a multi-step attack scenario.

Reactive attack analysis is the process whereby responders analyze IoC for TTP of an unfolding attack in order to stop the attack and to find appropriate responses.

Beyond the details of multi-step attacks, glancing through the high-level categories (the column headings in the of ATT&CK matrix in Fig. 5.1 on page 119) may offer a useful mental classification system of the various types (and, implicitly, the attacker's desired effects) of attacks, without which, as I've noted, no security architect can practice. ATT&CK may offer a leg up for beginners, as well as filling in attack categories and exploit types for those who are more experienced.

I've been using ATT&CK's column headers in my threat modeling classes. (My addition of ATT&CK column headers is relatively new. I hesitate to declare it a success. Still, I offer this new experiment in case it may help.) Class participants often know one or a few attack types before they attend the class. As they practice applying attacks to systems (threat modeling the fictitious systems we use as examples in the class), glancing through ATT&CK's column headers helps participants go beyond what they know. The column headers are a prompt for consideration of attacks with which class participants are less familiar.

ATT&CK could provide an industry-wide organizing principle, which is presently lacking. Many threat modeling programs rely upon Swiderski and Snyder's STRIDE‡ (Spoofing,

---

* ATT&CK™ may be found at: https://attack.mitre.org/wiki/Main_Page
† https://mitre.github.io/attack-navigator/enterprise/
‡ Swiderski and Snyder, 2004.

Tampering, Repudiation, Information disclosure, Denial of service, Elevation of privilege) method, which may have been the first enterprise-wide threat modeling approach; it was invented and used at Microsoft®.

STRIDE is interesting for a few reasons:

- It was the first published attempt to make threat modeling accessible to development communities.
- It finally gave security and development some common language to discuss potential attacks.
- It's easy to understand, especially for developers with little security knowledge.
- It has become security industry "folklore," in that nearly everyone who's had any experience of threat modeling has heard of it.
- STRIDE is often treated as though it were a canonized standard; it isn't and has never been.

However, STRIDE has some significant problems when taken beyond its intended purpose: an initial opening for developers to grasp the importance of considering how their software may be attacked. STRIDE provides a gateway to the art of threat modeling software that is currently under development.

> I had a great conversation with Frank Swiderski about the broad adoption and durability of STRIDE. It was never intended to become an industry standard. It was a beginning, and a good one (in my opinion).

Most importantly, STRIDE is far from comprehensive; a glance through the ATT&CK column headers ought to show the range of attack types that may have to be considered. STRIDE is fairly tightly focused on application and operating system development for developers of these types of software. STRIDE may be less applicable to other types of software.

Because of STRIDE's prevalence, threat model findings are often couched in STRIDE terms. I've seen numerous models in which the many complex attack vectors that have been considered are tortured into conforming to one or more of the six STRIDE categories. Why is this even useful? (In my experience, conforming all attacks to STRIDE provides zero value and may, in fact, obscure details necessary to build effective defenses).

Plus, impacts (Information Disclosure) are mixed with techniques: Spoofing. The DREAD rating system[*] (Damage, Reproducibility, Exploitability, Affected, Discoverability) is supposed to take care of ratings; risk rating is not supposed to be implicit in the STRIDE collection. But in practice there's a mental conflation with STRIDE that makes evaluating risk more difficult; even finger-to-the-wind guesses are hampered by intermixing technique with impact.

However, STRIDE does provide something that the ATT&CK headers don't: an indication of the technical things that attackers do to systems. Thinking about this problem, I had been casting about for this next level of classification for a couple of years.

One excellent place in which one may play with technical attacks is Adam Shostack's card game, "Elevation of Privilege."[†] I believe that when Adam teaches, he has participants play the game. We used it a bit in the first term of Michele Guel's National Cybersecurity Award (2011)–winning education class, Security Knowledge Empowerment (SKE), at Cisco (Michele Guel

---

[*] https://en.wikipedia.org/wiki/DREAD_(risk_assessment_model)
[†] https://social.technet.microsoft.com/wiki/contents/articles/285.elevation-of-privilege-the-game.aspx

Initial Access	Execution	Persistence	Privilege Escalation	Defense Evasion	Credential Access
Drive-by Compromise	Scheduled Task			Binary Padding	Network
Exploit Public-Facing Application	Launchctl		Access Token Manipulation		Account Manipulation
	Local Job Scheduling		Bypass User Account Control		Bash History
External Remote Services	LSASS Driver		Extra Window Memory Injection		Brute Force
Hardware Additions	Trap		Process Injection		Credential Dumping
Replication Through Removable Media	AppleScript	DLL Search Order Hijacking			Credentials in Files
	CMSTP	Image File Execution Options Injection			Credentials in Registry
Spearphishing Attachment	Command-Line Interface	Plist Modification			Exploitation for Credential Access
Spearphishing Link	Compiled HTML File	Valid Accounts			
Spearphishing via Service	Control Panel Items	Accessibility Features		BITS Jobs	Forced Authentication
Supply Chain Compromise	Dynamic Data Exchange	AppCert DLLs		Clear Command History	Hooking
Trusted Relationship	Execution through API	AppInit DLLs		CMSTP	Input Capture
Valid Accounts	Execution through Module Load	Application Shimming		Code Signing	Input Prompt
		Dylib Hijacking		Compiled HTML File	Kerberoasting
	Exploitation for Client Execution	File System Permissions Weakness		Component Firmware	Keychain
		Hooking		Component Object Model Hijacking	LLMNR/NBT-NS Poisoning and Relay
	Graphical User Interface	Launch Daemon		Control Panel Items	Password Filter DLL
	InstallUtil	New Service		DCShadow	Private Keys
	Mshta	Path Interception		Deobfuscate/Decode Files or Information	Securityd Memory
	PowerShell	Port Monitors			Two-Factor Authentication Interception
	Regsvcs/Regasm	Service Registry Permissions Weakness		Disabling Security Tools	
	Regsvr32	Setuid and Setgid		DLL Side-Loading	
	Rundll32	Startup Items		Execution Guardrails	
	Scripting	Web Shell			
	Service Execution	.bash_profile and .bashrc	Exploitation for Privilege Escalation	Exploitation for Defense Evasion	
	Signed Binary Proxy Execution	Account Manipulation			
		Authentication Package	SID-History Injection	File Deletion	
	Signed Script Proxy Execution	BITS Jobs	Sudo	File Permissions Modification	
		Bootkit	Sudo Caching		
	Source	Browser Extensions		File System Logical Offsets	
	Space after Filename	Change Default File Association		Gatekeeper Bypass	
	Third-party Software			Group Policy Modification	
	Trusted Developer Utilities	Component Firmware		Hidden Files and Directories	
	User Execution	Component Object Model Hijacking		Hidden Users	
	Windows Management Instrumentation			Hidden Window	
		Create Account		HISTCONTROL	
	Windows Remote Management	External Remote Services		Indicator Blocking	
		Hidden Files and Directories		Indicator Removal from Tools	
	XSL Script Processing	Hypervisor			
		Kernel Modules and Extensions		Indicator Removal on Host	
		Launch Agent		Indirect Command Execution	
		LC_LOAD_DYLIB Addition		Install Root Certificate	
		Login Item		InstallUtil	
		Logon Scripts		Launchctl	
		Modify Existing Service		LC_MAIN Hijacking	
		Netsh Helper DLL		Masquerading	
		Office Application Startup		Modify Registry	
		Port Knocking		Mshta	
		Rc.common		Network Share Connection Removal	
		Redundant Access		NTFS File Attributes	
		Registry Run Keys / Startup Folder		Obfuscated Files or Information	
		Re-opened Applications		Port Knocking	
		Screensaver		Process Doppelgänging	
		Security Support Provider		Process Hollowing	
		Shortcut Modification		Redundant Access	
		SIP and Trust Provider Hijacking		Regsvcs/Regasm	
				Regsvr32	
		System Firmware		Rootkit	
		Systemd Service		Rundll32	
		Time Providers		Scripting	
		Windows Management Instrumentation Event Subscription		Signed Binary Proxy Execution	
				Signed Script Proxy Execution	
		Winlogon Helper DLL			
				SIP and Trust Provider Hijacking	
				Software Packing	
				Space after Filename	
				Template Injection	
				Timestomp	
				Trusted Developer Utilities	
				Virtualization/Sandbox Evasion	
				Web Service	
				XSL Script Processing	

Discovery	Lateral Movement	Collection	Command and Control	Exfiltration	Impact
Sniffing	AppleScript	Audio Capture	Commonly Used Port	Automated Exfiltration	Data Destruction
Account Discovery	Application Deployment Software	Automated Collection	Communication Through Removable Media	Data Compressed	Data Encrypted for Impact
Application Window Discovery		Clipboard Data		Data Encrypted	Defacement
Browser Bookmark Discovery	Distributed Component Object Model	Data from Information Repositories	Connection Proxy	Data Transfer Size Limits	Disk Content Wipe
	Exploitation of Remote Services	Data from Local System	Custom Command and Control Protocol	Exfiltration Over Other Network Medium	Disk Structure Wipe
Domain Trust Discovery					Endpoint Denial of Service
File and Directory Discovery	Logon Scripts	Data from Network Shared Drive	Custom Cryptographic Protocol	Exfiltration Over Command and Control Channel	Firmware Corruption
Network Service Scanning	Pass the Hash	Data from Removable Media	Data Encoding		Inhibit System Recovery
Network Share Discovery	Pass the Ticket	Data Staged	Data Obfuscation	Exfiltration Over Alternative Protocol	Network Denial of Service
Password Policy Discovery	Remote Desktop Protocol	Email Collection	Domain Fronting		Resource Hijacking
Peripheral Device Discovery	Remote File Copy	Input Capture	Domain Generation Algorithms	Exfiltration Over Physical Medium	Runtime Data Manipulation
Permission Groups Discovery	Remote Services	Man in the Browser			Service Stop
Process Discovery	Replication Through Removable Media	Screen Capture	Fallback Channels	Scheduled Transfer	Stored Data Manipulation
Query Registry		Video Capture	Multiband Communication		Transmitted Data Manipulation
Remote System Discovery	Shared Webroot		Multi-hop Proxy		
Security Software Discovery	SSH Hijacking		Multilayer Encryption		
System Information Discovery	Taint Shared Content		Multi-Stage Channels		
	Third-party Software		Port Knocking		
System Network Configuration Discovery	Windows Admin Shares		Remote Access Tools		
	Windows Remote Management		Remote File Copy		
System Network Connections Discovery			Standard Application Layer Protocol		
System Owner/User Discovery			Standard Cryptographic Protocol		
System Service Discovery			Standard Non-Application Layer Protocol		
System Time Discovery			Uncommonly Used Port		
Virtualization/Sandbox Evasion			Web Service		

MITRE ATT&CK™
Enterprise Framework

attack.mitre.org

Figure 5.1 MITRE ATT&CK™ Matrix (*Source:* Reproduced with permission of The MITRE Corporation)

is Cisco Distinguished Engineer and 2011 National Cyber-Security Award Winner).* Playing the game, or at the very least, glancing through the cards, can provide a pretty comprehensive (if not always up to date) introduction to the techniques that attackers employ. Elevation of Privilege, to my mind, puts the meat on the bones of STRIDE.

> Michele, Vinay Bansal, and I were the first instructor team. Please see John Stewart's blog post about the program at https://blogs.cisco.com/security/baking-security-into-the-culture-at-cisco---a-tip-of-the-hat-to-the-security-knowledge-empowerment-team

However, I've found that there are too many cards to use when actually threat modeling a system. (Although, I wonder if Adam Shostack uses the cards in some effective manner in his threat modeling classes?) As far as I know, Elevation of Privilege wasn't meant for building attack scenarios; it's a teaching tool, for which it works admirably. However, if running through the deck helps threat modelers identify relevant attack possibilities, then please, by all means, use any and all tools available.

The Common Vulnerability Enumeration (CVE) isn't about attack types, it's an enumeration of all known (and reported!) individual exploitable conditions. Not the right information for threat modeling. These are not vulnerability *types,* but rather, vulnerability *instances.*

The Common Weakness Enumeration (CWE) is at the wrong level of granularity. CWE lists each particular case and variation of exploitable weakness. When I work through CWE, I find that I quickly descend into the weeds. Those "weeds" are critically important to understand, at least for a few examples, or one may not pick appropriate defensive measures. But, as I've stated, security architecture wields classes of attack, not their details.

I had high hopes for MITRE's Common Attack Pattern Enumeration and Classification (CAPEC) when Alan Paller (SANS Institute™) introduced me to it in 2008 or 2009. Though I was excited by the prospects, I found myself lost in the details of software weaknesses. Again, this was somewhat of a disappointment, and I left CAPEC to follow its useful course, whatever that might be.

In the intervening years, I've come to realize just how important an organization (of some kind) of attack types must play in threat modeling, particularly. None of us can carry around an encyclopedic listing of every weakness detail. Nor do we have the time to be running through long enumerations in order to ensure that we've covered the correct bases—that is, applied a comprehensive set of appropriate attack types to a system. Most practitioners, myself included, develop an internal organization that fosters far more rapid application of the right attacks to the right attack points and technologies. But, as I've already written, building an internal organization is a slow process—too slow.

After beginning to apply ATT&CK's column headers, I once again took a look at CAPEC's highest-level categories. A light went on: ATT&CK headers coupled to CAPEC top-level categories (Mechanisms of Attack) might just provide the set of relevant information to make threat modeling easier. And that's how I present these to my classes: ATT&CK column headers and CAPEC's categories linked together.

ATT&CK's column headers provide attacker intentions. CAPEC's categories provide the methods to achieve those intentions (see Fig. 5.2).

In Figure 5.3, I've drawn arrows between "Initial Access" and a couple of the techniques that attackers use to gain access to systems: "Collect and Analyze Information," then "Engage in Deceptive Interactions." These two mechanisms don't comprise the universe of "Initial Access"

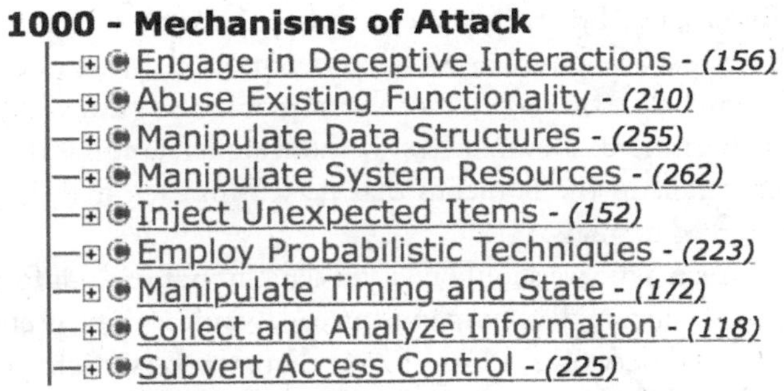

1000 - Mechanisms of Attack
Engage in Deceptive Interactions - (156)
Abuse Existing Functionality - (210)
Manipulate Data Structures - (255)
Manipulate System Resources - (262)
Inject Unexpected Items - (152)
Employ Probabilistic Techniques - (223)
Manipulate Timing and State - (172)
Collect and Analyze Information - (118)
Subvert Access Control - (225)

Figure 5.2 CAPEC Mechanisms of Attack

techniques, but they are commonly employed.* Likewise, "Execution" is gained through "Inject Unexpected Items" and "Manipulate Data Structures" (again, not an exhaustive set).

In order to keep Figure 5.3 readable, I used only two arrows and linked directly from only three of the categories. The relationships are more complex than those shown here. Still, I hope that this simple graphic demonstrates visually how ATT&CK column header intentions are achieved through the mechanisms (techniques) in CAPEC.

Attacks Types + Techniques == Exploits
Category
Initial Access
Execution
Persistence
Privilege Escalation
Defence Evasion
Credential Access
Discovery
Lateral movement
Collection
Exfiltration
Command and Control
...
1000 - Mechanisms of Attack
Collect and Analyze Information - (118)
Inject Unexpected Items - (152)
Engage in Deceptive Interactions - (156)
Manipulate Timing and State - (172)
Abuse Existing Functionality - (210)
Employ Probabilistic Techniques - (223)
Subvert Access Control - (225)
Manipulate Data Structures - (255)
Manipulate System Resources - (262)

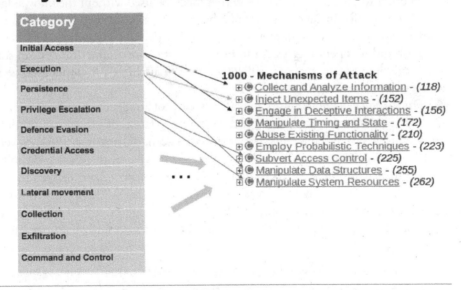

Figure 5.3 ATT&CK Headers Combined with CAPEC Categories

When building defenses, we want to prevent or increase the cost of prosecuting the mechanisms, thus preventing or slowing down ATT&CK's (attacker's) intentions (column headers). In order to build the correct set of defenses, it's helpful to understand what the attacker is

* A more comprehensive listing of Initial Access techniques can be found by perusing attacks that have been added to ATT&CK Navigator.

trying to achieve (intentions). Preventing successful prosecution of the mechanisms becomes the purpose of each defense. Defenses, as we have seen previously, are not tied one-to-one (1:1) to exploits. Some defenses close off several mechanisms, whereas others may solely warn that an attack technique has been tried. Nevertheless, without understanding the actual mechanisms (and sometimes, the details in the branches that lie within each high-level category's tree of entries), one will be forced to guess.

"Encryption is secure; maybe we should encrypt data in motion." Unfortunately, such statements too often are made during development. Instead, wouldn't it be useful to know that data are moving over untrusted networks? Or not? And that attackers might "Collect and Analyze Information" by "Subvert(ing) Access Control"? Now we know that bi-directionally authenticated TLS might be worth consideration as a defense mechanism. The attacker will have to "Engage in Deceptive Interactions" (Man in the Middle), which will raise errors on both sides of the connection if the X.509 certificates tendered during a TLS authentication exchange are being handled correctly. My sincere hope is that these two readily available resources, when combined in this somewhat unexpected manner, might provide that bit of organization and insight—the guidance necessary to properly identify those attacks that systems will need to resist. I'm using this paradigm regularly in my threat modeling classes; anecdotal evidence suggests that the approach is proving useful to attendees.

Taking an example that was given in Chapter 3, Architecture, Attacks, and Defenses, let's re-examine it through the lens of ATT&CK and CAPEC.

"In order to take over a machine so that it can be used without the knowledge of its ordinary user or owner (for instance, as part of a botnet), an attacker will have to piece together one or more steppingstones, system objectives, such that the attacker will gain sufficient privileges on the host and its operating system in order to install command and control software that will persist across restarts (reboots). The goals are the attacker's 'intentions' to be gained through prosecution of technical 'mechanisms.'

"For instance, a vulnerability that allows 'code of attacker's choosing' isn't actually sufficient until that exploitation can be coupled with an escalation of privileges in order take control of an operating system (and thus, the host). (In a scenario in which the attacker is starting at a high level of privilege, escalation is not needed.) In a situation in which the victim is not running at sufficient privileges to install high-privilege software, an attacker must not only execute code, but also find a way to increase privileges such that the attacker's command-and-control software can be installed and run. In this trivial example, an attacker might need to exploit as many as three or four system objectives in order to successfully gain persistent control of the machine:

1. Find a way to deliver the attack code payload.
2. Get the payload to run on the victim's machine.
3. From the 'code of the attacker's choosing' payload, exploit a second vulnerability that increases privilege level above that of the operating system's current user.
4. Establish communications with the attacker.
5. Potentially download additional code for permanence across restarts."

Of course, one may dig into ATT&CK to find the techniques used in each category (Intentions or System Objectives). Mitre's ATT&CK Navigator contains templates for many of the most well-understood attack sequences. By selecting a named campaign such as "APT1," the Navigator will highlight those TTP that the APT1 attackers employed. Exploration of well-known attacks could offer invaluable insight into how attacks proceed. It should be obvious through taking a look at just a few of Navigator's attack templates how multi-step attacks advance. An understanding that attacks often comprise a string or collection of exploitations is important, perhaps key.

In parallel, I believe that it is useful for practitioners to understand at least a few of the techniques described in each of the CAPEC mechanism trees. CAPEC entries describe the technical details used in each mechanism. By understanding in computer science terms (as we did in Chapter 3), we can more readily derive the right defenses to prevent or at least slow down the attacks.

A bit of study of both ATT&CK and CAPEC, I hope, might shorten the learning curve about attacks without which security architecture cannot be practiced. Combining the two organizing principles—ATT&CK highlighting that which attackers need to accomplish and CAPEC the techniques to achieve these goals—seems to help my class participants to widen their understanding of attacks. With these resources in hand, perhaps learners won't need to "shadow Brook for a year"!

5.2 Which Defenses for What System?

As we've seen previously, once we identify the attacks that we believe will be levied against a system, the next task is to build the best set of appropriate defenses. But how does one acquire this knowledge set?

One might take a "follow-the-herd" approach. There are plenty of standards one could follow: just do everything in the standard, as well as everything humanly possible. Venerable NIST 800-53 (revision 53ARev4[*]) contains 170 controls. Implementing each of these might be a way to play it safe, to avoid additional analysis. But it would be expensive to implement each of 800-53's controls well, probably prohibitively so. Plus, without additional analysis, there's no way to know which controls apply and which might be irrelevant in context.

NIST 800-53 is a hodgepodge of nearly everything that comprises information security's controls and processes. AC-5, Separation of Duties, is a design principle aimed at foiling fraudulent and collusive behavior. The idea is that it's harder to get a *group* of people to act fraudulently, especially when the group is not particularly cohesive. AC-7, within the same control family, Unsuccessful Logon Attempts, is a common abuse indicator: when attackers are attempting to brute force a password, there will be an unusual number of unsuccessful logons. The control is to limit the number of attempts, usually within some given time period.

For a very small company, separation of duties doesn't make much sense. Everyone already knows what everyone else is doing. A person behaving poorly will often get caught by the other principals, who usually watch each other's actions pretty closely. I call that "eyeball-to-eyeball security." It works reasonably well in small, tightknit, closely coordinating teams. Besides,

---

[*] https://nvd.nist.gov/800-53/Rev4/impact/HIGH

during the startup phase it is very typical for each person of the very small founder team to fulfill multiple organization roles. There aren't enough people to "separate" the duties between. But eyeball-to-eyeball security doesn't work well at all at enterprise scale, where formal separation of duties access policies apply.

Although a standard like 800-53 sets out a universe of information security typical practices, it does nothing to define what applies to particular contexts.

Still, I believe that in order to apply defenses appropriately, a practitioner would need to understand the function of just about every control named within NIST 800-53 and similar standards. Such standards, at the very least, set out the well-understood universe of stuff that people do to secure their organizations.

Something like the BSIMM™ (Building Security In Maturity Model)* software security measurement is also an example of follow-the-herd. In the case of BSIMM, the measurement is of companies that take software security seriously enough to pay for a BSIMM assessment. It's not (yet) a measurement of the universe of what organizations in general do or do not do. It's not a random sampling of organizations; there is no attempt at generating a statistically valid sample (though, to be sure, the designers have put a lot of thought into how to measure what they measure). BSIMM's measurement is of companies willing to pay for a BSIMM measurement—ergo, companies that care about software security.

I don't mean to imply that BSIMM tells us nothing. It tells us what companies that have sufficient resources already dedicated to software security are doing and evaluates how mature those practices are. That is certainly valuable: what do the leaders do and how mature are they at doing what they do?

What BSIMM does not tell us is how effective their software security programs have been at preventing harm from security incidents caused by issues in software that the measured companies have built or deployed. Is what BSIMM companies do effective? Since the total list of BSIMM companies is not public, there's no way to match known incidents against BSIMM participants.

Only a few BSIMM companies have granted permission to be named on the BSIMM website.† Without data on which companies have been through a BSIMM assessment, it's impossible to accurately correlate BSIMM participation to security incident occurrence. Measuring companies' software security effectiveness is actually trickier, because many incidents do not get reported publicly.

Still, in a back-of-the-napkin investigation of large security breaches, only two of the named BSIMM companies, JP Morgan Chase and Sony Pictures, had reported breaches. Both of these breaches were in 2014 and may very well have motivated these two companies to improve their software security practices, resulting in them joining BSIMM. From public sources, I cannot tell.‡

Although it seems quite possible that simply investing in software security, which I believe is clearly apparent by an investment into a BSIMM measurement, will generate sufficient security

---

* https://www.bsimm.com/about.html

† https://www.bsimm.com/about/membership.html

‡ If I knew anyone who was at one of these two firms, I wouldn't be able to relate what they may have told me, anyway. All BSIMM conferences (I've attended three and spoken at two) are strictly held under a Non-Disclosure Agreement (NDA).

practices and technology to keep one off the front pages, actually, that's not true. A company that was a member of a security-sharing forum to which I represented my employer for six years had a huge breach 10 years later. I remember them sharing their program. At the time, it seemed to me that they were taking security pretty seriously. Perhaps security was defunded after that. That particular Chief Information Security Officer (CISO) had long since left the concern for another role. I suppose I'll never know for sure.

But just maybe, the practices outlined in BSIMM constitute a fair sample of reasonable software security practices.

My point in all of the foregoing is that we do have examples of what organizations try. We do have pretty concrete descriptions of the sorts of controls that at least NIST thinks make up a robust security program. Familiarity with a few of the available standards might help someone new to defenses build the requisite knowledge to apply particular defenses to particular security needs.

When Michele Guel invited me to help teach her first SKE course, we based the course around the SANS Institute's introduction to information security course materials. The materials for the course appeared to me to cover a comprehensive collection of security situations and controls. If I recall correctly, course participants felt that they'd gained a fair amount of security knowledge, although, apparently, the homework that I'd added as security architecture practice was named "the hardest material in the course." Oops. Still, SKE did win that award. Michele keeps running the course. As an alternate approach to shadowing an experienced practitioner, surely there are similar courses available beyond what SANS offers.

A quick web search for Massively Open Online Course (MOOC) returns dozens of hits (I provide two example listings in the references*). There appear to be lots of offerings available to the willing student. I make no representation as to which MOOC might be any good. Obviously, a lot of MOOCs are for-profit operations. Buyer beware, always. Still, today, it's not that hard to find an introductory course in information security. Any decent survey course must include typical security controls and their application. Probably, for those living near to a university, college, or other post-high-school institution, such institutions also offer some intro to cyber security that might prove useful.

One other public resource may be worth considering. Each individual attack pattern in MITRE's CAPEC collection has a set of preconditions that must be met before the attack pattern can be exploited successfully. Although each attack pattern's preconditions aren't themselves defences, any tactic or control that removes a precondition is, in fact, a defense against that attack pattern. I suggest that if there is any doubt about what defenses may counter a particular attack, a study of the preconditions listed in its CAPEC entry may point toward the right set of defenses.

Whatever the media, one must eventually learn those controls (NIST 800-53 listing or similar) that will apply to the systems one will be analyzing. To be honest, depending upon the situation, I've been called upon to analyze controls that have included:

- Network restrictions
- Traffic analysis

---

* https://www.mooc-list.com/tags/information-security
https://www.coursera.org/courses?query=information%20security

- Memory protections
- Operating system privileges
- Coding practices
- Testing strategies
- Boot loaders
- Disk protections
- Network storage configurations
- Website configurations
- Administrative controls and restrictions
- Monitoring and logging

(The above list should not be considered exhaustive.)

Basically, I've dealt with a potpourri of the length and breadth of information security practices. Eventually, I fear that if one examines enough systems and organizations, one will encounter just about everything described in NIST 800-53 and similar at one point or another. I don't think that there's a quick path to such exposure. I'm lucky to have always had brilliant practitioners around me who could help me to understand the problems and help craft reasonable solutions within each diverse context.

Still, at today's level of engineering practice, please bear in mind that no substitute exists for peer review and mentorship. I offer the above as adjuncts and potential accelerators to readers' learning curves.

5.3 Threat Modeling: The Learning Method

As we have seen, attacks and their defenses provide a key foundation for security architecture, perhaps all of information security. I've discovered that practice in identifying relevant attacks, then applying these to defendable situations in order to figure out the appropriate defenses, is one of the best educational opportunities existing. When we shadow an experienced practitioner, that's what we're observing. As we attempt our first few analyses, in essence, this is what we're learning: attacks and defenses.

Hence, empowering learners to analyze their systems turns out to be the single most important practice that we can offer. The plus side is that nearly everyone who participates will get something out of the experience, even if many of them don't go on to pursue a security architecture role. As I noted previously, threat modeling practice provides a huge hack toward a culture of security, particularly for development organizations. If there's any magic in the world (and readers will have to decide for themselves on this point), practicing threat modeling may be one of the best—though of course, there's no actual magic in this. Rather, it's opportunity.

The "magic," such as it may be, seems to lie within an opportunity to see systems as the attacker sees them. I don't know who coined the phrase "think like an attacker." Still, that simple directive isn't enough. Most developers are too busy trying to think like their users, like the owners of the systems they're building, even trying to think in the way that a machine will interpret the code they're generating. Adding one additional, "think like a . . ." doesn't really help much and may be perceived as yet another burden laid at the feet of taxed developers.

But, taking time out for attack analysis does, indeed, help. It's even more useful if there's some structure to the analysis. I believe that this may be why STRIDE has been so readily adopted. STRIDE, despite its shortcomings, provides a structure to attack analysis. Structure, I believe, is the critical component. It perhaps doesn't really make much difference what structure is used, so long as there's a life raft for at-sea developers to cling to.

It also helps to include a diverse set of experiences when threat modeling, so long as the experts or more experienced leave sufficient room for everyone to try his/her/their hand at the analysis. If everyone gets some opportunity to try, the inclusion of folks who have more skill allows learners to observe discrimination between science fiction scenarios and relevant ones. It allows learners to reflect upon their attempts in contrast to those with more skill, but in a safe way, hopefully without someone telling them that they've made errors.

Most people can identify their own misconceptions just fine without pointing fingers. Shame doesn't make a very good learning environment. A lively and honest dialectic over the analysis is usually sufficient for learning to occur.

Obviously, if an organization is allowing learners—some of whom are completely new and perhaps as yet clueless—to threat model systems that are going to be subjected to attack, there has to be some amount of check to ensure that systems have an appropriate set of defenses. Mistakes will be made.

I've already described a lightweight governance model of peer review in this book (Chapter 4: Culture Hacking). Review boards, in my experience, too often turn into PhD oral examination-like experiences that close learning down far more than assist. These sorts of board reviews can also be terribly inflating for the board members as they try to fulfill their due diligence responsibilities. Although there is probably a place for architecture review boards for enterprise-wide changes or the truly innovative and very complex, review boards, when applied to most efforts, have too many poor side effects, including becoming a bottleneck process through which otherwise nimble efforts get slowed. I'm not a big fan of these, having sat on many during any number of the programs in which I've worked.

Instead, I've been able to refine the governance review process described in this book: one person with more experience and one person who's independent of the effort, who hopefully knows little about the system under review.

If the peer review committee can't agree, they get another more experienced person, until the most senior technical security leader is included. If they can't agree (and this has occurred maybe twice in all my years doing it this way), then the decision is escalated to management.

What I've used and hopefully described well enough in this book works. Threat models get completed while still fostering maximum learning opportunities. Besides, this process is fast. Most reviews take less than an hour, often more like 30 minutes. That's because all the leg work has already been completed, most of the attack scenarios have been defined, most of the attack surfaces cataloged, most defenses described. Experienced practitioners can glance through the completed materials quickly to identify any important misses.

By including someone independent in the reviews (and the original analysis, if possible; see the next section), effective cross-training occurs. Also, backup of personnel and knowledge occurs such that if some horrible accident should befall the original threat modelers, there's still someone around who's familiar with the system and its security who can pick up the thread.

Through analysis inclusion coupled to lightweight review techniques, organizations gain the maximum training and culture change benefits from threat modeling. However, there is a caveat to which organizations must attend: everyone involved has to understand that a threat model is one of the most sensitive analyses that will be generated. Threat models, and especially under-mitigated attack scenarios, are most certainly not social media candidates! "Loose lips sink ships." Or, at least, loose threat model "lips" offer attackers the very information that is required for successful system attack.

I find it's important to reiterate this message on sensitivity and the need for discretion regularly, repeatedly, and in multiple forms through multiple media channels. Process has incredible entropy, unfortunately. I've found that after a couple of generations, the folks enacting the process will not have had the reasons for its existence communicated well, if at all. A clever project manager or line manager will ask, "Why are we doing this extra thing that takes time and effort? It seems pointless." Which is why it's critical to regularly and repeatedly re-explain the purposes of established processes.

Long after a peer review governance process has matured, long since nearly every development team threat models as a matter of course, someone with influence will eventually question the efficacy of the work, will want to remove the task from required activities. It's inevitable. The wise program leader will have been keeping track of the defenses discovered during threat modeling and then implemented. Such statistics will ensure that those who question can be shown hard proof demonstrating efficacy. There is always churn. Always, there are counter-influences that will need to be addressed.

In any event, I've learned that threat modeling may be one of the most effective security trainings that exist.* Perhaps that's because participants have to put more of their security knowledge to use during an analysis. Threat modeling is a training opportunity as well as a culture shifter. Don't allow anxious security folks to hold your organization's threat modeling prisoner. Get everyone involved for maximum benefit. At the same time, build some sort of check on the results to ensure that the fewest possible misses and mistakes leak into production or release.

5.3.1 How to Escalate for Management Decision

I've mentioned issue escalation a number of times up to this point but haven't yet explained what it is, why it's important, or how to perform successful management escalations.

At the outset, it is important to understand that the need to escalate to management, often to executives for risk decision making, is not a failure. Escalations are an organic, expected result of a mature and robust security architecture program. Escalations must never be wielded as a punishment whenever there arises some conflict between security needs and other business drivers. In fact, escalation to management for decisions is a useful and much needed tool to work through apparently intractable conflicts.

I expect the architects who deliver security in my programs to occasionally find themselves in conflict with the people who produce software or who maintain software services (infrastructure and production). In the course of building and maintaining security, an issue will arise that must be dealt with immediately (or very soon) but for which the people charged with implementing the

---

* The other security training that I've observed to be highly effective is security assessment of third parties.

change haven't planned and don't have sufficient resources to address. These conflicts shouldn't come up very often, but I can guarantee that they will arise from time to time.

Practitioners who never have any escalations may not be standing up for security strongly enough. On the other hand, someone who is constantly in serious conflict with their development counterparts is very likely wasting precious security influence on matters which could be easily handled through negotiation and perhaps the grant of a time-limited exception.

I prefer to reserve escalations for issues that have been assessed as having high potential for exploitation and/or high damage. In other words, those high-risk items for which we cannot find a suitable solution to sufficiently protect a system and its organization are candidates for escalation. But there's no need for an escalation when everyone agrees on a solution. Escalation is for the (hopefully) rarer situation on which we cannot agree.

The underlying requirement for effective escalation must be that security will have absolute authority to rate risk. With that authority comes grave responsibility to rate risk fairly and consistently. In *Securing Systems*, Chapter 4, I offered a risk rating system based upon Factor Analysis of Information Risk (FAIR), an Open Group Standard. Whatever you use, your risk process must apply to a broad range of issues, be based upon firm risk methodology, and be repeatable and consistent.

Repeated inflation of risk ratings will earn the practitioner or program distrust and dismissal by the people who must make decisions based upon the ratings. One of my best tricks is to make managers who might be a part of escalations in the future aware of the many low and medium ratings I make. Visibility and transparency of ratings, especially of relatively minor issues, builds trust in the rating system's fairness and consistency. The visibility mechanism can be a simple "FYI" email; these notices don't have to be fancy or particularly formal.

Then, when a truly dangerous situation arises, those involved, having seen many reasonable ratings, will know intuitively that a higher risk rating is not an attempt at winning an argument, but rather, the rater's (my) considered, professional opinion about the importance of the issue at hand.

Further, it really helps to be able to back up a rating with a technical description of the effects of the issue, as well as being imperative for executive decision makers that potential damage (impact) be well explained in business terms. Chapter 4 of *Securing Systems* describes these needs in a fair amount of detail. If you have any doubt, please refer to that.

Having arrived at a defensible risk rating, and having determined that further interaction with implementers and their direct management will not arrive at a suitable solution, it's time to escalate. I keep contentious arguments with development teams, project managers, development managers, etc. to no more than two attempts to arrive at a consensus. A couple of, "yes, no, yes, no" interchanges is sufficient. I don't need to waste further time in lobbying, cajoling, begging for something different; it's already clear to me that we're stuck.

It's important that I never let those whose role is to meet budgets and deliver to a schedule decide a serious security issue's resolution. That's because there is a built-in conflict of interest: these people's bonuses, their promotions largely depend upon meeting the schedules that have been decided. Unless a line manager has near saintly understanding, she/he/they are typically going to refuse anything that gets in the way of agreed-upon delivery. That's their job! I would have it no other way. Because of this, though, they aren't the right people to make decisions that may affect, sometimes significantly, their precious schedule and budget.

The aim is to escalate to the person in the management chain who holds responsibility for the failure to fix's potential impact. In small organizations, this might be the CEO, Executive Director, Executive Committee, Security Committee, etc. That is, the escalation might have to go to the top. This is also true when a large company's brand is at stake.

For impacts that have been assessed at a group or business unit scope, the leader of the unit will be the correct choice for escalation, and so on down the management chain: the appropriate level within management will be directly proportional to the scope of the impact. Please see Table 5.1 for possible escalation levels. Because organizations vary widely as to the scope of such titles as Director and Vice President, it's impossible in a general explanation such as this to give you, the reader, a better guide than "scope of impact." Level depends upon the amount of organization hierarchy and how that hierarchy is built.

Table 5.1 Organization Hierarchy and Potential Impact Relationship

Chief Executive Officer	Critical brand or organization revenue impact
Vice President	Division or product line impact
Director	Group or product impact

Impacts limited to a single application can probably be decided by whoever has responsibility for services that the application delivers to the organization. These decision makers are sometimes known as the system's "owner" or "customer". Damage that might impede a business unit or functional group will necessarily go to that group's leader(s). As I wrote above, damage to the organization has to be decided by someone who can speak for the organization as a whole.

An additional benefit derived from working through escalations with decision makers will be a better understanding of the organizational risk tolerance. You may remember that risk decisions can't be made well without a grasp of organization risk tolerance. Working through escalations provides a view into which risks are worth taking and which are not. Over time and after repeated escalations, most security architects get a pretty clear idea about organizational risk tolerances. That knowledge then can be applied when rating risks to determine which items may need escalation. There's definitely a feedback loop between risk rating and organization risk decisions. It's worth paying attention to how these influence each other in order to escalate the correct issues and to rate accurately for the organizational context in which an issue resides.

5.4 To Accelerate: Cross Pollinate

One of the biggest accelerators of skill that I've found is working on problems outside of the areas in which one feels most skilled. That is, if someone has been focused on, say, endpoint applications, then any opportunity to work on operating system problems or cloud approaches and technologies provides learning benefit that may never be had from continuing to go deeper and deeper into the subtleties of application development.

"Outside" problems don't have to be entirely orthogonal to one's expertise. It will be harder for most application developers to leap completely into network architectures than to try and understand the issues of applications that have to be multi-tenant and horizontally scaled (perhaps elastically) versus what the person is already familiar with.

No matter how far away from current expertise the leap into new territory, the very act of considering new issues helps most people begin to separate implementation detail from structural patterns. As I've tried to articulate, understanding structure coupled to an appropriate amount of abstraction to obscure irrelevant detail is a critical technique of the practice of architecture.

In the same way, application of access controls will have various implementations, depending upon many factors, including organization and business context, desired security posture, trust placed into those entities granted access, the technologies available, and so forth. But access control serves the same general (architectural) purposes: to tie behavior to an object or entity and, perhaps, to reduce attack surface. By working with differing contexts, most people's minds develop perception both to the specifics and to a generalized pattern. It is generalized patterns that broaden our skills.

Or, to put it more bluntly: opportunities to analyze lots of different architectures increases analysis skill dramatically.

To accelerate the overall skill level of a security architecture program, one of the main tasks will be to give the security architect(s) lots of chances to work on architectures, especially threat models, with which they are unfamiliar.

If you want dramatic skill increases, cross-pollinate. Break down silo walls. Give people lots of chances to grapple with problems with which they are currently unfamiliar. This single undertaking is a powerful accelerator.

The other benefit will be a mounting sense of community. As learners build skill while interacting with new people, they build trust in each other. New lines of relationship get formed. The network of shared practices increases. This instills a sense of shared purpose, builds a community of practice. Working across project lines shouldn't be the only vector of shared practice. Still, sharing across knowledge areas builds upon other community practices you may introduce. The sense of contribution and execution together is a powerful community builder.

5.5 Build a Community of Practice

Inviting team outsiders to review isn't the only method for creating a community of practice. What are other methods? And why is a community of practice important?

A sense of community fosters belief in the shared purpose. For those who are motivated to contribute to something worthy of their time, something of substance, contribute to something that serves a grander purpose, a belief in a shared purpose can be very motivating and sustaining. Others may be more motivated by that very sense of shared purpose and support. I also find that when people see something happening, things actually being accomplished, joining becomes very attractive. Building community scratches each of these itches.

Communities also offer significant opportunities to increase skill and to integrate new skills through sharing with others. This aspect of "learning the trade" shouldn't be overlooked when creating an environment that fosters learning and creativity. While not every engineer likes to share, some can be encouraged to share what they know. The act of explaining to someone else why something does or doesn't work and how it can be accomplished is a key method for the integration of knowledge already acquired.

One of my main strategic initiatives is the creation of community. This is another powerful culture hack. Total team learning accelerates through the dynamics of shared sense of purpose and community. But also, as my friend Vinay Bansal (Vinay Bansal is a Distinguished Engineer at Cisco Systems, Inc.) once said to me, "Brook, we could move mountains together." Just the simple knowledge that others are going to support you when you're challenged or make a mistake, that you trust others to help you find the best solution to complex problems, that you can share your trials and tribulations, your joys and successes, makes most of us more resilient and oftentimes stronger.

But community doesn't simply spring forth without putting in some directed effort. It may be that engineers, many of whom tend toward introversion, can be a fairly difficult population with which to form community. Participants will have to stop working with their computers in order to interact. Following is a list of many of the techniques that I've used to foster a sense of community:

- Create a space for a community.
- Make sharing a safe activity.
- Share both successes and failures.
- Problem solve together.
- Allow diverse and even conflicting opinions.
- Meet regularly and predictably.
- Communicate to the community through multiple channels.
- Offer regular improvement training as a part of the space for the community.
- Model active listening.
- Give the community decision-making power over items which affect the community.

The community space can be virtual; I've created virtual community spaces five times, as of this writing. A community space can really help to establish trust, relationships, and a bond of shared experience. It helps to meet face to face from time to time. However, in-person meetings will usually be rare treats; most people in software development and security, at least currently, are used to working with people who are remote and are comfortable with virtual meeting environments. So long as the meetings commonly offer value to attendees, people will attend regularly. The key is that the community space exists and recurs predictably.

How does one create a sense of value in a recurring meeting? I won't claim that I have a patentable technique that always works. And, regrettably, sometimes at the virtual team meetings, one just has to take care of administrative business, which can be a community disintegrator (unfortunately). When I have significant business on the agenda, I always try to balance it with something of interest.

A great technique that I learned from another sphere entirely is to begin meetings with a short skill-building presentation or exercise. Nearly always, threat modeling a piece of a team's software draws lots of interest. If my community members are at least partially drawn from development teams, then one of their current projects makes a great subject of wide interest.

The team will present their architecture. Then, the entire community gets to analyze the architecture for attacks and defenses. These discussions become quite interactive, sometimes conflictual, which is fine so long as polite and professionally focused on the work at hand. Lots of participants have an opportunity to analyze and to speak. Dialogues between two people who don't agree should quickly be ended in favor of letting others try their hand at the analysis.

The presentations could also be about new pilots or experiments, new technologies, new processes that teams have invented, including strengths and pitfalls of the processes. If these presentations are kept short and to the point, they will be of interest to at least part of the community.

It's hard to find subjects that are of interest to everyone. Presentations about new process mandates and existing process or tool changes are often of reasonably broad interest, generally receiving strong engagement—the point being that by offering some opportunity for skill building and knowledge transfer, while every presentation will not be of interest to every participant, over time and through variety, many of the presentations are likely to be significantly engaging.

Shared problems are another important community builder. But, long reports of everything that each team is doing are boring, disengaging, and ultimately community killing. My strong advice is to avoid agendas packed with each team reporting in. Engineers go through plenty of those on multi-team projects in which periodic reports must be a part of the process. They don't need to do that in the security architecture community space.

Instead, open a regular and predictable time for any member to bring an issue for which they'd like help. This agenda item should be relatively unstructured. It also must be safe; I'll explain what I mean by "safe" below.

If there's an organizational history of emotional baggage around speaking up, or even negative consequences from bringing up problems, then the facilitator will have to address that history directly. I don't mean going over the history; I mean soliciting contributions, and then honoring these in some meaningful manner.

Dialoging—that is, when two or three participants go back and forth, essentially disagreeing with each other, or repeating the same, conflictual points—must be interrupted, usually with a simple act of thanking the speakers for bringing up the problem and then asking others for opinions. If everyone else remains quiet, then I will ask if anyone else cares about the issue. If the speakers or just a few participants are the only ones concerned, then the facilitator can move the agenda item or problem to a meeting just with those concerned, taking the conflict out of the community space. Or, if other participants remain silent, ask them why. This never fails to illicit contributions beyond those who've been taking up all the verbal space in the meeting. Sometimes, when quiet folks speak up, the group gets to hear an entirely new view that creatively opens a problem/solution set up. Responses to, "Why are you not participating?" can be very revealing.

However one chooses to facilitate conflicts and grandstanding, it's important that the facilitator remembers that the larger goal is not necessarily to solve problems, but rather, to create community trust and solidarity. Solutions may actually be better generated by a smaller group.

If a small group is going to be spun off to work on a particular problem, I make sure that the problem scope is understood. I also try to ensure that every viewpoint, even those quite divergent, is represented in the makeup of the group—as well as a couple of members who don't have a strong stake in any particular perspective. The group can then report back to the entire community when it has a proposal. The proposal will then be discussed, and perhaps eventually agreed to (or amended) by the entire community.

As I wrote above, any decision which affects the way that software is developed or the way that security is to be achieved should get community input and agreement. This establishes a shared sense of purpose, as well as some sense of control over how the work should be done.

I will note that even if I believe a particular way of executing a task is less than perfect, or maybe might not work as believed, I will still let the community decide and try. There's nothing like grappling with the consequences of a decision for learning. Plus, meeting the challenge as a community builds that necessary sense of shared task and shared responsibility: "We are all in this together."

Many years ago, two of our team members proposed a risk rating system that averaged the various risks. Our technical lead at the time, Steve Acheson, recognized the problem. But, being an experienced leader, he let the rest of us collect erroneous ratings until we could gather from the data that the arithmetic was incorrect: all of our ratings tended into a bell curve towards a center—the average. Doh!

Steve's leadership demonstrates just what I'm describing: even when it's an obvious error, the learning, as a group experience, may be more important than a period of incorrect results. I play a long game, just as Steve showed me so very long ago. I focus on long-term relationship goals and am often willing to sacrifice short-term gains in favor of community-related, strategic goals.

Establishing an empowered community of practice will deliver far more benefits than worrying over some poor arithmetic, as a team experiments, iterates, learns from the doing, and then pivots toward better solutions.

There is one caveat to the dreamy, people-oriented strategic description I've laid out just above. If your management is not 100% on board with the strategy, problems will ensue. As soon as I've received a technical leadership role, I go over my long-term community-building strategy with my direct management and their managers. Everyone needs to support the strategy or significant problems, likely misunderstandings, will occur. My first task is to ensure that we are aligned both with the strategy and the fact that along the way, there will be inevitable errors.

- Are we all willing to take those risks?
- At what level of risk should I use my influence to avert impacts?
- What level of poor decision making can we tolerate?
- What should I prevent with my leadership power and influence?

Once we have collectively answered these questions, I'm better armed to lead as well as to facilitate. I then have guidance on when to listen, when to let the community proceed, and when I need to step in and prevent negative impacts. Answering the above questions with my management allows the strategy to unfold rather more smoothly than might otherwise happen.

5.6 Support Learners' Errors

I noted in the community-building section that mistakes are going to be made; errors are a natural process of learning, and there has to be some room for making mistakes in the course of learning. Of course, mistakes are not confined to learning situations; everybody makes errors, whether of judgment, fact, analysis, or poor data composition.

One of the most effective ways to create a safe space for errors is to acknowledge my own. I have a number of stories about major errors I've made, whether involving programming, structuring things (architecture), or just poor judgment. If I'm in a leadership position and readily share my own failings, others will tend to feel safer based upon my authenticity. This is also a great technique for establishing bonds of trust: if I want the trust of developers, I'll often tell a story that highlights the difficulty of getting code right, because any experienced programmer has had to suffer through their own coding mistakes. We've all been there, done that. Admitting my own errors rarely fails to establish some sense of resonance, of shared experience among us, especially if I can generalize my error to the sorts of things that we are all likely to mess up.

Beyond the shared experience, it is critical for people to feel safe when seeking help. No matter the issue, it's important to focus on the problem and potential solutions—if there are no ready solutions, at least find reasonable approaches for gathering any required information so that we are trending toward potential solutions. So-called "blame storming" is useless. After all, everybody screws up sometimes.

Although having noted the uselessness of blame, if there's tension in the room around how a difficult situation has come about, if I had any part in it at all, I will tend to take all the responsibility for what has occurred.

I'll admit that this is somewhat of a manipulative tactic on my part. First, by taking all the blame, the group can move on to what we're going to do about it. Second, this is another community builder. The typical result is a bit odd and perhaps counterintuitive. Probably the sociologists or psychologists can tell us why this is—is it human empathy? Even so, for many people, once one person takes responsibility, other folks begin to see their part as well. By my taking all responsibility, I've made it safe for everyone to think about how they contributed to the situation. It's also very trust building for people to admit they've made an error or contributed to a difficult problem, so long as everyone is treated with respect. It may seem illogical, but taking responsibility for problems is very trust building in practice.

Occasionally, there will be someone who's more interested in blame than in problem solving. By my taking responsibility, I smoke these folks out. I need to know who they are, because they will stand in the way of community; people who are more interested in blame can be community challenges or even roadblocks. If I know who those people are, I can work around them and they don't get in the way of my trust-building strategy. They expose themselves, because other community members will be taking responsibility for their part in a problem while the blamers are busy pointing fingers. Don't you want to know about those whose interests are not aligned with your community of practice, with building great, highly motivated teams? I do.

It must be noted that anyone who continues to make mistakes, and especially the same errors repeatedly, also must be dealt with. I've heard many a really great leader say something of the order of, "It's okay to make mistakes. Just don't make the same mistake twice." I find that a little too strict. It can often take a few errors of more or less the same type to learn enough to avoid them.

Anecdotally, observing the many security architects with whom I've worked, it isn't all that uncommon to make similar errors more than once. However, if someone repeatedly makes the same errors, the other members of the community or their team will notice. Continual errors will have to be dealt with, potentially by the team. Someone with repeating errors will be a drag on the team's performance. I don't think there's any way to avoid that really dreadful management experience of telling someone they aren't working out.

I try not to think of the person as a failure or a mess up; rather, I prefer to think that the person may simply be in the wrong role. As I've noted in Chapter 2, where I detail the skills required in the practice of security architecture, one must communicate and influence—people skills. Security also involves the mental ability to see structures

> As I understand these two mental activities, the processing resides in different hemispheres of the human brain. Linear logic is processed in the left half, while mapping, relationship, and structural abstraction is performed on the right side. Individuals are typically stronger in one mode or the other; few are "ambidextrously" equal in brain processing modes. An architect must be able to work in both modes. More people, I think, are stronger with left-brain processing. Fewer individuals are stronger with right-brain activities.

and relationships, to identify patterns among the details that make up complex software. Architecture requires an ability to understand structure and to grasp relationships between components as well as the more obvious aptitude for logic and linear flow (see inset). These consist of two disparate thinking styles. Among the many people with whom I've worked, a fair sampling have struggled with the architectural requirement to map complex systems. Personally (and this is just my opinion, for what it's worth), I think perhaps the folks who've struggled with the structural and abstraction demands of security architecture may very well have been in the wrong role. At least, I prefer to be generous, so that's the way I want to look at this problem.

Occasionally there are people who don't really seem to care or who are not operating with the same integrity that the vast majority with whom I've been privileged to work. This may show up in repeated errors, often of omission as much as comission. One just has to face the dreadful task of asking them to leave so as not to drag everybody else down with them. I will say that the technical teams that I been a part of and have led are very attuned to this sort of behavior, even if they can't articulate what's wrong. Dysfunctional behavior makes teams dysfunctional. Unfortunately, however, it has to be faced. It's the downside of a leadership or management role. But happily, for me this is been extraordinarily rare. I mention it only for completeness.

While, as I've noted, repeated errors, especially if they are similar, is a red flag that something is wrong and must be attended to, errors continue to be a natural byproduct of learning and practicing complex skills such as those in security architecture. If we don't make a place for people to make mistakes, acknowledge them, hunt for solutions, and learn from them, we have failed in creating an environment that fosters learning, creativity, and innovation.

To paraphrase the famous saying,[*] "Wisdom comes from experience. Experience comes from making lots of mistakes." Whatever wisdom I may have gained is most certainly a byproduct of the many errors I've made.

---

[*] Terry Pratchett: Wisdom comes from experience, and experience often comes as a result of lack of wisdom. (https://inspire99.com/wisdom-comes-from-experiencebut-experience-is-lack-of-wisdom/)

5.7 Facilitate as Much as Lead

Instead of starting with policies and standards, instead of starting by issuing mandates, the first order of business is to build relationships, trust, a body and sense of shared practice. Hopefully, above, I've explained the benefits from these and how I go about fostering them.

One of the things that I learned facilitating large consensus meetings many years ago is the power that can be gained for the group if leadership isn't about making decisions, but rather, empowering the group to make them. For me, facilitation is actively guiding a group through a solution-seeking process toward the best decisions that we can collectively make. During that process, one of my focuses will be to ensure that most of the participants who have an interest get a chance to shape decisions. This is literally actively ensuring diversity.

Many years ago, when I was rebuilding a team which had suffered a lot of loss in a very short time, I focused first on establishing team relationships and trust. That means that I *facilitated* decisions and did not try to make any except the most urgent or most technically difficult myself. A new member of that team who came from a very different leadership style later said to me that he thought I didn't know how to lead because I rarely made decisions. However, a number of years later, when he saw the results of that careful and intentional team building, he acknowledged to me that, though he thought at the time that I seemed to be clueless, in fact, "you built a home for us."

If I could hand just one technique to other security architecture leaders, it would be my dictum to facilitate at least as much as lead; to listen at least as much as to speak; to use one's leadership in the service of the group; to use one's leadership to foster participation, along the way making sure that the quietest voices, the most uncertain voices, also have space and time to participate. This has been the greatest acquired skill that I brought to my leadership. And, whatever skill I may have as a facilitator, this has been the one key leadership skill upon which whatever success my teams have achieved has been built.

I feel so very lucky that I learned these facilitation skills so many years ago and that every single one of my managers (save one) have seen the benefits of my practice and not just allowed me to carry on, but rather have encouraged me to apply my facilitation skills to our collective work. It is one of the great joys of my career to see great teams come together and do amazing things.

5.8 Summary

I cannot promise the reader that each of the techniques described in this chapter will work for you. One security architect, many years ago, accused me of having a "cult of personality." Not sure exactly what that means; but most certainly each of us is one of a kind. Each of us must work with our own skills, limitations, and challenges.

In this chapter, I've tried to set out the things I attempt to do to create an environment in which the people I work with can grow into the very best security architects they can be, or at least find that they're not suited to the work and move on to something where they can be effective. Some of the items I've listed here very likely depend upon my particular strengths

Table 5.2 Summation of Actions Described in This Chapter[a]

Do	Don't
Encourage learning through mentors	Train exclusively via mentorship.
Offer learning opportunities through multiple learning styles.	Force all training via a single pedagogy or teaching/learning approach.
Build threat model attack scenario knowledge through public resources such as Mitre's ATT&CK™ Navigator™ and CAPEC™ categories.	Rely exclusively on security expert knowledge when threat modeling.
Build effective threat model attack scenarios by considering both attacker intention for each attack step, and also the technical mechanism used to achieve the intention.	
Empower and support learners to analyze systems for attacks and their defenses.	Restrict threat modeling to experts.
	Let security personnel hold threat modeling prisoner.
Use threat model reviews as a training opportunity. Include at least one person not familiar with the system under analysis.	Force all threat model reviews through an expert-laden, manual review board.
Record threat model requirements that have been implemented.	Measure security architecture efficacy by number of projects completed.
Escalate key risk decisions to an organization level that has sufficient scope and accountability for the potential impacts.	Allow people charged with implementation and delivery to rate and make important risk decisions.
Give security practitioners absolute final authority to rate risk.	Inflate risk ratings in order to force favourable decisions.
Give security architects opportunities to analyze systems outside of their usual purview.	Isolate learners strictly to their usual systems and away from other practitioners.
Build a community of security architecture practice: share successes, failures, challenges. Agree on processes. Give time for unscripted exchange, build trust and a shared sense of responsibility	
Admit to errors to model safety for mistakes and finding solutions.	Pretend to never make mistakes, and don't defend or excuse leaders' errors.
Use one's leadership in the service of building collective skill and shared responsbility.	Make all the decisions for everyone else.

[a] Table 5.2 is supplied in the hope that the table's summary statements provide a quick reference to the tips and tricks that I've outlined in this chapter.

---

and, shall I say, "madness"? But others listed here anyone can do. Try these things, whatever seems to apply to your situation, and see what works for you. Feel free to let me know what worked, what didn't work, what you don't understand or seems mysterious—what I haven't explained well enough for you to try. I'd like to be the best technical leader that I can be; I assume that you want to be the best security architect and leader that you can be. These are the things that I've done out of which great teams have formed who then have executed powerfully.

Perhaps I've just been lucky to have worked with such amazing people that despite anything I may have done the team members would've unified effectively anyway? Having trained literally hundreds of security architects, I am beginning to think that at least a few of these things might help create a beneficial environment for the teams that I've been privileged to lead. Your mileage, as always, may vary. Best of luck in your journey.

Chapter 6

Problem Areas You Will Encounter

6.1 What Does a Mature Practice Look Like?

The most obvious result one might expect from a mature security architecture practice has got to be "better"—that is, more secure, the program regularly producing readily securable designs. But since "more" and "readily" are subjective, non-quantifiable qualities, there seems to be a lack of definition of "mature" and an inability to measure "security built in from the start of projects."

Luckily, it isn't completely true that measurement is entirely squishy; I proposed a few measures in *Core Software Security* and *Securing Systems* which I will reiterate below. Still, I do expect that over time, software's ability to resist attack will improve. Let me share my experience of that change first before diving into skill and programmatic markers of maturity.

6.1.1 Do We Add Value?

As I've written in *Securing Systems*, one of the first signs that a security architecture program is gaining traction will be that the program's clients—that is, software developers, research and development, and engineers—regularly seek security architects' help.

"My first measurement for the program itself, and for each security architect, is whether the architect is being included in the relevant architectural discussions? In short, are architects being invited back repeatedly by the teams? Are security architects sought after? Do people call them when there are issues to solve? When they have security questions?" *Securing Systems*, p. 378

You will know that your architects are successfully providing value because those who develop your software will be reaching out, regularly. This is a bellweather of both individual performance and program effectiveness.

6.1.2 The War Is Over

As partnership grows, the battle over whether or not security is important, whether to enact the Secure Development Life Cycle (SDL), should disappear. That doesn't mean that there will be no conflict! Conflict between competing business needs is normal, healthy, and, frankly, inevitable. Below, I address some tricks that I use to manage conflict for the benefit of all, rather than sliding into endless frictions around, "Is security really necessary?"

Still, the change that should manifest in a mature program will be when conflicts are not about whether security is important or not; conflicts won't take place about whether any particular SDL task is effective or not. [Although, as I noted in a previous chapter, it is seemingly inevitable that someone will question each of the SDL's activities, at some point or other, even long after they've become well established.] Instead, when conflict arises, it will be about the security work itself: Is a particular solution or course the best or most appropriate? When should we schedule a fix or mitigation? Out of a number of possible treatments, which one provides enough benefit for the effort involved?

These are the sorts of discussions that we must have. No utopia exists where these issues don't come up. At least, I haven't yet had the pleasure of working in that organization. Plus, security folk don't necessarily have the fullest business picture; that's why it is essential that we keep an open mind and open ears to understand and incorporate the other business pressures that must be attended to. These sorts of hard decisions are why software security is a collaborative sport and will remain so for the foreseeable future.

You know that your program has gained some maturity when you no longer have any (many?) fights over whether security itself is the issue, whether or not security is among the important attributes that an organization's software must exhibit.

6.1.3 Optimum Tool Use

At first, most programs will try to tackle so-called "low hanging fruit"—that is, the easy issues. Quite often, easy issues will also be those that automated tools, such as static or dynamic analysis for security, will find (see *Core Software Security* for more information about these kinds of tools).

But one of the biggest problems I've continually encountered is that the tools haven't been sold to nor set up for the development process: they've been aimed at security. But security mustn't be the sole users or controllers of these types of tools. I know that I'm being quite heretical with my approach. That is, I do everything in my power to acquire effective tools that will at least solve some issues easily and without much noise or friction. Then I hand the tools over to development while teaching teams how to use them. Then we, security people, get out of the way and let development take it from there, trusting that they want to find bugs as much as anyone else.

A common phrase among application security teams is, "Trust but verify." It's that "but" in the phrase that rankles me and which I believe to be completely wrong-headed. If you must verify someone's work, then you don't really trust them to verify their own.

As I've pointed out numerous times in this work and others, there's no way to ensure that one's code is bug free without trying to verify its correctness. Programmers already know this, deep in their bones. Verification is part and parcel of producing working software. Why not give developers workable tools to verify the security implementation too? I propose, "Trust *and* verify." The "and" changes the phrase from distrust to a partnership.

Unfortunately, security tooling, as I've said from many a presentation stage since somewhere around 2007, can be wickedly difficult to configure and tune to eliminate or reduce false positives and results that require human analysis to validate. Instead, I've proven several times that if the tools return mostly high-confidence results, developers will adopt tools readily.

My friend Ryan Ware (Senior Security Researcher at Intel®, Inc.) once ran a series of side-by-side comparisons of well-regarded, commercial static analysis tools on a Linux kernel project. He couldn't get a better result than 15 percent fidelity—the remainder of the findings were false positives. That is a terrible result, frankly.

To fully understand Ryan's experiments, one must take into account that operating system kernels must do a lot of strange things that applications don't need to do (the kernel does them for the application). Those strange or unexpected actions often look quite similar to security issues. Kernels also usually must perform a fair number of very *dangerous* things; that is the nature of system code. Kernels are notoriously difficult to secure. So it's not all that surprising that tools written for general software might have difficulties with the odd code that often winds up in a kernel. Still, the point here is that even after significant tuning the tools specifically for that kernel's code base, tool fidelity was quite low.

I've gotten much higher fidelity out of static analyzers. But that is only after I abandoned the security team approach, which typically sets the tools up to find as many issues as possible (for due diligence reasons). When security dictates the tool "policy," or set of checks, they typically choose the broadest collection of checks. That makes sense when the people who will qualify the results have significant skill in identifying actual issues and are getting paid to perform that task; security code reviewers and security researchers often have those skills. As a result, the tools generate a lot of noise, but the noise isn't that much of a problem for security professionals who have the skills to winnow out false positives and to validate low-confidence findings.

However, the typical developer doesn't have the skill to qualify the real issues versus the false positives. That's why we want our code run through an analysis tool in the first place: there just aren't that many supremely talented secure coders. Although most developers are willing to learn something about secure coding, they likely won't have the time or the interest to become gurus. Hence, I've recommended for a long time that coders also get help from security tools. But, many of these tools return thousands of findings every time they're run over a complex build. Developers typically don't have time to go through those thousands of results to find the ones that actually need to be fixed.

This is where security's approach and development's needs are wildly divergent. Development wants to quickly identify any issues that the tool can actually find with high confidence. In most tools, that is a very different set of checks than the wide net security teams tend to cast with security tools.

My big learning in this area was sometime around 2004 or 2005. We had a huge portfolio of web applications, very few of which had been scanned for web issues. Another architect and I met twice a week for months, racking our brains over how we might start identifying vulnerabilities within thousands of applications and then managing somehow to get the findings fixed. One day, after one of our meetings when we had discarded yet another concept, I had a realization that it was the high-confidence findings we needed to chase. Once we'd identified a tool to implement, it took just about five minutes to figure out what the set of high-confidence checks would have to be. That program, called Baseline Application Vulnerability Assessment (BAVA) is still running successfully. I've based every tool implementation I've done since 2005 on BAVA's obvious success. (See inset.)

> Hilariously, I proposed the name "BAVA" as a joke. We also had a deeper, manual analysis, which we dubbed, "DAVA," so I made a joke about doing the "BAVA, DAVA dance." Perhaps unfortunately, the name has stuck through these 15 years, as of this writing.

Coming into a subsequent leadership role, the teams had been running static analysis on their code for a few years. But, because most teams had not tuned the analyses, one team had 72,000 findings, and another 46,000. Can you, my reader, guess how many the development teams actually fixed?

If you guessed "zero," you would be correct. No development team has time to pore through thousands of findings searching for the few really important ones. However, when I left that role, every team was getting useful results from the code analyzer that had once been ignored. The trick was to get the vendor to tell me that tool's set of checkers returning the highest fidelity results. In that tool's case, it has a set that'll deliver at least 85 percent or better real issues (that is, a false positive rate of ≤15%). That level of noise is tolerable for most development teams.

Once coders start getting some effective assistance in finding coding issues out of a tool, they start to learn secure coding from their mistakes, just like learning other coding patterns and semantics from compiling and other tests. Often, I see development teams then start to play with the aggressiveness of the checkers, until they find a workable balance between finding issues and tolerable noise.

Give development control over the tool's policy or rule set. Start them with a known set of high-confidence checkers. If they never stray from that, at least those issues will always be removed from the code. But, after teams have confidence that the tool delivers real value, they'll play with settings to find the optimum balance between issues and noise.

Security must give up control of this resource and, instead, empower development teams to verify security (trust *and* verify), just like developers must verify other aspects of the code they generate. Security departments will have to trust that developers will do their best. First, we have to train coders how to code securely and then give them security tools that generate valuable results.

6.1.4 You Know That You're Maturing When

With help from decent, well-configured tooling that fits organically within the natural development workflow, in multiple organizations I've seen the number of relatively easy-to-find issues decrease. At several of my jobs, we kept metrics on issues; we could correlate successful tool implementation against a decrease of these issues in released software.

Another feedback loop will be what external researchers find. As our tool strategy unfolded, external bug reports stopped finding many of the obvious issues. Reports were rarer, finding issues much more difficult to identify—the sorts of issues that tools cannot find (i.e., design issues). For code bases with a long history, many of those design issues will be within the legacy code, designed against an earlier threat landscape which will have typically contained fewer and less sophisticated exploitation techniques, since attack techniques are continually added and improved.

As coders find and remove the issues discovered through tightly configured and tuned analysis tools, I've seen a dramatic shift in the sorts of issues that arrive through external reports (that is, from security researchers and bug hunters). Analysis tools that have been focused on high confidence tests will likely be finding many of the issues that are easier to identify. Issues that are trickier to identify—those issues that require complex analysis—are the types of issues whose identification tends to be more difficult to automate. Hence, in general, high-confidence tests will be focused on the easiest-to-identify issues (though this is a broad generalization, not a hard and fast rule).

Because of the correlation between ease of identification with ease to automate and a higher analysis fidelity, the result will be that, at first, a code analysis program will be removing easier-to-find issues. As a result, externally originating issue reports should reflect the gains being made in code security over time. A maturing program ought to see a decrease in external reports of simple-to-find issues. Over time, researchers will have to work harder; the issues being reported will gain complexity and technical difficulty.

Of course, a few simple issues will continue to be missed by testing, thereby getting released in production software. We have already covered the basic fact of software development life: a few bugs will inevitably get missed by even the most rigorous testing regimen. However, the easy-to-find issues will decrease as a software security program matures. Plus, complexity and technical sophistication of issue reports by penetration testers and security researchers should increase as the program matures.

In fact, this is exactly what I've seen over time in my programs: as development teams become more successful at removing issues for themselves and at designing for the security principles revisited below (and explained previously in this book), those who probe the software for issues have to look harder—often a lot harder. The replacement of easy-to-find issues with more challenging ones is a measurement of a maturing software security program.

6.1.5 *"Nothing Proves Architecture Like Nothing"*

A program that quickly addresses the easy-to-find issues, using as much automation as possible, leaves itself time to develop a secure design (security architecture) program. As I've noted, security architecture takes time. Plus, the results will take a relatively long period to manifest. I like to quip that, "Nothing proves an architecture like nothing." What I mean is, over the life of a system,

- If it's had a minimum of incidents.
- If it's resisted most known attacks, and the successful ones haven't caused a great deal of damage.

- If the system design has been flexible enough to accommodate most of the changes necessary to fulfill the system's goals, security and otherwise.

Then one may safely say that one has reaped "the long tail of architecture." ["The long tail of architecture" is a phrase coined by my friend Srikanth Narasimhan, Cisco® Distinguished Engineer.] Nothing horrible has happened. Nothing happening doesn't occur by accident; nothing terrible occurs because the system was architected and designed well. One of my favorite presentations phrases is, "Nothing proves architecture like nothing." That is to say, we've reaped the long tail of architecture over the lifetime of a system when there have been no major incidents, security or otherwise.

As I noted at the beginning of this chapter, measurement of mature programs can be tricky. Taking my little architecture joke at face value, one might think that one is measuring "nothing." But nothing could be further from the truth (if you'll pardon a play on words?)

We can measure architecture success in the negative:

- There have been a low number of major security incidents over the lifetime of a system (or better, none).
- Expected attacks have been thwarted.
- New, unanticipated attack techniques have been slowed down sufficiently to be stopped before major damage.
- Successful exploitations have been contained to minor impact.

I have helped with systems on major web platforms that have delivered the above results. I know that achieving "nothing" is within the realm of the possible. Experience suggests that such results were achieved through diligent and coherent architecture practices such as I've suggested in this book.

I want to repeat my software security principles. These principles define the behavior that secure software will exhibit:

- Be as free as humanly possible from errors that can be maliciously manipulated—ergo, vulnerabilities.
- Have the security features that stakeholders require for the intended use cases.
- Be self-protective; resist the types of attacks that are expected to be aimed at the software.
- In the event of a failure, software must "fail well"—that is fail in such a manner as to minimize consequences of successful attack.
- Install with sensible, "closed" defaults.

You will see the above principles begin to emerge in the behavior of your software as the security requirements that you specify get implemented and begin to populate your software releases. As your software exhibits these behaviors more and more over time, then you have achieved an understanding of security architecture as well as having achieved a practice of applying information security to systems.

Contrary to what most users and even many developers assume, security is a systems property emerging from the totality of system behavior. When the software produced in conjunction with your security architecture program exhibits the above behaviors, then I suspect that your program is relatively mature. That doesn't mean that all problems are solved, of course.

6.1.6 Get It in Writing!

"Security architects who document their recurring patterns, who provide the solutions to those patterns, and who help to get those solutions built into the available services and software from which projects may draw will increase the scale and velocity at which the organization's development teams can operate." *Securing Systems,* p. 331

I don't like repeating the same security requirements over and over again. I have known practitioners who believe that repeatedly demanding that developers hue to a company's policies and standards is the essence of their role. I would find that boring work, personally. I want to document the standard methods and technologies thoroughly; I want standard services, say an authentication system that is part of the application infrastructure, to become ridiculously easy to implement such that, as Steve Acheson used to say, "[M]ake the secure path the easy path."

6.2 Typical Problems Programs Encounter

In this chapter, I hope to explain to you what I have done to meet some of the typical problems I encounter. What I find validating is that as I speak with other security architects whose programs are well underway, the same set of issues comes up, over and over again. While your set of challenges may not match mine exactly, I think you'll find at least a few of yours described here.

- Scaling to large or complex development portfolios
- Assessments taking too long, negatively impacting development schedules
- Visibility into what's been completed and into challenges
- Governance for consistency and completeness
- Quality control
- Late engagement
- Friction with developers; developers not cooperating
- Isolation and "battle fatigue"

I shall try to address each of these areas in turn, though maybe not as linearly as I've presented them, since there are profound dependencies. The problem-to-solution set do not map 1:1.

6.2.1 Scale

As I've noted already in this book and others, there is a deficit of experienced cyber security personnel. There exist far fewer candidates then there are jobs. And the situation has existed for quite a long time. When I was asked to take up Cisco Infosec®'s first application security architect role, they had been looking to fill the position for about 18 months. That was in early 2001. Things haven't changed much in the intervening years.

Hence, attempting to build an army of security architects through hiring is likely to take quite a long time. Even hiring a small team will take a significant time, perhaps as long as it took to find me to fill Cisco's application security architect role. Perhaps longer, because there are more positions now than there were then. Of course, there are more practitioners, as well.

Still, my LinkedIn® account receives requests for security architects every week, sometimes every day. One of my dearest friends in the industry has already spent months trying to build a 60-member security architecture team. It can be a very long haul, indeed.

At Cisco, it soon became pretty obvious to me that we weren't going to find all the architects we needed. Plus, in hiring contractors for such a key role, there's often significant ramp-up time to get a feel for an organization's risk tolerance, the existing services and limitations of the infrastructure, an organization's policies and standards, application delivery mechanisms, and the rest of the complexities of designing, generating, and deploying software. In *Securing Systems,* I called this information, "the Three S's." In my humble experience, it's impossible to threat model unless the analysis is grounded in the Three S's. Contractors quite often can't come up to speed fast enough within their contract period, even if they are massively experienced. That was our experience at Cisco.

For the foregoing reasons, Michelle Koblas and I racked our brains for some other way to get the staffing that we needed. I wrote a bit about the story in my blog, "brookschoenfield.com":

> "Teams of empowered, decentralized 'partner' security architects spread across a development organization and integrated into delivery teams. Certainly, a few organizations have had 'security champion' programs. These are not the same thing, at all. The original idea here was to train, empower, mentor, coach, and create a community of security architects by capitalizing on the interest and skills of an existing system/software architecture practice.
>
> "I originally pitched the concept to Michelle Koblas in 2002 or perhaps it was early 2003?—Ferris Jabri program managed the first successful team with me and Cisco Infosec's 'Web Arch' team. Kudos go to Michelle (originally), Nasrin Rezai, and John Stewart for strongly supporting the original experiment. Enterprise Architecture kept telling us that we had to wait. Ferris literally said, 'We're just going to do it, Brook.' We then proved the concept admirably. Thanks for your fine leadership, Ferris.
>
> "A key differentiator is empowering each virtual team member as a formal part of the security organization. That is, each member has the policy powers[*] for security and must perform the due diligence role typically reserved to Infosec. These are not simply 'red flag' spotters, but fully functional security architects. Such a program has to accompany the empowerment with training, mentoring, continued coaching, and support. In fact, without ongoing support and air cover for hard prioritization and risk decisions, the virtual team will ultimately fail. Another key difference is the creation of a community of support among the partner team. Participation is a critical factor, as well as an inducement to perform the work (beyond having 'security' on one's resume)."[†]

As I noted at my blog, there's a big difference between mandating that a development team member report about security issues and concerns to a central security team and empowering one or more members of the development team to become the team's security architect.

When the approach is to appoint someone, the designated person quite possibly doesn't want to do the job. Importantly, the security role may quite likely place that person in conflict

---

[*] That is, power to enforcement security policy and standards.

[†] http://brookschoenfield.com/?page_id=217

with the rest of their team. Furthermore, if the appointed security eye isn't given power, influence, or skills, they aren't being given much incentive to carry out the role. I might go so far as to suggest that someone whose job is to watch others might be considered a spy by those others. That role doesn't really sound very appealing, and too often, isn't to the appointed "spy."

At the other end of the spectrum, what I've done four times now is actually offer the necessary training and support for development team members to become security experts in various areas, one of which we hope will be a path to becoming a security architect for their team.

We do everything possible to empower the developer security architect. We empower them to enforce standards and policies. We empower them to escalate risks for decisions. But, because escalations might bring an on-team member into conflict with their own management, we don't hesitate to pick up tricky escalations and run with them for our satellite security architects. In this way, the people fulfilling this role are both empowered and protected; we never want to place one of our security architects in conflict with their own management.

The "carrot" for people who pick up this role is that they can truthfully claim that they have fulfilled the role of security architect. Because for many organizations security is a premium skill, there is often a bump in pay somewhere in the near to medium future for these people. People who have fulfilled the satellite security architect role as I've outlined here actually have performed the work. A significant number of them continue on to become security architect leaders.

Of course, not everyone who goes through the program and does the security architecture work chooses to continue in security as a career. That's okay. If they've gained nothing else, they will bring their security knowledge to whatever role they may fulfill in the future of their career. Generally, that will be a win in whatever roles they fill.

There are couple of challenges that satellite programs will tend to encounter. The foremost is that as people go through the program, fulfill the role, they will be hired away into other organizations. There will be staff turnover. I learned the hard way that my program would have to account for some staff churn. Which also means that there are always new people to train.

I'll take up the visibility problems below.

It was John Stewart (CSO of Cisco Systems, Inc.) who taught me that on an annual basis or so, one must reinvigorate the empowerment of the program with executives. His tactic is to thank directors and vice presidents for their support of the program; this works perfectly while maintaining the critical management relationships that are necessary in complex organizations.

Unfortunately, occasionally there will be an executive or director with significant influence and power who doesn't want to support the program. That's where my executive's support will be critical. Without that, any difficult director can wreak havoc, at least in their department or group. We avoid placing our satellite architects in the line of this kind of fire. The central group has to take over in order to protect the people that the program depends upon to execute the work.

I don't have any magic pills or silver bullets to give you that will ameliorate damage that an uncooperative director can cause. The best I can offer is to quickly push this up to supportive executives higher in any organizational hierarchy. It is really a management problem, not a security or security architecture problem.

I can never forget the time that I was trying to advise a director who was questioning why her teams had to execute the company's required SDL tasks assigned to them. At a meeting to discuss her team's SDL tasks, she said to me, "Did I give you permission to speak?" That had never happened before and has never happened since. I don't think she realized that I was one of the CSO's most senior security architects. Nevertheless, at most high-tech jobs, we simply don't treat each other in this manner. A high-tech workplace isn't a hierarchical classroom. We are cooperating together to find the best solutions given business realities. Problem solving usually requires collaborating very closely and considering very diverse viewpoints.

Luckily, my manager was also in the meeting and immediately used our private chat session to assure me that the director's behavior was severely out of line. That misbehavior was escalated up at least to the Vice President level at the company. The director left the company not very long after that. I didn't try to find out if it was because of what she had done to me particularly. But as I say, in those sorts of situations about all you can do is enlist your supportive executives' help. At least they can give you cover so you can get your job done.

6.2.2 Assessments Take Too Long

As the pace of software delivery increases, security tasks, especially tasks depending upon human analysis such as threat modeling, may be seen as too time intensive to complete.

"With DevOps, you have to move super-fast. There can be no 'manual' in that process. If you don't have automation, you'll never be successful."[*]

There may be resistance to performing any human analyses, which get described as "old fashioned" or even unnecessary. Curiously, developers just might be right! Whether or not manual analysis will be necessary depends upon architecture and technology stability.

Consider the situation in which engineering is adding to or changing the processing of an existing architecture and platform. Let's say that the structure of the system and its technology dependencies haven't changed and aren't going to be for the foreseeable future. Let's also assume that a thorough threat model has already been completed. With that completed threat model, the system's security requirements are understood. Let's assume that the requirements generated through the threat model have already been implemented. Let's also say current development is diligently implementing those security requirements or standards that must be coded (see inset). Finally, let's assume that the build and deployment systems have also had their security worked out and implemented.

> Requirements like never using memory after it's been freed and ensuring that memory copies cannot exceed the receiving buffer's length are usually coded, not consumed as a service or implemented within infrastructure.

In the case I've outlined in the previous paragraph, I don't see a reason to perform any additional threat modeling analysis. None of the triggers for review have fired. From a threat modeling standpoint, the only trigger that might require further analysis would be some kind of significant shift in the threat landscape—a never-before-seen attack technique that applies to the system under development.

Shy of some shift in threats or technologies, developers would be correct to argue that manual threat modeling under these circumstances won't be fruitful. I didn't make this situation up. I actually threat modeled in a situation as described. There were no additional security requirements. Nor should that organization have further analyzed their system. Nothing about the threat model was changing.

---

[*] Romeo, n.d.

For situations where security architecture will add value, there are ways to speed analyses up. The triggers for a threat model or threat model review are:

- Architecture (development) is new; there's no existing threat model. [And the development will require a security posture. Not all development has security requirements.]
- Architecture (structure) changes (adding, changing, removing functions or components).
- Adding/removing/changing a security feature or implementation.
- Adding or changing code whose function is believed to be critical.

As my friend (and terrific security architect) Chris Romeo said in the quote above, everything that *can* be automated should be.

If development is constrained to a well-understood and defended set of technologies, languages, infrastructures, and platforms, I believe there's significant benefit to automate at least part of the threat modeling process. The security requirements can be scoped and bounded such that many basic requirements will be identical for sets of applications—maybe all.

As an example, imagine generating new business logic for applications that will run in a carefully designed and managed cloud platform. In this case, the application programmers will be defended, as least in part, by what's been built into the platform. Because applications will be generated to fit within a set of standards, much of the security architecture analysis should have been spent on making the "easy path the secure path."

> Steve Acheson encouraged me to design for "make the easy path the secure path" in 2001. As far as I know, he originated this design principle.

Cisco Infosec's Web Architecture team (Web Arch) built our systems and processes in exactly this manner: web application teams had to implement a limited set of security requirements that were well defined. The easiest path to deployment had the fewest security needs because a great deal of what was required was already built into the infrastructure into which web applications were typically deployed. Because application teams were only responsible for a few security requirements, developers were relieved of the burden of implementing most of the required security controls. Much security defense was simply inherited or consumed. Use of services such as authentication were a check box at deployment; appropriate configuration files were auto-generated by the deployment infrastructure.

In the above example, developers aren't required to perform a great deal of analysis, particularly manual analysis. In a tightly constrained environment, hewing to standards will take care of a lot of, perhaps most, ongoing security needs. In such systems, questionnaires/surveys about use cases and technology uses will be sufficient for much new development. Commercial requirements tools might help generate the needed requirements surveys. I personally know of three very successful implementations of commercial requirements survey tools for precisely this purpose. These three implementations are at major, Fortune 1000 companies.

Where development is less constrained, but there are still well-understood patterns, perhaps because various implementation elements can be reused (let's call them "ingredients"), automation might still be applied, at least for those systems that will be consumed by additional development as ingredients.

At the time of this writing, there are two commercial threat modeling tools that allow users to enter architecture patterns (visually) and then attach security requirements to these. Both of the commercial tools come with deep and broad libraries of typical architecture patterns and the ideal set of defenses for those patterns.* As far as I know, each tool has a significant collection of customers. That alone indicates to me that threat modeling automation is coming of age.

In the afterward of *Securing Systems,* I mentioned that there existed at that time a new commercial tool. Now there are two, both with a customer base. Though each tool is significantly different from the other, some feature convergence has occurred. To me, that demonstrates a maturing of the market, as customers come to understand what features they will need for a successful implementation. I find this very hopeful. It is obvious from the tools' successes that a market for threat modeling automation exists and can be met.

Alongside the commercial offerings, there are three open source or freely available threat modeling tools available. (See inset.) Whether one or more of these will get the development attention that's required to capture sufficient architecture patterns and their defenses remains to be seen.

> There are also two open source tools that deal with other aspects of threat model automation: automatically triggering reviews via UML changes and automating test scripts based upon threat model requirements. I believe both of these are also useful in a DevOps development shop.

Microsoft®'s Threat Modeling Tool (TMT) is freely available. However, my experience among the 120 (or so) security architects in my last team suggests that TMT's results are often idealized and lack context. I have not counted the number of times that a security architect new to threat modeling has generated a TMT threat model, only to be overwhelmed by the number of TMT findings. She/he/they will then bring me the results through which we'll prioritize the findings that will provide real-world protections, versus the many that aren't contextually impactful. This is only my personal experience. My senior security architects would each have also had to perform such reviews. My guess (and it's only a guess) is that too many insignificant findings is a typical result from even simple TMT threat models. Hence, while TMT provides a gateway into threat modeling analysis, its results tend to produce too much noise to be taken without further analysis and prioritization.

My present opinion is that at least the commercial tools offer significant help wherever:

- Typical architecture patterns similar to those already included in the tool are employed (these can then be consumed without further configuration).
- There is a discreet enough set of unique patterns that these can be input into a tool within some reasonable period of time (that is, before the patterns become obsolete).
- There exists a discreet enough set of locally built or defined defenses that these can be reasonably input into the tool (similar to architecture patterns, above).

As I've been saying in some of my conference presentations, why do we need to keep reiterating obvious and well-known defenses, like those that have been part of coding and architecture standards for a long time? For instance, OWASP (Open Web Application Security Project) has generated dozens of excellent web application programming and design documents describing how to prevent typical web vulnerabilities. A threat modeling analysis isn't required to identify these; they've been identified for years. Nearly every reasonably complex web presence will need to deal with most if not all of the issues contained in the OWASP materials.

We know for certain that a default, unhardened operating system should never be connected to the Internet. Continually repeating that hosts must be hardened isn't necessary. The

---

* *Disclosure:* I'm friends with the founders of each of the companies, but have no financial interest in either.

Center for Internet Security (CIS) hardening guides have been there for years; there is no need to invent a new, local hardening guide (except for an entirely new operating system that CIS hasn't yet seen).

Plus, these sorts of requirements will be a part of the commercial threat modeling tools, will be included in content for some of the survey tools, and may even have been captured by one or more of the open source or free tools. Security architects shouldn't, in my humble opinion, have to repeat such well-known security practices, *ad nauseum*. That's not where I want to spend my analysis time.

Using these kinds of standards or tools that include these standards will surely speed development, perhaps immensely for those projects using typical architectures. We must, if I may offer a strong opinion, relieve the burden of manual, one-at-a-time analysis from development teams wherever and however we can. There are still plenty of tricky security problems to go around!

"'While many development teams resist embarking on a threat modeling effort, there's no need to delay. As with many aspects of DevOps, starting quickly and integrating often are the keys to success,' said NCC's Michlin. 'Threat modeling can be done in a half-day session, and it will give both developers and operations teams more insight into the project.'"*

I would add to Ms. Michlin's wise observation to ease threat modeling analysis through the artful inclusion of threat model tools whenever investment in time and/or money will return on the investment (as described above).

Reserve manual analysis for difficult, atypical, and unique problems. Either purchasing or documenting the well understood will eliminate unnecessary analysis to improve velocity and agility. Besides, repeating "escape your web inputs" and "validate the adherence of your messages to expectations" is boring: these security defenses are well described in multitudes of literature, standards, and in all the tools. As Cristoph Kern did at Google®, make it impossible to release code that doesn't adhere to the obvious security standards.

Instead, let's focus on one-of-a-kind problems and designing build/deployment systems that ensure defensive code. That will surely be faster.

What do I mean by "unique" or "one of a kind"? Imagine that you have a customer authentication system that was built in 2004 (15 years ago, as of this writing). In 2004, computer virii and worms were a major focus. Web attacks encapsulated within application messages were a cutting edge in the threat landscape. Reverse engineering tools were nowhere as powerful as they are today; network packet capture was a state-of-the-art security analysis technique (it still is, but tools have matured significantly).

Imagine that you're the security architect who identifies several credible attack scenarios against this legacy mechanism. But you are constrained by business's need to continue to use a great deal of the business technology that depends upon the customer identifiers. You are given no grand investment to redo the entire suite of systems. Still, in your professional opinion, by today's standards, the authentication system is weak; you believe that you are one customer compromise, perhaps two, from the authentication system's failure.

I didn't make the foregoing example up; I encountered a very similar situation a few years ago.

Situations like my example that don't conform to standard problem patterns are where a security architect can be of enormous help. Finding improvements each of which will

---

* Michlin, n.d.

significantly increase the overall robustness of the authentication system, but none of which is outside the capabilities and the budget of the developers working on the service, is (and was) an interesting challenge (see inset).

At the same time, I could raise the risk of leaving things as they were. I could (and did) advocate for building a much more resilient set of services in parallel to making incremental improvements to the legacy (existing) system.

Presumably, assigning an experienced security architect who would both advance the state

> For the example customer authentication system, the incremental improvements that were implemented were additional entropy used to construct the identifier, an update to its cryptographic strength, and improvements to the strength of storage protections.

of the art against a changing threat landscape while also helping to build services resistant to the broader range of attacks that had become possible over the life of the legacy system proved worthwhile for the organization. Problems like these are where experts can most profitably be applied. There isn't a tool in existence that can perform this analysis; it's got to be a human (at least at today's state of the art).

How can we improve the velocity of security assessment? We must eliminate needless manual processes in favor of collections of well-understood engineering patterns. My comment is nothing more than standard engineering practice. Where there's a proven method or technique, describe it, then apply it. It doesn't really matter how the knowledge is packaged: a standard, a book or other literature, a training course, within a commercial or open source tool. The point is, we can increase the speed of what we do if we don't rely on human analysis to repeatedly identify that which we already understand to be required.

There is one final comment about speed I'd like to make: threat modeling doesn't have to take a long time. As I've noted in this book, if an inexperienced team finds just one requirement that significantly improves a security posture, this is a win and should be celebrated as such. This implies that threat models needn't be the long, exhaustive exercise often promulgated by software security programs. Rather, get developers thinking about credible attack scenarios. Over time, they will likely get better at the analysis, identify more scenarios that apply, and thus identify more security requirements.

These early analyses can be short and discreet. Start with those well-understood and well-described attacks against similar technologies and systems. Most developers are familiar with at least a few of these. When threat modeling is performed as a group activity, the analysis benefits from varying team member's attack knowledge. They'll consider more attack types. I've seen this pooling of attack knowledge play out again and again in my participatory threat model classes.

Importantly, threat modelers needn't invent new attacks. Apply those attacks that have been successful in the past against systems similar to the system under analysis. Plus, detailed knowledge about how each attack works isn't necessary. Threat modeling works best when types of attacks, classes of attacks, are considered (as I've described in Chapter 5, Learning the Trade).

Thus, threat modeling doesn't require a penetration tester's knowledge of attacks. It's enough to know that memory conditions can be manipulated in C and C++ (or any language directly handling memory addresses), or that there have been virtual guest escapes to take over the host running the virtual environments. We don't need the details because the next exploit will be somewhat different, anyway.

Finally, in order to assure some quality and completeness, make a practice of peer review (as described in this book and *Securing Systems*). These reviews are really short! From experience,

I can tell you that a two-hour review is quite long. Usually, for many systems, the review is 30 minutes, an hour at most. Nearly everyone can devote an hour to helping teams complete their threat models.

Thus, where human analysis must be applied, it can be kept quite manageable and discreet.

"It makes no difference if, for example, a threat model is produced as the result of a whiteboard session with the development team, is written out as a narrative in a Microsoft Word document, or is produced with the use of a specialized tool, such as the SDL Threat Modeling Tool."[*]

Unless compliance requires a particular, formal threat modeling document to be archived, in my experience, allowing teams to use their most organic approaches will encourage teams to actually build threat models. Requiring that teams produce some long, exquisitely detailed document that no one actually reads or works from only discourages the analysis that we need them to perform.

"In my experience, the minimum documentation necessary to prove that a security assessment has taken place, and to achieve implementation of the security requirements, will be the security requirements document. If nothing else is produced, the requirements document can even imply a threat model. That is, the security requirements document can stand as evidence not only of the assessment, but of the threat model from which the requirements were derived." *Securing Systems*, pp. 369–370

My opinion and experience have not changed since writing *Securing Systems*: the most important document generated by a threat model, at least for the purposes of developing secure software, will be the security requirements document.

It's also handy to have some sort of visual indication of the system's structure (data flow diagram or logical architecture). For more complete documentation, I also like to list the attack scenarios that have been considered credible. If there's a requirement to capture risks from threat modeling, then a risk assessment of the likelihood and potential impacts from each credible attack scenario is also useful.

Other than for compliance to some regulation, I don't find further documentation necessary. A picture of a white board with a list of attack scenarios with estimates for occurrence and impact ought to be sufficient to document what's been considered; the security requirements speak for themselves.

Keeping documentation lightweight and natural to the analysis will speed things up, sometimes considerably. Years ago, my friend Eoin Carroll would spend weeks on graphing the various layers of each project's threat model. Most teams no longer have the luxury of waiting that long for results. His threat model diagrams set my high bar for understandability and clarity—they were absolutely amazing documents. But they weren't easy to generate. Besides, in iterative development processes, the threat model is subject to change as development proceeds. One doesn't want to spend too long on the documentation because it may be obsolete before it's been completed.

For velocity:

- Make the easy path the secure path.
- Use standards wherever possible; automate the use of standards.
- Apply expertise only to those problems requiring it.
- Integrate with the natural flow of development.
- Keep documentation appropriately lightweight.

---

[*] Microsoft, n.d.

6.2.3 Late Engagement

I hear from security architects about being engaged with projects toward the end of the effort, sometimes very close to release of the software, go-live, or production. At every security conference and every class, architects will complain of the same late engagement problem. I can speak to the ongoing problem from personal experience, just as much as from hearing my colleagues in other organizations complain about it.

In fact, one of my stock jokes for secure design or security architecture presentations is to remark about development teams asking, "Bless my project before go-live." I often get a lot of nodding heads and quite a few chuckles from the security folk. Anybody who's been around for a while has experienced this problem at least some of the time, if not regularly and repeatedly. Based not on scientific, but rather entirely anecdotal, evidence, late engagement appears to me to be rampant. At nearly every consultation with experienced architects, they ask me what to do about recurring too-late engagement.

This problem is at least in part a function of too much separation between the security practitioners and the development effort. Cultivating security architects who are more closely tied to each development effort, or better, placed on each development team, will allow security tasks to more closely follow the development process organically. Hence, a satellite program is one of the ways to address this problem.

Of course, the satellite program must train and support these new security architects so that they understand what security tasks (SDL*) are appropriate to execute throughout the development process. Failure to help the satellite architects understand the entire SDL will continue to create problems such as late engagement.

But there's another trick I use which has never failed to end a vicious cycle of late engagement, at least with the team with whom I've engaged. Let's say that a team comes to me a short time before the development cycle will end. They ask me to create a threat model. At that point, if the team is completing testing, the code has already been frozen, and the design has been implemented, so the only good a threat model can provide is to identify under-mitigated risks that will go into production. It is generally highly unlikely that production release will be halted, even in the face of a major security miss.

What I do is ask the team and their management what they will do if we were to identify a nasty security risk or problem. Will they hold their release so that the issue can be addressed? Will they ask for an exception? Would they be willing to put such a security item onto the top of development tasks for the next release? I get the team to grapple with this problem *before* I perform any analysis whatsoever.

Somehow, thinking through the situation the team created by engaging with me late causes them to consistently engage early from then on. This has never failed to change the dynamic.

Then, we agree on the timing of any SDL tasks for the next and future revisions. Once having been through a fire of their own making, I've never seen a team that continues to engage too late. See if this works for you.

Many times, when I've tried to engage early, I'm told by the architects of a team that they haven't "finished the architecture yet. We'll engage when it is complete." There is an awful

---

* Please see my chapter, The SDL In the Real World, in *Core Software Security* for more information about SDL tasks and where they best fit during a development process.

myth that threat modeling cannot be done until all the structures of a system have been set. Unfortunately, after all the structure has been set is far too late. Building a model with the potential to change the architecture after a great deal of hard work has been put into thinking that structure through should seem obvious to my readers, I would hope.

The model has a huge potential to add elements, possibly to move them, possibly to think through connections and data storage. If the security analysis occurs after all the other work, then either it invalidates that effort, or whatever schedules and budgets have been based in the work are very likely to change, and not in a good way: more stuff to be built.

As I say in my classes, "Start the threat model as soon as there's sufficient structure to analyze." Even a couple of functions, when put together, will probably require some security thinking. Threat modeling must iterate as a key part of any architecture or design work. It's fine when using any of the iterative development processes to allow the model to iterate right along with, as a part of, the ongoing unfolding of the software.

Threat modeling is rarely that useful when performed exactly once, at a particular point in time. That's because throughout development, things change regularly, sometimes constantly. Modeling once, too early, and continuing structural change will be missed. I've already noted the pitfalls of attempting to threat model too late (above). Further, when we freeze the threat model, this hamstrings the ability of developers to meet problems—security problems included.

Ultimately, a frozen list of security requirements that cannot be amended as a part of the creation and implementation process will ultimately not get built at all. I learned this lesson the hard way early on as team after team in pre-production reviews would tell me that my frozen requirements could no longer be built as described because of other changes to the software that occurred throughout development.

Instead, today, I advise iterating security just like anything else that's been required. As teams learn about how to implement, security implementation is likely to improve, just like other parts of the software. Of course, this works a lot better with satellite security practitioners embedded in the team who can respond to changing conditions as they occur. Another point in favor of satellite software security architects.

Obviously, by starting security analysis right alongside other early thinking, early engagement, that long-sought ideal will automatically be achieved. But I like to get started even earlier!

When I was asked to provide technical leadership for Cisco's web products, there was very little engagement except for infrastructure improvements. There had been little formal security architecture practice, though at least one of the products had security-savvy people on each key team. It sounds perhaps worse than it was. Actually, I learned a lot from those people; they invented some truly innovative security solutions. Even so, my task was to build a formal security architecture practice, an SDL, and to figure out how to make it work with these products (of which there were eventually nine).

Curiously, one of the product's sales team was encountering a lot of questions about the product's security that they couldn't answer. To respond to those security questions, the salespeople started to invite me to their customer meetings when these were focused on our product's security. I believe I interacted with around 50 enterprise customers over a period of about six months.

Those sales meetings often included the product's product managers, those people responsible for guiding the direction of product development. As our product managers began to understand my role and the value I was bringing to these customer interactions, they started to engage me and my team as they were defining each set of new requirements. I call those the "high-level security requirements."

Once security architecture was routinely engaged early by product management, our timing problems disappeared. Since high-level requirements were included with effort descriptions from product management to development, continuing security engagement was organic from the beginning of effort on through the development process. Our engagement timing problem had been solved through a profound demonstration of value up front, even before formal development began.

That early in the requirements process, requirements don't have to be particularly specific. I tend to think of these high-level requirements as security strategy statements. What security building blocks will need to be architected and then designed to achieve the organization's and the system's security goals? What security features will the system's stakeholders expect? At this early stage, there's no need to identify particular implementations. That will be done later, during architecture discussions.

Of course, requirements such as "product will be secure" are absurd. I'm not making this requirement up: I've seen that exact sentence in a product requirements document more than once, I'm afraid to say.

Early on, knowing that authentication and authorization will be required is probably enough. It may be obvious that data will cross untrusted networks and thus require protection (usually, encryption). Really early on, it was sufficient to identify the sorts of security features that stakeholders will require and not much else. It's pretty simple, really. The important thing is that security engagement will have already begun before a single architecture diagram has been drawn or a single line of new code written. That's truly early engagement.

If you can hook into product management, you will solve your early engagement problems. But gaining their trust may take some effort. I got lucky through that series of customer meetings. In subsequent roles, I've been forced to work harder at building relationships with my product managers such that early engagement unfolds naturally as a part of the product management process.

Ultimately, an appropriate timing for security engagements will end up being a relationship problem. Development teams are very good at overlooking anything that doesn't make engineering sense. They are good at disinviting anyone who takes more effort than the value they deliver. This tendency to ignore is why just mandating rules doesn't usually solve many of these problems, particularly the timing ones.

Executives can declare repeatedly that security engagement will be early. Policies can be drafted explicitly demanding early engagement. The SDL can get published with specific activity timings. And yet, I've seen far too many organizations that have done each of these and still complain of late engagement—engagement so late that nothing can be done for the development effort except to get exceptions and waivers approved.

I still believe that a mature organization will document its SDL clearly and then set expectations for execution of the various tasks in the SDL as clear as humanly possible. But the ensuing collateral that results from drafting an SDL is for reference, not culture change. In my very humble experience, relationships and trust, not policy mandates, deliver early engagement.

Please take a look at Chapter 4, Culture Hacking.

- Empower a community of practitioners.
  - Corollary: Accept all offers of help.
- Build a community of practice for practitioners. The practices will be based upon the SDL.
- Offer obvious value through the behaviors you want to encourage.
  - Corollary: Reward the behaviors you intend.
- Use my consequences trick (described above) on teams that keep operating in the old way (i.e., engaging late). Ensure that those teams understand how you can't help them as well as you might have (or at all).

Problems such as late engagement don't change quickly. I find that I have to play a long game, continually working toward the culture changes that foster security while addressing behavior that cannot work, including too late security engagement.

Isolated Security Practitioners

Sometimes security practitioners, especially those who are "federated"—that is, assigned to a security role from outside the security team—feel alone. It can be a very lonely role, having to call out security problems as a lone voice among others who aren't focused on security and may even experience security as a blockage to getting other priorities accomplished.

Those security people who don't report into a central security team have dual responsibilities. It's important to understand a couple of potential conflicts:

- The person's manager may not understand the security role well, or at all. The manager may have little understanding of the value to security of the person's work.
- Others on the development team may experience security needs as one person's opinions, not as a required set of functions and activities assigned to every development effort.
- In order to meet budgets and schedules, development managers may try to silence the security person, since security requirements may impact deliverables.
- The security person may feel conflicted when there's disagreement: their manager and team versus security. A person involved in such a conflict is likely to believe that they are caught in a crossfire and have divided loyalties.

Any of the above experiences can lead to feelings of alienation and isolation on the part of security practitioners, especially so-called "satellite" or "federated" security architects.

One-way communication from a central security team to their satellites will not help any of the above situations. One-sided communications instead are likely to increase a sense of isolation, of being forgotten, of being asked to sit in an organizational "hot seat" for security's sake.

In my humble experience, one of the best methods to address isolation is the formation and sustenance of a community of practice, as described above and in Chapter 5, "Learning the Trade." If there is a vital community, practitioners are supported, interact regularly with their peers, solve individual and collective problems together, and generally come to understand that each is not alone and can get help whenever needed.

Importantly, I try to remind everyone who has a security due diligence role for the organization to avoid wasting precious influence on issues of low impact (i.e., lower-risk items). Low-risk issues are prime candidates for the use of exceptions. I like to say that "exceptions are my friends" and "exceptions are my favorite tool." When a development team refuses to fix an issue, for whatever reason, offering an exception normally will transform the interaction from a disagreement to problem solving, from "you must fix" versus "no we won't," to "when can this get fixed and how will we fix?"

Exceptions are a tool to maintain relationships and trust in the face of divergent priorities and interests. Performing the duties of a satellite security architect puts practitioners into conflict with their teams—the very people with whom the security architect must get along if she/he/they are to be effective. The security architect must have influence in order to foster open-minded exploration of risks and development priorities. Hence, one of the main tasks for those who are building and running a federated security architecture program will be to protect satellite security architects' influence.

Obviously, coaching satellites on people skills must be a part of the program. In addition, tactical use of exceptions will make an end-run around the built-in conflicts of interest inherent in a federated approach in which security practitioners are appointed from within development team members.

Managing contentious escalation is another technique that we've used to protect security architects from conflicts with their own teams and management chains. When a member of the federated team must stand up for a security fix while their own manager, perhaps even the management chain, are resisting, this can be deadly for the security architect, since her/his/their employee performance rating and perhaps bonus all depend upon the goodwill of the manager. While we would hope that managers are mature enough to understand that their employee is merely performing assigned duties, quite unfortunately, I've seen far too many managers that believe that the employee is supposed to agree with whatever the manager believes. Disagreement on the part of the security architect can adversely affect eligibility for promotions and other advancement and perquisites that the manager controls.

A solution to this built-in difficulty will be for the central team to take over the situation. In this way, the manager and her/his/their employee will no longer be in conflict. Generally, the central security architecture team will have a different management chain and thus, will be independent of any direct line-management pressure to conform.

> When setting up a security architecture organization, it is critical to consider the necessity for management independence of at least some security architects, usually the central team or the most experienced resources who will lead the program.

Because at least some members of the central team will be independent and perhaps relatively more senior in the organization hierarchy, these people are in a much better position to escalate for management priority decision making or risk assumption. There is no conflict of interest because the central team will have been hired to identify significant issues, to seek solutions, and to raise risks for appropriate decisions. Basically, this is just the sort of thing (beyond technical leadership) that senior team members have been tasked with.

A senior central team member (senior security architect) can identify a correct decision maker. They will then interact with that person(s) to seek appropriate priority, resource allocation, and risk determination for the issue that's being escalated. In this way, the satellite security architect has been protected from any side-effects from trying to do the right thing around a security issue that has become contentious.

Please see Section 5.3.1, How to Escalate for Management Decision (on page 128), for more information on management escalations.

6.2.4 Skill Churn

If you make sharing, mentorship, and teaching a requirement for promotion, these will become organic. Each successive generation of security architects will take a cue from their ancestor architects to nurture the next generation, and so on through successive generations of security architects.

Even in an organization that incentivizes loyalty and cultivates long-term employment, there will be people who leave. No matter how careful hiring practices are, some number of candidates won't work out for one reason or another; it's a fact of hiring that not every person, even when appearing to be qualified, can perform each role's responsibilities well enough, can't seem to grow into some particular role. Security architecture, as you may have seen in earlier chapters of this book, requires technical capabilities, business understanding, and a strong dose of interpersonal skill.

The following story, quoted from *Securing Systems* (pp. 374–375), I hope will highlight the error of believing that every senior engineer must then become an architect.

> "At one organization that I worked for, as their architecture practice began to mature, management and HR made what I consider to be a fatal mistake. Since architects are generally more senior than engineers (though not always), HR (and engineering) assumed that the technical growth path was from engineer to architect for everyone. Since in order to be a competent architect it's usual for a person to have been an engineer for quite some time, it seemed intuitive that as engineers matured, they would move on to architecture. The new technical growth path at that company, in attempting to account for the emergence of architecture, went from engineer to architect to senior architect to enterprise architect.

> "But there's a flaw in that logic: Not every person is comfortable with the kind of horizontal thinking that architecture typically requires. In fact, plenty of people become engineers because they like the linearity that engineering typically applies. I'm not saying that architecture doesn't require linear thinking. It does! But architecture also requires patterning, relationships between components, lots of abstractions. Plenty of engineers simply aren't comfortable with the amount of ambiguity that occurs in the practice of systems architecture. For long periods of time, you don't know the details of many of those little boxes in the diagram. You have to be comfortable with that.

> "Furthermore, as I stated above, architects tend to be leaders, which means, to be blunt, architects have to work with other people. Other people have to like working with an architect. There are a great deal of 'people skills' involved in a typical architecture role. There are plenty of engineers who don't particularly enjoy working with lots of people and, even more so, with people who disagree with each other and with that engineer. I like to say, 'If you don't like working with people, security architecture is not for you.'

> "At the organization that I described, as soon as the architecture role was opened up as the single technical growth path, one unit immediately promoted fifty engineers to the architect role. Many of these engineers had been in line for promotion for quite a long

time. Once the architect role opened up, it seemed natural to management to move these engineers upward in the new growth path.

"You can perhaps see the problem. A number of those people, although perfectly wonderful engineers, weren't very good at thinking about complex relationships and flows between systems. And a number of the same set of individuals didn't like interacting with people all that much. For a few years, it was a mess.

"In that situation, there were numerous 'architects' who didn't have the capability, perhaps not the aptitude, for what the architect role requires. And remember, these people were senior to a lot of the engineers with whom they were working. That means that even though architecture decisions might not be the best possible solutions, those working underneath these new architects might have to implement something that was not ideal. Indeed, some of the engineers could see the mistakes being promulgated by the new architects, which led to a loss in confidence in the architecture practice.

"This one mistake caused a three-year halt in the development of what eventually was an industry-leading enterprise architecture practice. It took several years to filter out those folks who would never gain the right skills or who didn't have the temperament, while at the same time having to wait for the development of those who would take the places of the poorly promoted lot.

"Since our security architecture program depended upon the capabilities of the enterprise architecture program, our growth and maturity was somewhat stymied for those same three years. Indeed, we had to deal with a good deal of disruption and outright incompetence during that time. It wasn't fun. Not everyone can be an architect. Not every security person will be successful as a security architect. The lessons from those three years are burned into the way that I select candidates for the architecture role."

One of the tasks that a security architecture leader or manager must face is the eventual need to help someone who isn't working out to find another role somewhere else. Which means that a new person will have to be found to fill the vacancy.

At the same time, as security architects grow in skill and experience, they will be offered positions elsewhere. Security architecture is a very competitive career space at the time of this writing. A job change can often be accompanied with inducements such as additional salary and increased organization level. These can be very hard to pass up: significantly more money, equity in a fast-growing company, and a bump in level, say from Manager level to Senior Manager, or even to Director or Principle Architect/Engineer. People will move on no matter how Human Resources tries to remain competitive and no matter how much people like working for an organization and with a particular leadership.

Hence, in my experience, a program must continue to invite new people in, then to train them. Experienced people need to be given expanding scopes of responsibility and authority, as well as greater technical challenges. It's important to maintain explicit and implicit paths to growth.

This includes the top technical position. Of the four programs that I've built, I've left each one better than I found it. I've attempted to groom at least two people who could step into my shoes should something sudden happen to me. And, I've purposely stepped aside so that one of those people could try their hand in the top leadership position.

While my strategy might not work for everyone, my leaving allows the next technical leader to try her/his/their hand as a leader; it removes any "glass ceiling" from preventing growth. It might be hard on an organization and program in the moment, but if I've done my job correctly, although there will be a shift in style to a new leader, the program should survive and function into the future.

My point is that there must be a possible and visible growth path for everyone, or skill loss will be too high for the program to maintain and survive.

Also, by fostering generations of teachers and mentors, the program can organically deal with the inevitable churn that security programs today must face.

6.2.5 Exceptions

Exceptions are your friends! They should never be used as punishment or as retribution. Exceptions are one of the powerful tools that security has to meet the inevitable conflicts that will occur between business drivers, development objectives, and security demands. These differing needs must and will come into conflict from time to time. The wise security architect must prepare. Usually, the solution set can include an exception to relieve friction and to shift the discussion to solutions.

Exceptions are agreements, with management sign-off, to allow a risk to exist for a specified period, by the end of which a mitigation will be released. More importantly, exceptions are a key to moving from a win/lose conflict to a win/win solution. Development gets to put off immediate work on the basis of a firm promise to complete the needed security fix within an agreed-to time period. The conversation moves from "Yes you will/no we won't" to "How can this be fixed and when can that fix be completed?" The second conversation is the one I want to have.

Furthermore, I know, in point of fact, that there are many times that needed security changes cannot be delivered immediately due to other contingencies. The important variables to factor into decisions are risk without mitigation, the expected reduction in risk from mitigation, the difficulty of fix, any expected business gain from the mitigation (even as watery as customer goodwill), and resources required to complete the work. Once these have been estimated, a reasonable balance between immediate risk taking and eventual fix can usually be found.

I've already described the process for escalation in this chapter. The same rules apply for exceptions: the deciders probably shouldn't be those who are directly biased toward a particular decision (development mangers, project managers, product managers, developers, etc.). Deciders have to be high enough in the organization to have a broad view and to have the authority to take on risk for the scope of the potential impacts. I'm never afraid to escalate upward to find an appropriate level for decision making.

Even minor exceptions build trust, as I've already described. I keep these really simple and fast, so that decision makers aren't deluged with insignificant problems. Often a quick phone call with an email documenting risks is sufficient for low-risk issues.

At the end of the day, using exceptions to move conversations to solutions rather than arguments is a powerful tool that I've wielded to great effect for many years. Granting exceptions demonstrates to partners that I'm willing to negotiate fairly, compromise, and, most importantly, to understand their problems and to factor those into our mutually agreed upon solutions. That process—that is, using exceptions—has proven to be an effective tool to establish successful relationships that are strong enough to meet the really big challenges that will eventually show up in the form of a critical security issue.

6.2.6 Fostering Innovation

One of the frictions that may frequently arise between security needs and developers will be a desire by developers to explore new techniques and technologies. Often, when a new approach is "hot," developers will want to get that technology into production as soon as possible; also, if developers implement the new technology, they will do so, ad hoc, organically, perhaps without much of an overarching plan or architecture. And there is a tendency to assume trust, both of the tool's capabilities as well as everyone involved, giving a broad swath of people high privileges for convenience sake.

From a security perspective, every unknown change must be considered as potentially risky until proven otherwise. After all, security people typically have a due diligence responsibility to their organizations to either mitigate harmful risk to conform to the organization's risk tolerance or to make unmitigated risks visible to decision makers. A risk, once identified, cannot be simply left unattended. Security's role is to bring digital risks to within organizational tolerances.

Developers are apt to perceive security's hesitancy as standing in the way of perfectly legitimate exploration intended to improve things. Which is, as far as I'm concerned, a reasonable objective. Still, a lot of unintended damage can be done by a developer or anyone else. There's truth in both positions in this case, hence the resulting organizational friction when this conflict appears.

People should be exploring new technologies. At the time of this writing, new programming languages have been developed, new technologies to build, deploy, and maintain software are invented or improved almost daily. The aggressive pace of innovation is especially marked for software running in virtual environments, often hosted where cloud services are high leveraged. Recently, there has been a nearly relentless creation of new software appearing to offer greater automation potential.

DevOps offers a philosophic shift and also softens the technical differences between writing software and operating software. The philosophic shift is that writing software and running it is a deep partnership which has a common goal: successful software that behaves as intended (and, presumably, specified).

It used to be that the skill set for developing software was fairly distinct from that of operations. Writing and testing code differs from observing the metrics and behavior of that same code. Whereas operations people usually wrote some automation, the complexity and algorithms were different and orders of magnitude less complex than many that have to be employed to produce commercial software. The languages were different: scripting and shell languages for administration versus third-generation, structured programming languages used to produce applications or operating systems.

But that wall has collapsed. For instance, operations folks use Python; lots of commercial code is written in Python, to name just a single scripting language in wide use today. Furthermore, new DevOps tools code operations rather than having to script them or manually perform tasks, as these used to be accomplished. DevOps folks have to code; it's just that the code does operational things like build loadable images, start the images, test out new code in a subset of cloud instances, etc. DevOps breaks down old distinctions that are no longer applicable between coder and administrator. Everybody codes; they just solve different problems with software.

Hence, DevOps' implementation of new technologies may appear to security to be nearly relentless; every time I turn around, it seems that there's two or three new tools of which I've never heard and that may present more attack surface. If the DevOps implementers fail to carefully consider security when choosing and deploying new technologies and tools, then the opportunity to introduce unprotected attack surface is very high. Security folk know this, in their bones, live and breathe the consequences, daily. It should be no surprise that the natural reaction to this pace of innovation might be to try and slow it, to try to get just a bit of control around it.

I don't think that just saying, "No, you can't try that new technology," works very well. There are good reasons to architect our build and deploy systems. I hope that I've articulated well enough security reasoning for architecture versus organic growth in this and other works.

To relieve this friction, that inevitable tension between innovation and improvement and the need to have time to design security appropriately, there must be a space in which experiments can proceed unhindered.

One solution might be to provide an experimentation space for each developer to play in. That space might be a sandbox provided by a cloud provider. I've seen this work effectively, at least, anecdotally.

At the same time, innovators probably also need a facsimile of production to which to bring likely candidates that have been discovered and qualified through developer exploration. Since the facsimile environment wouldn't have production data and could be well isolated to avoid leakage, its security control might be considerably looser than environments used for actually building, deploying, and running software for business or customer use. In this way, that long-sought-after experimentation space could be fostered with minimal security implications.

The facsimile environment mustn't also be one of the test environments. Otherwise, there will be conflicts of interest between use of the resources for tests and unfettered (or lightly constrained) experimentation. Also, every part of the build and deploy chain will usually have security requirements. These needs will very likely get in the way of innovative play. The facsimile play area needs to remain reserved for the purpose of experimentation, I believe. It will drift from facsimile every time a new technology is introduced, so it really wouldn't be suitable for dual purposes.

The other necessity has been expressed elsewhere, by many others, so I don't believe this is anything new or revelatory: management must budget time for research and exploration for every developer. You can't discover if you haven't time.

There is another key to ensure that innovation actually occurs. Experimenters must share everything that's been learned—the good, the bad, the ugly. If a tool or new technology appears to be promising, everyone will want to know about it. Planning for potential inclusion will be seeded by the learning gained through experiments. At the same time, if experimentation demonstrates that something isn't going to be beneficial, others won't want to waste time repeating the same experiments. A regular, periodic, predictable forum for reporting on experiments not only highlights interesting new technologies, but also generates the excitement necessary to support potential changes to production services.

The whole point is to encourage use of new tools, but in a safe way.

6.3 Dealing with Chaotic Elements

It's a plain fact that at work, we have to collaborate with people with whom we probably wouldn't interact given complete freedom of association. Even the best hiring managers occasionally bring people in who behave unpredictably, for whatever reason.

Personally, and this probably just stylistic, I rather enjoy working with people whose thought processes are unique, even idiosyncratic. Sometimes, similarly unique emotional styles might be coupled to idiosyncratic and original analysis. I'm willing to take others' idiosyncrasies if they are willing to work around mine.

Whatever your stylistic preferences, the larger your team, your organization, the more likely you're going to have to deal with people who sometimes appear to be a chaotic element—that is, unpredictable in the workplace.

Obviously, if someone is significantly hurting the ability of a team to deliver, that's a management problem. Other works deal with this situation in detail. I won't address how to manage workplace behavior problems here.

However, there is a single type of destructive behavior that I believe does merit a comment. A person who is working solely for their own benefit and advancement, who believes that promotion is a win/lose competition, who sabotages others can be very difficult and destructive to the community spirit I've outlined in this book. My dear friend and mentor, Roddy Erickson advised me many years ago not to give disruptive, dishonest people my authenticity. They will wield as a weapon whatever honesty and vulnerability is given them. [Roddy Erickson no longer works in technology. He had worked on the early DARPANET and was one of my early programming and computer science mentors.]

The problem I find with ignoring such destructive and dishonest behavior is that I've seen such people turn on anyone who is achieving success beyond what the competitor can tolerate. I've seen some truly gifted people become embroiled in terrible personnel wars that were entirely manufactured to destroy their work. Becoming a target can severely impact one's ability to get things accomplished.

My method, once I realize that a workmate is not functioning with integrity, is to appear to them that I'm their strong supporter. I don't actually have to do much; words of support are often sufficient to convince such people to direct their aggression elsewhere. Then, I proceed with my own objectives.

Quite often, such people have over-promised what they can deliver. The lack of delivery will often result in one of two things: the whole charade crashing down on the destructive person and they leave, or (and I've seen this several times), the person declares victory on the first successful milestone and uses that as a stepping stone for their own advancement to a different role, leaving the mess for others to clean up.

I've watched such people go from architect through the grades to vice president in the space of a few years. This can be a very "successful" strategy, if what one is after is title and status. That's not my definition of success. But at least the destructive behavior disappears on its own volition. Good riddance.

In any event, if your career lasts long enough, you are likely to run into unique, idiosyncratic people, at least a couple of whom may well lack integrity. I find that it's useful to smoke these out in order to protect myself and my programs from their path of destruction.

6.3.1 *There Are Differences*

We have to stop jumping from threat modeling to penetration testing to secure coding as though these are all equivalent. They are not. Each of these activities is a discreet dimension of software security, especially when software security is considered as a wholistic problem. Each technique at this state of the art is quite distinct from the others.

- **Threat modeling.** In this work, I've tried to explain that threat modeling is an analysis used to uncover likely attacks, rate the relative risk from successful compromise, and, based upon that analysis, build defenses intended to prevent or dissuade attackers, or, at the very least, slow attackers down sufficiently to discover the attack before serious damage occurs.
- **Penetration testing.** Penetration testing refers to manual security testing, usually by a highly skilled tester who employs, as close as possible, the same tactics, techniques, and processes (TTP) as those that real-world adversaries will use.
- **Secure coding.** Securing coding and its corollary verification steps such as manual code review and static analysis for security testing (SAST) is concerned with not introducing unintentional effects into code as it is written, which will allow attackers some leverage to prosecute their goals—that is, vulnerabilities.

I was listening to a presentation by (supposedly) software security thought leaders at a major conference. Even these purported experts substituted these three activities as though they were equivalent, rather than addressing distinctly different problem areas of software security. It appears as though there is still considerable confusion, despite works such as *Core Software Security*, for which I drafted a chapter, which explains the detailed differences between the many activities and tasks that make up a robust and rigorous software security program.

I hope you, the reader, see that each of the foregoing approaches provides a significant addition to releasing self-protective software. But these address different aspects of the problem space:

- Identifying the security requirements that should be built *before* these have been implemented
- Ensuring that what is coded doesn't also create attacker leverage
- Proving that the security requirements are functioning as intended and providing additional assurance that no unintended behavior has leaked through secure coding activities

Threat modeling happens early in development and continues so long as changes are made to structures and design.

Static analysis won't identify most design issues. It's focused on code quality, implementation errors.

Penetration testing is intended to offer some proof both that the threat model was correct and that any security analysis techniques have not left something important unaddressed. It takes place very late in a development lifecycle, when a system is nearly complete or even after release.

It is a major error to confuse these important techniques. Worse is the tendency to believe that software security can be handled with any particular approach by itself. Software security is a multi-dimensional, multi-variate problem whose challenges must be addressed by a collection of overlapping techniques and analyses that must be enacted throughout a development process, whatever that process may be.

6.3.2 Translate and Generalize

"Customers never come with problems; they always come with solutions."

—Joerg Reichelt, Senior Security Architect, Cisco Systems, Inc.

My friend Joerg Reichelt captures one of the key problems for anyone who must translate customer/client feedback into stuff that will actually get built—that is, requirements. It is a truism that changes will too often be offered as, "Here's what I want you to build," rather than, "I need . . ." Particularly, security folk will often want encryption everywhere data is stored or exchanged, typically not thinking through the thorny problems of key protection, which today is the more difficult problem: we have encryption standards that, at least until quantum computing fulfills its promises, appear to be quite sufficient to achieve reasonable confidentiality protection.

One of the skills that we must acquire is the ability to translate backwards from the customer's solution to a customer need. Take for example, a customer request of a Software as a Service (SaaS) that all cloud processing for that customer be encrypted by the customer's keys, which the customer will hold.

I've heard this very encryption request multiple times over the years. Such a solution honors the due diligence responsibility to maintain confidentiality throughout the exposure that must occur as a result of allowing sensitive data beyond security controls under the direct governance of an organization. Intuitively, encryption appears to be the ideal solution.

First, data cannot be processed if it is encrypted and the keys are not available to decrypt. Furthermore, if data must be decrypted at every stage of processing, the processing time required for decryption will be significant, probably far too costly, especially when considering the performance cost of retrieving keying materials. Plus, will the customer even trust the SaaS to handle the keys at all, even if only using a customer key once to produce an intermediary key for the processing?

The translated request is for careful protection of confidentiality during SaaS processing. That's what the customer wants. Encryption is their solution. Obviously, if the data must be processed in some fashion, there will have to be compensating controls such that confidentiality is appropriately protected.

In *Securing Systems,* I offered a design paradigm for confidentiality protection for precisely the confidentiality during SaaS processing problem:

"Similar to network encapsulation, each tenant in a multitenant application will be assigned either a header preceding data or a header and footer surrounding data. The encapsulation identifies which tenant the data belong to and ensures that each tenant's flows remain separated during processing. Only a particular tenant's data may flow through a chain of processing intended for that tenant just as a single TCP message will be routed to a single IP address and a unique TCP port number. The encapsulation must be designed such that no tenant's data can be mistaken for another's. Figure 11.3 represents this data encapsulation visually.

"Usually, the tag that identifies the tenant is a token tied to the tenant's account, not the actual tenant name or other public or well-known identifier. In this way, the application has no notion of tenant identity. The tag is 'just a number.' Some other, separate process is used to tie processing to the tenant. "Better than using 'just a number,' perhaps a predictable number, is to

Figure 11.3 Multitenant Data Encapsulations

introduce unpredictability—that is, entropy into the calculation of the tag token. In this way, should the application be breached and one or more flows become compromised, the attacker will have more difficulty associating an unpredictable number to the vendor's clients.

"A step above utilizing a high-entropy token would be to add a bit of indirection into the tag. A separate store might associate a client account to the hash. A second temporary storage (perhaps in memory?) would associate the tag token to the hash. At this point, an attacker must breach the hash-to-client store and the token-to-hash store. These should be kept in segregated processing units, perhaps separate network segments? Capture of the flows delivers nothing but a bit of data that is being processed. Wiring that data back to a client would require several more attacks, each successful.

"I've seen a data store that used the above scheme to store customer data files. Although the files were all comingled on disk, they were stored under the token name. There were tens of thousands of individual files, each named by some high-entropy number. The number-to-hash store resided outside the data layer. The hash-to-client store was in yet another layer.

"At this company there was 24×7 monitoring of data administrator activity. An alert would be generated should any customer file be accessed by an administrator account (administrators had no business reason to look at customer files).

"Essentially, administrators who had access to the client/hash store didn't have data access. Data administrators couldn't access the client key. In this way, customers were protected from each other, from the accidental comingling of data, and from accidental or malicious administrator access. A shared application must be designed to keep tenants' data separated sufficiently, both in processing and storage." *Securing Systems,* page 316–317

Not only must a specific solution be understood as a request to address a problem or missing requirement, but also, it often occurs that the analyst must generalize from one particular customer or client's problem to a solution that will address multiple customer needs (many of which may have been communicated as specific solutions which address only that customer's needs). One must scry into the particular and specific, the local and unique, for that which will enhance functionality across user or customer needs. I often ask myself, "What missing or incomplete function underlies or enables all of these requests?"

In the above example, the customer request was generalized into a need for robust data separation during processing and storage whose controls include separation of duties, data encapsulation techniques, cryptographic hashes, and indirection such that attack cost is raised significantly for both external attackers and privileged insiders. But the data remain processable and highly performant, reaping the benefits of SaaS while also providing confidentiality. The customer request has been translated and generalized. What's been built is not specifically what's been requested, but rather what can be built to achieve the result: confidential and processable.

6.4 Summary

Table 6.1 Summation of Actions Described in This Chapter[a]

Do	Don't
Consider whether or not a security architect is actively included in development team meetings by invitation.	Measure security architect performance by the number of projects completed or the number of requirements generated.
Establish a baseline suite of tests for each security validation tool, in which each baseline test produces high confidence, low false positive results.	Attempt to lower risks by demanding that developers use an overly broad set of each tool's tests, especially when these are known to produce significant false positives or whose results will require concerted human analysis and security expertise to validate.
Give developers the ability to add tool tests above the baseline. Let them find a workable balance between tool aggressiveness and noise in the results.	
Keep track of the types and complexity of externally reported issues.	Rely on external bug report totals or CVSS scores in place of risk analysis.
Measure the lack of attack success and impact.	Equate number of attack attempts or number of vulnerabilities to "risk."
	Measure the effectiveness (or lack) of a security architecture program by counting successful exploitations.
Make the secure path the easy path: automate consumption of security services and document repeating requirements.	Waste skilled resources on repeating the same security requirements over and over again.
Scale up to demand by training internal people to become security architects.	Attempt to hire large security architecture teams.
Hire a few security architecture leaders who are also passionate about teaching.	
Empower "satellite" security architects as local members of Infosec/security.	Ask satellite people to become security spies on their teammates.
Invigorate and empower the program by annually thanking executives for their support.	Waste time on disruptive, oppositional mid-management.
Take over escalations when carrying forward will place the satellite person in conflict with their own management.	
Review threat models based upon changes that have security implications.	Waste time threat modeling stable systems (when a thorough threat model's requirements have been implemented).
Employ threat modeling automation for repeating and stable architectures whose requirements are well understood.	Relay solely upon threat modeling automation for complex, one-of-a-kind, and innovative analysis.
Threat model attack scenarios known to have been successful against similar systems and technologies.	Fantasize about attacks that require techniques not yet invented.
Keep threat model documentation appropriately lightweight.	Waste time on visually stunning, detailed threat model documents unless there is a business reason for them.

(continues on next page)

Table 6.1 Summation of Actions Described in This Chapter (cont.)

Do	Don't
Shift consequences from too-late security engagement to developers and their management chain.	Attempt to solve secure design issues after a development cycle is nearly complete.
Allow the threat model to grow and refine throughout and as a part of design work.	Rely on interjected, single point-in-time threat modeling analysis, especially performed after architecture has been considered complete.
Collaborate with product management and similar functions as new development is still in ideation.	
Create and maintain a security architecture community of practice.	Rely on top-down, central Infosec-to-others communication channels.
Grant tactical exceptions to shift conflicts over development priorities.	
Establish a possible and visible growth path for every security architect, at all levels of skill.	Assume that every engineer will mature into an architect.
Provide spaces in which engineers can experiment, innovate, and try new technologies. Encourage use of new tools, but in a safe way.	Make innovation so difficult and constrained that experimentation isn't worth the effort or experimentation occurs sub rosa, evading policies to prevent it.
Pretend to support efforts by low-integrity people who work only for their own advancement and sabotage others.	Get into conflicts with low-integrity individuals if at all possible.
Generalize customer feature requests into changes that will benefit a collection of customers.	Accept customer feature requests as given without further analysis.

[a] Table 6.1 is supplied in the hope that the table's summary statements provide a quick reference to the tips and tricks that I've outlined in this chapter.

You may not encounter all of the above problems. Still, I discuss organizations' problems on a regular basis. I see the same problems crop up over and over again. Indeed, it may be true that as a program matures, at least some of what I've outlined must appear as a result of the maturation process.

I hope that solutions that have proved useful to my programs help you to craft your most effective program; let the foregoing be a starting point for surmounting your challenges. Please let me know how well these work, or not.

Appendix A

Heartbleed Exposure, What Is It Really?

Posted on April 17, 2014, at http://brookschoenfield.com/?p=213

> *"Heap allocation patterns make private key exposure unlikely."*
>
> Neel Mehta, discoverer of Heartbleed

In the media, there's been a lot of discussion about what might be exposed from the heartbleed OpenSSL attack. It is certainly true that very sensitive items can be exposed. And over thousands of test runs, sensitive items like private keying materials and the like have been returned by the heartbleed buffer overread.

A very strong case can be made for doing exactly as industry due diligence suggests. Teams should replace private keys on servers that had been vulnerable, once these are patched. But should every person on the Internet change every password? Let's examine that problems by digging into the details of exactly how heartbleed works.

First, heartbleed has been characterized as an "overflow" error: "Heartbleed is basically a buffer-overflow vulnerability". This unfortunately is a poor descriptor and somewhat inaccurate. It may make better media copy, but calling heartbleed an "overflow" is a poor technical description upon which to base a measured response.

Heartbleed is not a classic buffer overflow. No flow control or executable code may be injected via heartbleed. A read of attacker chosen memory locations is not possible, as I will explain, below. A better descriptor of heartbleed is a "buffer over-read". Unintentionally, some data from memory is returned to the attacker. To be precise, heartbleed is a data leak, not a flow control error.

In order to understand what's possible to disclose, it's key to understand program "heap" memory. The heap is an area of memory that programs use to store data. Generally speaking, well-written programs (like OpenSSL) do not to put executable code into heap (that is, data) memory[1]. Because data and execution are separated, the attacker has no way through this vulnerability to execute code. And that is key, as we shall see.

As a program runs, bits of data, large and small, temporary and more or less permanent for the run, are put into the heap[2]. Typically, data are put wherever is convenient at the moment of allocation, depending upon what memory is available.

Memory that's been deallocated gets reused. If an available piece of memory happens to be larger than a requested size, the new sized piece will be filled with the new data, while adjacent to the new data will remain bits and pieces of whatever was there previously.

In other words, while not entirely random, the heap is filled with bits and pieces of data, a little from here, a little from there, a nice big chunk from this session, with a bit left over from some other session, all helter-skelter amongst each other. The heap is a jumble; taking random bits from the heap may be considered to be like attending a jumble sale.

Now, let's return to heartbleed. The heartbleed bug returns whatever happens to be on the heap just above the 16 bytes that are required for the TLS heartbeat packet. The attacker may request as much as 64K bytes. That's a nice big chunk of stuff from the heap; make no mistake about it. Anything might be in there. At the very least, decrypted data intended for application processing will be returned to the attacker[3]. That's certainly bad! It breaks the confidentiality supposedly gained through the TLS encryption. But getting a random bit is different than requesting an arbitrary memory location at the discretion of the attacker. And that is a very important statement to hold in mind as we respond to this very serious situation.

An analogy to Heartbleed might be a bit like going fishing. Sometimes, we fish where we can clearly see the fish (mountain streams) or signs of fish (clearer lakes), or with a "fish finder" appliance, that identifies fish under the surface when the fish aren't visible.

Heartbleed is a lot more like fishing for fish that are deep in a turbulent lake with no fish finding capability. The fisher is guessing. If she or he guesses correctly, fish for dinner. If not, it's a long day holding onto the fishing rod.

In the same manner, the attacker, the "fisher" as it were, doesn't know where the "fish", the goodies are. The bait (the heartbleed request) is cast upon the "lake" (the program heap) in the hopes that a big fish will "bite" (secret "bytes" will get returned).

The attacker can heartbleed to her or his heart's content (pun intended). That is, if left undiscovered, an attacker can continuously pound the other side of the connection with heartbleeds, perhaps thousands of times. Which means multiple chunks of memory will be returned to the attacker, as the heap allocates, deallocates, and moves data around.

Lots of different heap chunks will get returned. There will likely also be overlap between the chunks that are returned to the attacker. Somewhere within those memory chunks are likely to be some sensitive data. If the private key for a session happens to be in one of those chunks, it will be exposed to the attacker. If any particular session open through the OpenSSL library happens to a contain a password that had been transmitted, it's been exposed. It won't take an engineering genius to do an ASCII dump of returned chunks of memory in order to go poking about to find interesting bits.

Still, and nonetheless, this is hunting for goodies in a bit of a haystack. Some people are quite good at that. Let's acknowledge that outright. But that's very different than a directed attack.

And should a wise and prepared security team, making good use of appropriate security tools, notice a heartbleed attack, they will most likely kill the connection before thousands of buffers can be read. Heartbleed over any particular connection is a linear process, one packet retrieved at a time. Retrieving lots of data takes some time. Time to respond. Of course, an unprotected and unaware site could allow many sessions to get opened by an attacker, each linearly heartbled, thus revealing far more of what's on the heap than a single session might. Wouldn't you notice such anomalous behaviour?

It's important to note that the returns in the heartbleed packets are not necessarily tied to the attackers' session. Again, it's whatever happens to be on the heap, which will contain parts of other sessions. And any particular heartbleed packet is not necessarily connected to the data in a previous or subsequent packet. Which means that there's no continuity of session nor any linearity between heartbleed retrievals. All session continuity must be pieced together by the attacker. That's not rocket science. But it's also work, perhaps significant work.

I'll reiterate in closing, that this is a dangerous bug to which we must respond in an orderly fashion.

On the other hand, this bug does not give attackers free reign to go after all the juicy targets that may be available on any host, server, or endpoint that happens to have OpenSSL installed. Whatever happens to be on the heap of the process using the OpenSSL library and that is adjacent to the heartbeat buffer will be returned. And that attack may only occur during a TLS session. Simply including the vulnerable library poses no risk, at all. Many programs make use of OpenSSL for other functionality beyond TLS sessions.

This bug is not the unfettered keys to the kingdom, unless a "key to the kingdom" just happens to be on the heap and happens to get returned in the over-read. What gets returned is entirely due to the distribution of the heap at the moment of that particular heartbeat.

Cheers,

/brook

These assertions have been demonstrated in the lab through numerous runs of the heartbleed attack by a team who cannot be named here. My thanks to them for confirming this assessment. Sorry for not disclosing.

Notes

[1] There are plenty of specialized cases that break this rule. But typically, code doesn't run from the heap; data goes onto the heap. And generally speaking, programs refrain from executing on the heap because it's a poor security practice. Let's make that assumption about OpenSSL (and there's nothing to indicate that this is NOT true in this case), in order to make clear what's going on with heartbleed.

[2] The libraries that support programs developed with the major development tools and running on the major operating systems have sophisticated heap management services that are consumed by the running application as it allocates and deallocates memory. While care must be exercised in languages like C/C++, the location of where data end up on the heap is controlled by these low-level services.

[3] That is, intended for the application that is using OpenSSL for TLS services.

Appendix B

Developer-Centric Security

Previously published at http://brookschoenfield.com/?page_id=256

Security practitioners, implementers of at Secure Development Life Cycle (SDL), I urge you ask yourself the following question:

What am I doing to enable developers to innovate securely while they are designing and writing software?

The developer-centric manifesto attempts to crystalize this question into the follow precepts:

- Enable development teams to be creative and to innovate
- Ensure that developers have as much specificity as possible to "deliver security correctly"
- Build tools for developers to check for correctness
- Deeply participate such that security earns its "rightful place"
- "Prove the value" of security processes and tools

As I wrote in *Core Software Security,* developers, development teams must execute the SDL. Delivery of security is not executed by security people. Besides, there aren't enough of us to scale to the tens of thousands of developers who design, code, and validate the millions of lines of code upon which we in the Internet Age depend.

We can let security's dependence on developer execution lead to ever more restricting policies, standards, and mandates – but in doing so, we strangle the very innovation that is our collective lifeblood, organizational mandates, and upon which we have become dependent.

Or, we can

- Think like an attacker and a developer—thus providing the bridge between security and development
- Consider how to become part of existing work flows—thus avoiding creativity crushing interjections
- Become deeply engaged in the process, become supporters not stoppers
- Listen, always listen—sometimes, security might just be wrong

The basic idea behind developer-centric security is that trying something new engenders mistakes and errors. Bugs and/or design flaws are inevitable. Security ought help to find the errors, ought to help refine designs, rather than wagging a nagging finger about having made mistakes.

For instance, imagine if security code analyzers ran "like a compiler". Imagine that the results could be trusted like those from an industrial-grade compiler, that is the results had very high confidence. And, imagine if security analysis was trivially easy to integrate into the developer's workflow. That would be a start and a fairly radical departure from the tools of today (though, as of this writing, some vendors are finally reaching towards this ideal).

Let's start a movement. You have an open invitation to contribute, refine, and practice developer-centric security.

Appendix C

Don't Substitute CVSS for Risk: Scoring System Inflates Importance of CVE-2017-3735

Previously published at https://securingtomorrow.mcafee.com/other-blogs/mcafee-labs/dont-substitute-cvss-for-risk-scoring-system-inflates-importance-of-cve-2017-3735/ by McAfee Labs on Nov 24, 2017 This blog was co-written by Brook Schoenfield and Damian Quiroga

I am a wry observer of vulnerability announcements. CVE-2017-3735—which can allow a small buffer overread in an X.509 certificate—presents an excellent example of the limitations of the Common Vulnerability Scoring System (CVSS). This scoring system is the de facto security industry standard for calculating and exchanging information about the severity of vulnerabilities. The problem is that CVSS is used for far more than it was intended.

For many organizations, security tools, and risk assessments, a CVSS score has become the security industry's shorthand substitute for risk scoring and impact rating. In fact, many organizations measure their ongoing risk posture by counting the number of unfixed vulnerabilities and their associated CVSS scores.

The McAfee Product Security Incident Response Team (PSIRT) uses CVSS Version 3.0 as an important tool to assess vulnerabilities. McAfee PSIRT augments CVSS with other risk analysis techniques, similar to Microsoft PSIRT's Exploitability Index and Security Update Severity Rating System.

CVSS is useful, but must not be confused with deeper risk assessment. Strictly relying on CVSS for vulnerabilities such as OpenSSL's CVE-2017-3735 is likely to cause incident responders to focus their organizations' resources on patch cycles that may be unnecessary. In addition, PSIRT credibility and influence may be squandered on low-impact, low-probability issues. Due to the sheer volume of issues being discovered and reported, PSIRT must remain focused on those that have a high probability of exploitation and whose organizational impact or attacker value make them worthy of exploitation.

But as we shall see from the following analysis, a vulnerability itself, taken out of context, cannot be equated to risk. Furthermore, CVSS has an inherent problem in that the impact is averaged against the exploitability: From the attacker's perspective, this is a mistake, because threat actors exploit vulnerabilities to suit their goals, not just because something is easy.

For those readers whose sole interest is assessing OpenSSL CVE-2017-3735, this issue, I believe, should be rated as a low to very low risk. Although easy to perform, exploitation does not offer an attacker much of value. The most likely impact will be cosmetic within a text display. Plus, the code in which CVE-2017-3735 occurs is not called from OpenSSL's protocol and cryptographic functions,[1] but is rather confined to the display of an X.509 certificate, typically for users consumption. (Certificate display does not take place as a part of typical cryptographic functions.)

Taking either of the competing published CVSS scores for this vulnerability, 5 or 7.5, at face value is misleading. Without further analysis, one might be tempted to raise the risk from CVE-2017-3735 beyond its rather minor impact. That is why I decided to investigate further, including reading the offending module's code on GitHub. The CVSS measure of CVE-2017-3735 provides a situation where accurate scoring does not match the likelihood of exploitation and increases the score above what a risk analysis would probably reach.

Although it is true that attackers must choose exploits that lie within their technological capabilities—namely, exploits that are easy enough to ensure success—the first concern will nearly always be, "What will the exercise of this vulnerability achieve for me?"

In other words, what matters is the impact or result from the exploitation that is key to choosing a particular attack, not its relative ease or difficulty. If a vulnerability advances the attacker's goals, then it will be considered for use. If there is nothing to gain, the vulnerability will not be exploited.

Limits to CVSS

Attackers exploit vulnerabilities that further their goals: That is a key point when assessing the potential for harm of any vulnerability. In this analysis, we will take a closer look at CVE-2017-3735 for its potential value to attackers. Along the way, we will also examine some of the limitations of CVSS as it applies to this vulnerability.

I do not mean to assert that CVSS is not an important tool for assessing vulnerabilities. I have worked with CVSS since before Version 1 was published; CVSS is key to prioritizing initial responses to vulnerabilities as they are released. CVSS may comprise one component of a robust risk rating method or approach.

I like to characterize CVSS as "potential severity." A CVSS score, when fairly calculated,[2] can indicate what any vulnerability might harm. CVSS scores are particularly useful for triage, before a deeper analysis.

The McAfee PSIRT makes use of CVSS as a core component of incident response, just as many organizations PSIRTs do. As a CVE Numbering Authority, McAfee PSIRT must calculate a CVSS score for every published vulnerability. In practice, nearly every potential issue is scored as a critical foundation of PSIRT's robust risk assessment.

Still, despite the importance of CVSS to vulnerability triage, it is a mistake to confuse a CVSS score with a risk rating, as we shall see.

CVE-2017-3735 has had two competing CVSS scores published.[3] The difference is in the rating of the impact: Integrity = High or Integrity = Low, resulting in a combined score of either 7.5 or 5.3 (in CVSS Version 3.0). In either case, both scores earn the exploitability rating of 10, because the issue may be exploited over a network without authentication.

- CVSS = 7.5 CVSS:3.0/AV:N/AC:L/PR:N/UI:N/S:U/C:N/I:H/A:N (From: https://nvd.nist.gov/vuln/detail/CVE-2017-3735)
- CVSS = 5.3 CVSS:3.0/AV:N/AC:L/PR:N/UI:N/S:U/C:N/I:L/A:N (From: https://nvd.nist.gov/vuln/detail/CVE-2017-3735)

How can there be two CVSS calculations? Why is one calculation High and one Low? Plus, is Integrity the correct impact parameter?

We can answer these questions by analyzing what the vulnerability allows.

The vulnerability is a buffer overread. An attacker may read one more byte from program memory than should be allowed. The attacker's advantage of the unallowed access is directly related to where that extra byte exists. After looking at the code on GitHub, it appears all buffers in that module are allocated from program heap memory. Although running programs can exhibit macro patterns in their heap allocations and deallocations, generally, we can assume that any allocation may reside wherever it is convenient for the program memory manager to grab a piece of memory sufficiently large to support the request. This introduces an element of entropy (randomness) into any particular allocation. Each allocation may come from any portion of heap memory; there is no guarantee of a particular address.

Because a particular address cannot be guaranteed, an overread will get whatever bytes happen to be larger than that allocation's required size.

Whichever data happen to be at that address is what the overread vulnerability will retrieve. Buffer overread exploitation can be a fishing expedition; there are no guarantees of the data retrieved, though there may be macro patterns in programs in which runtime processing is relatively consistent from run to run. The data returned depends on how lucky the attacker is. We saw the same situation in the Heartbleed overread vulnerability.

Just One Byte

For CVE-2017-3735, the overread is precisely a single byte. That is a very small payoff for the attacker, especially considering that there is no guarantee of what that byte might contain.

Furthermore, even if this were not an overread but rather an overflow (which it is not), a single byte is not enough space for malicious code to allow an attacker to exit to a command shell. A buffer overread does not allow an attacker to push code into a program heap. It allows an attacker only to retrieve data (a single byte) that the attacker should not have reached.

Although we may be surprised some day by a clever attacker's ingenious use of a single byte, today we see no way that anyone can benefit.

If CVE-2017-3735 allows an attacker to retrieve only a single byte, then why have CVSS scorers used the Integrity impact rather than Confidentiality? Heartbleed, a heap buffer over-read that returned nearly 64KB to the attacker, impacted Confidentiality. Attackers retrieved data they should not have been able to access. Yet CVE-2017-3735 has been scored on Integrity. There is a clue alongside the description.

Because I do not have access to the graph of code calls to the vulnerable IPAddressFamily routines, I cannot confirm the following educated guess. However, typical cryptographic and protocol implementations do not dump certificates to text; primarily users do. Which indicates that an attacker does not retrieve the extra byte. Instead, the extra byte is converted to text in the IPAddressFamily certificate extension's human-readable dump. Thus the integrity of the text representation of an X.509 certificate has been impacted. With this understanding of the impact, scorers have used Integrity rather than Confidentiality.

If the attacker retrieves the text dump, is there a way to track back from various text irregularities to the value of the extra byte? I have not looked at a range of dumps to confirm or deny. Perhaps this is either not possible or not a productive approach.

If there is any way to retrieve the data byte, then the proper CVSS score would have to be Confidentiality = Low rather than None, which would increase the CVSS score to either 6.5 or 8.2, depending upon Integrity's value, Low or High.

A CVSS score of even 5.3 gives a luster of importance to CVE-2017-3735 that it does not deserve. Any of the potentially higher scores suggest the wrong direction, which is probably why scorers refrained from including the potential for a confidentiality impact. Still, we should analyze this score to understand the strengths and limitations of CVSS. If scored for all impacts and the ease of exploitation at 6.5, CVSS indicates that this is an important vulnerability that should be addressed in a timely manner. Yet if my analysis is correct, CVE-2017-3735 should not move to the top or even middle of anyone's work queue. Patch it in due time, through scheduled update cycles. Nothing more.

The potential impact from CVE-2017-3735 is probably not significant in the vast majority of OpenSSL's use cases. Integrity = Low, maybe Confidentiality = Low, too. Attacker utility = None.

In fact, the most often published description for CVE=2017-3735 indicates the trivial nature of any impact: "The most likely result would be an erroneous display of the certificate in text format." (See References.[4])

After reading this analysis, I hope it is clear that CVSS fails to account for the complete situation with respect to CVE-2017-3735.

Unequal Weights

As we mentioned, the exploitability and impact scores are each weighted equally (actually, averaged). From the attacker's view, this is inaccurate.

Attackers do not equally exploit every vulnerability. More important, attackers do not choose to exploit a vulnerability simply because it is easy to exploit. They have no time for that;

attackers are trying to achieve their goals, whatever those may be. Anyone prioritizing vulnerability responses needs to keep this in mind as we analyze.

The following published description for CVE-2017-3735 is, at the very least, misleading and erroneous, considering the single-byte heap buffer overread affects only a user-initiated text dump:

"Successfully exploiting this issue will allow attackers to bypass security restrictions and perform unauthorized actions; this may aid in launching further attacks."

There are no "security restrictions" involved in a certificate transformed to text. Further, a single byte is insufficient to enable "launching further attacks" even if the issue were more than an overread: The attacker cannot gain control of program memory through this flaw.

Quite often, organizations have hundreds or thousands of vulnerabilities to examine. To which should they respond first? Which response should get the most resources? Which of the perhaps dozens of vulnerabilities announced in any week or month can be allowed to remain open in the face of limited resources?

These are fundamental questions that every organization must answer, probably every day. One way to prioritize is to begin assessing the potential impact to the organization and the potential utility to the attacker. These two dimensions are more important than how easy or difficult a vulnerability is to exploit, although that also important information once we determine that a vulnerability is significant.

Calculating CVSS helps practitioners identify those items that warrant deeper analysis. Unfortunately, due to the way that a CVSS base score is averaged across the exploitability and the impact dimensions, CVSS in some instances fails to sufficiently assess risk, especially in cases where utility to an attacker appears to be relatively insignificant.

The McAfee PSIRT uses CVSS as a critical tool for triaging vulnerabilities and for gauging response times. Still, CVSS is no substitute for a deeper risk analysis when it is warranted.

Notes

1. We did not have access for this analysis to an OpenSSL code graph, which would have allowed a definitive examination of calls to the vulnerable code. However, it appears from a cursory examination that the module is primarily called upon user instigation, from command-line tools, not during protocol processing.
2. There are numerous cases of scores being inflated or deflated to fit the agenda of the scorer. How can cross-site scripting scores range from 1.8 to 9? That seems impossible, but a simple search will return that range of scores from Mitre's CVE data.
3. Vendors may calculate alternate scores for their products, which will be dependent upon particular vendor circumstances.
4. One published description seems to vary considerably. The following does not seem to match our reading of the code or the behavior of a single-byte heap buffer overread: *"Successfully exploiting this issue will allow attackers to bypass security restrictions and perform unauthorized actions; this may aid in launching further attacks."*

Security Architecture Smart Guide:

Just Good Enough Risk Rating: A proven method for rapid risk assessment

Brook Schoenfield, Enterprise Security Architect, Autodesk, Inc
Vinay Bansal, Senior Security Architect, Cisco Systems, Inc

1. Problem

Information security and risk departments are typically charged with assessing the information security risk of systems. The result of these assessments is generally some sort of risk rating that can be used to set priorities and make decisions about what exposures to accept and which to mitigate.

However, in the absence of a body of long-term actuarial data covering the many variety of information security incidents and losses, assigning risk values has been fraught with individual interpretations and stylistic variations. Indeed, the risk avoidance appetite of the assessor can greatly influence the rating of risk. This leads to experienced practitioners delivering different, perhaps wildly different risk ratings about the same system. Further, risk ratings for information security risk typically lack repeatability and do not generate comparative values.

There has been a general lack of agreement about which variables must be included within an information security risk calculation. The problem of risk components is further complicated by products that offer "risk calculations" based on only 1 or 2 of the required terms[1]. For instance, "risk" might be based upon threat and exposure, or vulnerability and hypothetical impact (usually of the worst case possible). The misuse of the term "risk" does not help the practitioner sort through myriad data points to calculate a repeatable and quantified risk measurement.

A number of risk models have been put forward in order to address these problems. Some of these are very easy to use, but do not address the basic problems stated above. Other methods assume that data has been gathered about assets, values, vulnerabilities, threat, and exposure that would be encyclopedic for any but the smallest organization. Such an effort is typically beyond the capability of an enterprise information security team who are typically faced with constantly changing inventories, newly arriving vulnerabilities, incomplete knowledge of threats. Other vendors have offered risk presentation systems. Several that the authors have investigated do not, in fact, rate risk. Rather, these methodologies address some portion of what must constitute a risk rating. For example, a method may only address attack types. Products for storing "risk" often require a significant investment not only to purchase, but to gather and assess risk, as well as requiring significant data entry demands. Once an investment has been made in one of these tools, the effort to keep the assessments updated is a nontrivial and constant task.

What is needed is a reasonably robust, fairly lightweight, inexpensive way to gain repeatability and consistency in risk ratings across practitioners and assessed systems. This guide explains Cisco's Just Good Enough Risk Rating (JGERR)

---

[1] The arithmetic for these calculations is also typically nonexistent or inappropriate. The authors have seen canned ratings for each vulnerability found, simple addition, and even averages over the terms.

tool. JGERR has been in use for 8 years. It is used enterprise-wide at Cisco Systems Incorporated for web infrastructures and applications and for assessing risk for new extranet connections. It is in use by more than 40 practitioners, day in and day out. While far from perfect, JGERR combines knowledge from several leading risk rating methodologies into a methodology that can be used in the absence of a sufficient base of statistical data about information security incidences and losses. JGERR can be implemented for any area within information security. It is lightweight and easy to use.

The methodology presented in this guide does not claim to calculate true risk. It is the authors' belief that the commonly promulgated equation[2] for insurance risk is currently impossible to calculate with any surety in all but the most narrow information security circumstances. JGERR provides instead, a risk rating result that can be used in the absence of an ability to calculate risk accurately.
The rating results are intended for prioritization in order to bring risk within a desired posture. The results should also be useful by management to understand gross risk trends, as well as provide some basis for tracking the work of the assessors[3].

2. Scope

The risk rating methodology described in this guide may be applied to any discreet area for which information security risk assessment and rating is required.

To apply this methodology, it is recommended that the area to which the method is applied be well enough bounded such that the question set that is developed in the implementation is specific enough to deliver meaningful and comparable results within that arena. The questions upon which ratings are based can become so generic as to not capture meaningful results. Further, the more generic the questions get phrased, the more interpretation is required in order to answer them. Implementations must balance generality versus specificity such that results provide an opportunity for sufficient repeatability.

For instance, the example given here does not purport to apply to every area within the broad range of information security risk assessments. Rather, the

---

[2] Risk = Probability * Annualized Loss. There simply is not enough data about the dollar value of losses and how often these occur over a wide enough population in order to calculate the standard risk equation.
[3] On this last point, care must be taken to remember that not every project or system will have a lower risk rating at its end from when it started. There are many reasons for risk rating to increase during the development of a system; the increase can even be dramatic. Despite the foregoing caution, most projects moving through a mature risk practice will have either a flat risk rating from beginning to end or will have ratings lowered through the project development lifecycle as information security controls are applied.

questions were developed specifically to address risk and loss areas of web infrastructures and applications. These questions make assumptions about the security controls that have been built into the local environments on which applications are deployed. Indeed, applications that hew to these standards will generally have a lower residual (unmitigated) risk than applications that have been deployed on one-off environments where security control compromises have been made.

These factors must be taken into account in this methodology. Organizational assumptions about what is more risky and what is less become embedded into the rating form. This is a natural part of capturing practitioner and tribal knowledge into the form's questions and into the ratings.

Implementation of this method is best scoped to a particular area of assessment. Multiple discreet versions of the questionnaire may be applied to the various areas that come under assessment. Using unique, focused instances of the method for each discreet area of assessment still allows the risk results to be comparable across the areas.

2.1. Sector
[X] General (Potentially applies to all sectors)
[ ] Government
[ ] University

2.2. Security Practice Domain
[X] Architecture
[X] Engineering
[ ] Operations
[X] Risk Management

2.3. What functions does it pertain
- Risk assessment and risk rating

3. Known Risks

Any attempt to capture tribal and/or practitioner knowledge is always limited by the capture process, which is, by its very nature, insufficient. The very act of distilling wide experience into a set of questions will always miss something. Further, corner cases are hard to capture. And, decisions must be made about priority, importance, and inclusion/exclusion. Information security is such a broad field, that something will always be left out, either intentionally or unintentionally.

There is a risk when applying this method that risks will be missed. That is why there is a "thumb on the scale" area built in for an experienced risk assessor to add in additional factors not canonized within the questions that have been included in the rating. Still, giving assessors this capability also then brings with it a risk of mis-use in order to force particular result scenarios. That is, if risk is rated high, an engineer or architect might force a set of security controls that overly reflect her/his personal risk appetite. To combat this abuse of power, the authors have insisted in practice that any "thumb on the scale" additional risk receive positive peer review before being used in the resultant risk rating. The details of the peer review process are beyond the scope of this guide.

There is a risk that unconscious assumptions about what is risky and what is preferable can creep in and rig this rating system towards higher or lower ratings results. In fact, the first two versions of this methodology had exactly these problems. Getting these assumptions to be more conscious and apparent in the questions was a part of the refinement of the method.

It is crucial that the ratings from the two values being calculated be kept separate in order for ratings to approximate a risk calculation. Threat, vulnerability, and exposure can be mixed together in questions, but must not be mixed into questions for impact and loss value. These two calculate different values whose arithmetic properties must be clearly separated. That is, the questionnaire dealing with the impact analysis must not include any assumptions about what is less or more vulnerable, what the threat landscape is, nor the controls in place. Impact questions must be solely about loss, though they do not have to be about monetary values only, since the results will ultimately be rated. However, this method will work fine if assumptions about threats, exposure, and vulnerability are conflated into the "technical" analysis questionnaire and rating. The conflation, as long as it's understandable, deliberate, and captures organizational understandings, will not harm the method's results.

4. Prerequisites

It is assumed that any organization contemplating use of this solution already has in place an information security risk assessment practice.

Typically, risk assessments are applied to:
- Applications and similar new projects
- Changes to running systems
- Infrastructures to support operations
- Etc.

It is assumed that the organization has at least a few experienced risk assessors who have practiced within the area to which the method will be applied.

While this methodology does not require any investment in tools or products, it does require an investment in time and attention of those who will distill the local risk knowledge, the organizational information security policies and standards, the risk practice, and the organization's risk posture preferences into the questions to be used during assessment and rating. In our experience this is a part time task which took the originators and practitioners not more than 20-40 hours, stretched over a period of 2 months. In addition, in the two successful implementations with which the authors are familiar, there are periods of peer review, comment, and refinement stretching over a few weeks and additional hours before the methodology is ready for production use. While not trivial, this effort should be within the reach of most information security departments.

Once canonized and put into use, the questions and ratings should be reviewed at least once each year against organizational, threat, and vulnerability changes.

It is assumed that an organization already has the following information security processes:
- An information security team
- A risk assessment practice

5. Required Artifacts

a) A risk rating spreadsheet whose questions capture assessors' understandings about what is risky and what is safer for a particular area. This artifact is developed by the assessment team(s) before being used[4].

b) An architecture diagram of all the components to be used for any system under assessment

c) Data flow diagram across all components of the a system under assessment

d) Data sensitivity rating of the most sensitive data within each flow and to be handled by each component of the a system under assessment

e) Information Security Policies

f) Organizational technical standards to which systems must comply

6. Step-by-Step Problem Solution

The risk rating calculated by this methodology uses 2 terms: an estimated attack vector and a scaled size of impact. These 2 terms are multiplied in order to get the risk rating.

estimated attack vector * *scaled* size of impact = risk rating

---

[4] Capturing and rating local and industry practice into a series of rated questions is a non-trivial task. Doing so is likely to take several iterations. Senior risk assessment staff, along with project management will probably need to be assigned to this task.

The estimated attack vector is actually a combination of several fundamental components that are typically combined within the term representing probability. Since, as has already been stated, Information risk assessors do not have the statistical data to estimate true probability, we must calculate a number between 0 and 1 to replace true probability term. And that number must represent as many of the factors from which probability might be calculated as we can estimate in a repeatable fashion. The good news is that experienced risk assessors do this every day as mental arithmetic. The difficult part is teasing this information out from mental arithmetic. Gathered attack vector knowledge is transformed into a series of discreet questions, each of which has a multipart, scaled, series of responses: multiple-choice questions, essentially.

For Cisco's web application assessments, a five bucket scale was chosen.

Both terms used to calculate the risk rating are 1 based. There is no 0 loss and there is no 0 probability – there is always some loss value and some risk.

The scale for the attack vector term is:

$$\text{Attack Vector (``technical exposure'')} = 0 > N < 1$$

And the scale for impact is:

$$\text{Individual impact} == 1 >= N <= 10$$

Impacts are summed for an impact rating of

$$\text{Total impact} = 10 >= N <= 100$$

Each of the 5 choices is evenly distributed[5] across the range, 1-10, with appropriate arithmetic to calculate the attack vector term, 0-1 (see below for details).

1. 1
2. 3.25
3. 5.50
4. 7.75
5. 10

In the following table, our definitions for each term that must be expressed in the attack vector term for the risk rating. It is the authors' assumptions that each of these situations without the presence of the other conditions is not risk. There seems to be a good deal of confusion amongst security practitioners about what

---

[5] There is nothing special about this distribution. The scale might be biased low or high, as required. The actual number distribution is less important than the consistency of use. In fact, Cisco's distribution was biased high for years.

risk actually means. Some methodologies equate threat to risk, in others, vulnerability is equated to risk, the assumption being that the very worst exposure and threat preexist simply because the exposure and risk are known to exist somewhere. This of course, is the safest course. But it does not get us closer to calculating risk for a particular situation. That is why we insist upon the existence of an exploit of the vulnerability ("exploit"), a threat agent that is motivated and has sufficient access to exploit the vulnerability, and that the vulnerability is exposed enough for the threat agent to exploit it. In other words, each of these factors is dependent upon the presence the other factors before an information security attack can be promulgated.

Vulnerability	Any weakness, administrative process, or act or physical exposure that makes an asset susceptible to exploit by a threat
Threat	A potential cause of an unwanted impact to a system or organization (ISO 13335-1)
Exposure	The potential damage to or loss of an asset from a given threat a vulnerability after consideration of existing controls
Exploit	A means of using a vulnerability in order to cause a compromise business activities or information security

Exclude[6] vulnerabilities that are not exposed or do not in the present or the foreseeable future have a motivated threat capable of exploiting the vulnerability. Doing so will help to keep the questionnaire short and focused on the area that is

---

[6] The authors do not mean to suggest that vulnerabilities that cannot be exploited should not be attended. That is a matter of organization policy and standard. We are suggesting that in order to keep the risk questionnaire lightweight, it is good practice to focus on prioritized attack vectors as defined here.

under assessment. We believe that this is critical to the success of the methodology. It is important to bear in mind that it is quite possible and even preferable to build multiple questionnaires, one for each area of technical expertise and assessment.

In this method, the business impact questionnaire is designed to be completed by a project manager working for the business that is driving a project. The questionnaire should be easily understandable by a project manager or other non-technical person. We removed as much information security jargon as we could. We ask questions that the project manager will likely know or which he/she can easily get answered by the sponsors of the project.

The attack vector, or "technical" questionnaire is designed for a trained information security assessor. This person may not have deep risk assessment skill. But the person will have a working knowledge of the sort of attacks that are currently being promulgated against systems in the domain under consideration. The assessor will have some understanding of the typical controls that are built into underlying infrastructure and the kind of controls that are typically required for applications. Further, the assessor should understand how these typical controls are applied to particular architectural patterns. Due to this pre-requisite training, we were able to generalize the technical questions considerably, as well as to shorten the questionnaire.

In order to build our questionnaires, we use the following process:

- *Distill* assessor *expertise*
- *Document typical* exceptions to standards
- *Transform* knowledge into assessment questions
- *Scale (bucket-ize)* responses
- *Gather* impact scenarios
  - *Repeat transformation and scale*
  - *As for attack vector term*

6.1. Distill Assessor Expertise

Interview your current experts who assessed typical projects coming through the area of focus of the questionnaire.

- What typical vulnerabilities do they look for?
- Which vulnerabilities to exclude?
- What threats are considered the most important?
- What are the typical exploits of the most important threats?
- One of the greatest weaknesses contained within local infrastructures in systems?
- What is protected particularly well?

- Which types of vulnerabilities are not exposed to active threats that are currently or projected to attack your systems?

Don't limit yourself to the questions posed in this guide. The object of this process is to discover and document the accumulated knowledge base from your experts. What are they most concerned about? What are they least concerned about because there's enough extant mitigation to discount successful compromise? And, it is important to gather understanding of what lies between these 2 extremes in relation to your systems. Those attack vectors that lie between the two poles (presented above) will become the buckets, the questionnaire choices that you will rate in order to generate the threat, vulnerability, exploit, and exposure combined term. You are trying to distill your attack vectors from worst to best-case scenarios.

6.2. Document Typical Exceptions To Standards

An additional gold mine of technical understanding are the security exceptions written for projects. Repeating exceptions indicate areas of weakness that aren't well defended. Those types of exceptions written only once generally indicate the inability or unwillingness of a particular project to meet organizational standards. These tend to be local. However, exceptions that occur repeatedly can point to areas where compliance is too difficult or expensive. As such, these point to weaknesses in the defense-in-depth capabilities[7]. These can be captured into the questionnaire.
If your infrastructures are fairly mature in that they deliver basic security controls to the hosted systems, you may choose to simply note whether exceptions exist as one of your questions. Your buckets (multiple choice responses) could then list the types of exceptions from none to most risky.

6.3. Transform Knowledge Into Assessment Questions

Each question does not have to encapsulate an entire attack vector's composite terms. One question may model active threats that have got some level of access. While another question might focus on exposed vulnerabilities at which you know there are active attack attempts.

For instance, if you have a population of unremediated cross-site script errors and you have a business driver to protect your web visitors from the effects of these attacks, then one question might focus on the presence of these vulnerabilities. Or, you might combine all input validation attacks into a question. Or, you may simply ask (as we did), "Are there known

---

[7] Not only should these exception types be included in the questionnaire, these also make a case for a change in security direction to close the holes, to make it easier for systems to comply. After all, an organization creates its standards for good reason, presumably.

vulnerabilities exposed in the application?" In this way, you can generalize all vulnerabilities.

At Cisco, the person answering the attack vector questions is always a security assessor who has had significant training. Hence, we were able to generalize the questions against the assumption that the responder is familiar with typical web based attack patterns. Your questionnaire may have to be more specific depending on what assumptions you can make about the responder/assessor.

Cisco's Web application Attack Vector (technical exposure) questionnaire uses the following questions:
1. How much exposure to attack is there?
2. Are there known vulnerabilities in the application/project or associated infrastructure?
3. Are mitigation or workaround ("hardening") techniques implemented to minimize the risks or vulnerabilities inherent in the infrastructure?
4. To what degree do you suspect deployment of this application/project in its current form would increase the security risk to other systems, applications, resources or projects in the event of a successful compromise?
5. How is entitlement accomplished?
6. How much security review has this application/project been through?

The authors stress that you must not mix impact with attack vector. The two terms' questions must remain distinct in order to generate a value that reasonably equates to risk. As written above, the two terms cannot be mingled or the calculation loses its ability to mimic a statistically based risk calculation. Cisco chose to use separate worksheets, filled in by different persons in order to achieve this separation of terms. None of the questions representing attack vector mention the size of the impact. And the questions describing possible impacts do not describe any of the terms that are combined for an attack vector.

6.4.   Scale (Bucket-ize) Responses

In order to derive buckets for your questions, start with binary choice:

•   What is the best case situation in relation to the question being asked?
•   What is the worst case that can be encountered?

For the sample question, "How much exposure to attack is there?", placement within an environment completely out of control or knowledge of Cisco and its security team was deemed the worst case scenario. This condition was then combined with a situation where serious inability to apply required security controls might exist: where a formal executive signed risk assumption has occurred into the follow worst case response:

- Offsite with an unreviewed ASP or other 3rd party, or contains significant exceptions or risk assumption.

Likewise, the best-case scenario is:

- Purely internal on a InfoSec-approved architecture

Having arrived at best and worst cases, degrees of exposure are filled in to derive the intervening series of buckets that fit the scale.

1. How much exposure to attack is there?
    a. Offsite with an unreviewed ASP or other 3rd party, or contains significant exceptions or risk assumption
    b. Internet Facing on a non-hardened or unknown architecture and/or without layering or with significant exception or risk assumption
    c. Internet Facing on an InfoSec-approved standard architecture
    d. Purely internal on a non-standard architecture or has exceptions
    e. Purely internal on a InfoSec-approved architecture

The responses are then put through the following calculation to create a composite attack vector rating:

$$\frac{{}_1\sum_n \text{(attack vector choices)}}{\text{Highest possible score * Number of questions}}$$

6.5.   Gather Impact Scenarios

To build a list of impact assessments, repeat the attack vector process, this time focusing on the types of business impacts that successful security compromises can have. Stress business terms. These must include financial impact. But we believe that the list of impacts must also include dimensions that are difficult to quantify.

Cisco's Web application focused business impact questionnaire contains the following questions:

1. What is the value of this application to company, i.e how much money will it save or bring in to the company in a fiscal year?
2. What critical company systems would the failure of this application impact?
3. What audience would be affected because of an interruption or compromise?
4. Does this project deal with any of the following personally identifying information (i.e. are there any privacy issues)?
5. What is the expected future lifetime of the system

6. Rate the criticality on this application for the continuing operation of your business.
7. Disruption of this application would have what sort of effect on the company's customers?

Again, as in the attack vector questionnaire, decide how many buckets will be useful (Cisco uses 5 for both sets of assessment questions). Choose the best-case scenario as the minimum value and the worst impact as the maximum. Then, fill in the buckets in between as ordinals of impact.

Following is Cisco's first impact question with it associated responses. We ask the project manager or business sponsor to estimate with a best guess the appropriate value[8].

1. What do you estimate the dollar damage to company would be if the data was modified, stolen, destroyed, or subject to unauthorized disclosure?
   a. A) Catastrophic (>=$400 million)
   b. b) Serious loss ($50-400 million)
   c. c) Significant Loss ($5-50million)
   d. d) Loss ($500K to 5 million)
   e. e) Minor loss <= 500,000 USD

As Cisco has grown, so the impact bucket ordinal responses have had to be revised. It is our working theory that as long as the scale remains the same, the bucket sizes can be changed to meet changing circumstances of expansion or decrease.

Arithmetic for deriving a 5 bucket distribution between 1 and 10 is as follows:

> Array of Impact buckets = from 1 to 10, last bucket + ((10-1)/4)

1 is a minimal loss, while 10 defines a maximum loss. Responses are scaled to 5 buckets, giving 4 divisions between 1 and 10, or

> $(10-1)/4 = (9/4) = 2.25$

The algorithm derives the following scale:

---

[8] An experienced project assessor can often spot inflated or deflated impact estimates based upon experience with systems of a similar type and size. Choosing the appropriate level of impact is sometimes a dialog between assessor and business sponsor. The responses on the impact sheet should be cross-checked for appropriateness to the overall system under assessment.

1. 1
2. 3.25
3. 5.50
4. 7.75
5. 10

Every loss to a system will have impact, no matter how trivial. The least total impact is 10 (1 * 10 responses). The greatest impact (catastrophic) is 100 (10 * 10 responses).

$$\text{Total Impact} = {}_1\sum{}_n (\text{responses})$$

6.6. Combine Terms

Estimated Attack Vector * Scaled Size Of Impact = Risk Rating

Attack Vector is "AV"
Impact is "I"

The risk rating is then

$$(0 < AV < 1) * (10 >= I <= 100) = \text{Scaled Risk}$$

Or, precisely in the Cisco spreadsheet:

$$\frac{{}_1\sum{}_n (AV)}{10 * \text{Number of questions}} * {}_1\sum{}_n (I) = \text{Scaled Risk}$$

Where:

Attack Vector ("technical exposure") = $0 > N < 1$
Impact == $10 <= N >= 100$

In the spreadsheet, the total is color coded to make it easy for the assessor to spot those assessments that will require action and those that signal projects of less information security interest.

Total Scores:		
Technical Exposure		0.55
Impact		62.20
Total Risk		34.21
Additional Security Risk Factor (0-40)		0.00
Composite Risk		34.21

Composite Risk Legend	
Low	0 - 20
Medium-low	15 - 34
medium-high	35 - 64
High	65 - 84
Severe	85+

6.7.   Additional Factors Outside the Questionnaire

Obviously, no short questionnaire can cover all of a complex domain for which risk assessment is performed. JGERR has built in a place for risk factors understood by the risk assessor but that fall outside of the questions that are being asked. Additional factors may be discovered during a security review. Or, the system under review may contain components that fall outside the typical scope of analysis. We call these "risk multipliers". In order to account for corner-case situations, there are four generic, open-ended fields into which the risk assessor may place a "finger on the scale" to increase the risk rating.

Are there any factors which are specific to this project that raise the risk significantly?
Factor 1 -please attach documentation about this factor
10) Factors cause this project to have additional very high risk.
8.4) Factors cause this project to have additional high risk.
6.4) Factors cause this project to have additional medium risk.
3.4) Factors cause this project to have additional low risk.
0) There are no factors

Including a space for the unforeseen and the corner case came from literally thousands of applications of the methodology. Over time, it became apparent that an experienced assessor has a more holistic understanding of risk that any automation. Somehow, that experience had to be incorporated into the risk rating

However, including an open-ended space with which to influence risk ratings is a tremendous responsibility that cannot be taken lightly. Therefore, only trained assessors are allowed to add additional factors. Further, the following conditions must be met before an additional risk factor can be added to the score:

- Additional risk factors must be formally documented
- Additional risk factors must be justified in writing
- Additional risk factors require peer review of at least 2 other assessors
  - One of the peer reviewers must be at the most senior level
  - One of the peer reviewers must be outside the sub-team directly involved in the business area of the project

If there is consensus that there is an additional factor that cannot be scored through the questionnaire and there is consensus about the size of the addition, then the additional factor is accepted.

Total Scores:		
Technical Exposure		0.85
Impact		66.00
Total Risk		**56.32**
Additional Security Risk Factor (0-40)		**14.80**
Composite Risk		**71.12**

7. Recommended Project Gate Initiation Point
At Cisco, risk assessments are performed upon Security Architecture engagement and just prior to go-live. The engagement may begin either before[9] the Execute Commit project gate or just after, when formal architecture and design work begins.

8. Other Smart Guides Referenced
None at this time.

---

[9] On particularly complex, critical and high-risk projects, earlier security engagement is preferred in order to identify security issues as early as possible. But such early engagement is typically not required for more standard projects.

9. Industry Standards Referenced

- ISO 13335-1

10. Public Domain Tools Referenced
- None at this time.

11. Taxonomy/Definitions

Vulnerability	Any weakness, administrative process, or access or physical exposure that makes an asset susceptible to exploit by a threat
Threat	A potential cause of an unwanted impact to a system or organization. (ISO 13335-1)
Exposure	The potential damage to or loss of an asset from a given threat and/or vulnerability after consideration of existing controls
Exploit	A means of using a vulnerability in order to cause a compromise of business activities or information security
Attack vector	A credible threat exercising an exploit on an exposed vulnerability

Impact	The overall (worst case scenario) loss expected when a threat exploits a vulnerability against an asset

12. Other Materials Referenced

- CVSS: Vulnerability, exposure, some impact: technically focused
- Microsoft Threat Modeling: Exploit, exposure, some threat modeling
- Bruce Schnier's attack tree methodology
- FAIR: Contributes significantly to Just Good Enough Risk Rating.
- The Security-specific Eight Stage Risk Assessment Methodology
- LAVA

13. Publication Date, Version, Authors, and URL where to find document

Date	Version	Author
2011/09/11	0.1d	Brook S.E. Schoenfield Vinay Bansal
2012/02/07	1.1b	Brook S. E. Schoenfield Vinay Bansal Michele Guel

1. **Other Contributors to the Methodology**
   - **Rakesh Bharania & Catherine Blackadder Nelson, concept originators**
   - **Vinay Bansal & the Cisco "Web Arch" team**
   - **Jack Jones & FAIR**
   - **John and Ann-Marie Borrelli & the KnowledgeConnect Security Sharing Forum participants**
   - **An unnamed trust researcher at RSA 2002**
   - **The Information Security Risk Methodology working group at Cisco Systems, Inc:**
     - **Doug Dexter**
     - **Marc Passey**
     - **Richard Puckett**
     - **Jim Borne**
     - **Brook Schoenfield**

Appendix E

Threat Modeling's Definition of Done

Awaiting publication by IOActive, Inc. blog at https://ioactive.com/resources/blogs/

I'm frequently asked, "How do you know if a threat model is complete?"

Unfortunately, threat model analyses can become quite non-linear, often recursive, despite our best efforts to torture the process into a sequence of discreet steps. It might seem, on the face of it, that an analysis might go on forever, taking into consideration ever more complex, labyrinthine, even baroque attack scenarios. The fact is that while an analyst can definitely play the "what if" game nearly forever, after a certain point there's little payback for the additional effort.

A threat model exercise is as much a journey through guesses firmly based on study and experience as it is an exercise in applying engineering certainties. In other words, the analysts' imaginations are an important input to the process. This is why setting boundaries around attack scenarios is critical to limiting flights of paranoid fantasy; there must be exit criteria for the threat model if other development tasks are to be addressed[*].

It's important to understand that threat modeling represents a perceived attack tree and collection of defenses for an ongoing, "living" system. Systems exist in an ecosystem that is subject to changes – sometimes sea changes.

System structures change; threat actors are creative and adaptive; research opens new techniques of attack. Each of these can and should trigger a threat model review[†]. In a sense, a threat model is never "done," since change is constant.

Still, for any particular threat model exercise, guidelines do exist to determine when "enough is enough."

---

[*] Some of the other development tasks will likely depend upon the output of the threat model.

[†] "Review" is my carefully chosen word, and does not indicate a complete rework. The model may be reviewed with consideration to changes in the inputs to the model.

My definition of threat modeling is "a technique to identify the attacks a system[*] must resist, and the defenses that will bring the system to a desired defensive state." Whether you like that definition or not, it suggests built in constraints to an analysis:

Identify attacks that a system <u>must</u> resist

Identify the defenses that will bring the system to a <u>desired</u> state

In my definition, "must resist" implies an enumeration of *relevant* attacks. This is a constrained list, not an open-ended enquiry. "Relevant" in this context indicates that some types of attacks won't or can't be considered against the system under analysis.

It may be useful to point out that exploits are specific to computer language, often also memory utilization, operating system, even component and version or build of that component. Indeed, exploits tend to match vulnerabilities one-to-one. If any of the contextual conditions change, a new exploit has to be generated.

With defenses, there are also limits. Many systems needn't defend against every potential attack, even if building a comprehensive and complete defense was possible given most organizations' resource limits.

One of the most important rules for building defenses is that any three (sometimes even two) well-placed persons can circumvent any technical control[†], so that number makes for a very natural constraint: don't attempt to prevent 3+ individuals from circumventing security controls where the individuals hold an ability to add their privileges together in collusion. It's a waste of time. In such circumstances, stick with the standard practice of separation of duties. Couple that separation of duties alongside monitoring of those actions that have a potential for collusive behavior. That's about the best one can manage against privileged actors working together to circumvent security controls.

"Desired state" in the threat modeling definition cited above indicates that near-perfect security may not be necessary. Depending upon the fielding organization's risk tolerance and the business context of the system, sophisticated attacks might not be relevant, that is, the organization does not feel a need to protect against such attacks. This should be an obvious stopping point for a threat model analysis: attacks requiring high technical sophistication and/or high complexity need not be defended against.

While recent events have certainly pointed towards a world where any digital system might be a target of any actor, there often exist limits beyond which an organization need not go.

---

[*]   "System" is defined broadly, encompassing any collection of digital and human processes that taken together provide a complete set of the functions under analysis. A system could be:
- A piece of code intended as a part of the bootloader (in which case, the threat model would necessarily also include all the bootloader code for the machine).
- A set of processes running in user space on an operating system (in order to create a proper threat model, a system must include those operating system functions that provide the infrastructure and runtime upon which the application is loaded and runs.
- A set of globally distributed cloud-based services.
- An enterprise and all of its infrastructure, digital functions, etc.

The term "system" is meant to be inclusive, such that whatever digital processes are being threat modeled are categorized as a system.

[†]   The fact that manipulation or impersonation of persons with the right set of permissions can circumvent technical controls was the premise of the long-running television series, "Mission Impossible." The later series of movies don't hinge on this same gambit, however.

For instance, consumer anti-malware software typically does not protect against highly targeted, sophisticated, state-sponsored attacks. That's because the consumers who count on these products would at the worst be collateral damage to some other target. And indeed, those who can count on being a state agency target don't usually rely on consumer-grade software for their protection. Hence, when threat modeling such software, the analyst may discount nation-state attackers and their technically astute techniques, focusing instead upon cybercrime, which has a rather different exploitation model and risk tolerance.

Even sophisticated attackers have their limits. Amongst the exploits leaked from the NSA and CIA in April 2017 ("Shadow Brokers" leak) was a piece of code that identified the presence of a particular anti-malware vendor's products. If the product was running, the attack did not proceed. Apparently, compromise against this defense was too much trouble, even for the USA's premier spy agency.

The constraints for attack enumeration are as follows:

- The risk tolerance of the organization owning/fielding the system
- The risk tolerance of the system's users (if any)
- The capabilities, goals, expended effort, and risk tolerances of the enumerated set of threat agents who will wish to attack
- The trust/risk profiles of the system's components, including infrastructure(s) and external entities
- The runtime/execution environment(s)
- The existing defenses (including infrastructure defenses and services)
- The highest sensitivity of data flowing through and being processed
- The probability of a particular attack scenario being low enough to be discounted (probability might rise over time as new attack techniques are identified)

While somewhat creative, a threat model must be grounded in hard data. Obviously, those active attacks that can be exercised against the system under analysis will be included.

Furthermore, an analyst draws attack scenarios from relevant past exploit/vulnerability pairs even if such vulnerabilities have not yet been found in the system. It's important to understand that even the most rigorous testing, as Edsger Dijkstra so famously quipped, "proves the system has bugs, not that it doesn't." If there have existed exploitable vulnerabilities in any component within the system under analysis or within similar components and technologies, even though these conditions have already been fixed, then the analysis must assume that at least a few similar issues will likely be found at some point in the future.

The analyst need not worry about particular exploit details[*]. Instead, it's sufficient to know that, for example, there are numerous forms of web input injection that allow an attacker to misuse a web server's content to attack the web server's users (such as Cross-Site Scripting attacks).

Another example would be consideration of attacks that can escape a virtual runtime environment (that is, a virtual machine or container) to take control of the host operating environment[†] (a

---

[*] However, an understanding of the mechanism of exploitation of at least one example of each particular type of attack helps to identify appropriate defensive measures.

[†] CVE-2019-5736 is a guest escape for Linux containers that was announced February 11, 2019. Failure to account for the possibility of such a vulnerability left many implementations vulnerable. Those implementations that used a specific defense were not vulnerable.

hypervisor or operating system). This attack scenario is called a "Guest Escape" attack. Nearly every virtual runtime has experienced at least one guest escape vulnerability. Failure to account for the eventual appearance of a guest escape leaves open the potential for harm at the point in the future when such a vulnerability has been discovered.

The above scenarios are not fictional. Such attacks have been successful recently. While we may wish to gaze into our crystal balls for future attack types, the here-and-now threat landscape offers adversaries plenty of opportunity for malfeasance; a threat model must account for that set of known attacks whose exploitable conditions have been found in the past in the technologies under analysis.

An analyst may stop enumerating attacks when:

- The attack scenarios seem demonstrably more complex than other methods of compromise that are easier and more readily available
- The required preconditions lie well outside the range of normal or typical configuration and usage
- Significant inside assistance (for externally-originated attacks) is required to proceed. (Insider threat is a special category that requires careful analysis across an organization. It rarely should be tackled one system analysis at a time. Separation of duties are often determined on a per-system, per-function, or per-privilege basis.)
- Where no exploit exists for a particular vulnerability, or the vulnerability is not exposed for remote exercise or research (it's important to periodically revisit the threat model in light of new developments)
- Attack scenarios start to border on the ridiculous, the strained, or the dubious, or depend upon computer technologies that have yet to be invented (i.e., "science fiction")

An analyst may stop specifying defenses when:

- Each defense has some overlap of protection with at least one other defense
- Each significant* attack vector is covered at least partially by more than a single defense

Admittedly, the criteria for completing a threat model are qualitative, as they will be for the foreseeable future. Still, the above set of guidelines and constraints can help to define some sense of completion, and provide the ability to declare "enough is enough" when an analysis bumps against one or more of these barrier conditions.

It's important to remember that a threat model exists within a context of constant change. Hence, in a very real sense, a threat model is a living analysis of a system being implemented or running within the dynamic context of maintenance, updates, and changing threat conditions. As such, "completion" can be seen as the end of a threat modeling exercise or review; a threat model can rarely serve its purpose as a one-time exercise.

However, these very real boundaries, when met, signal that a round of analysis has reached a termination point – a "definition of done."

---

* For more stringent security postures, each attack scenario must be mitigated. "Significant" is meant to mean those attack vectors whose successful exercise will cause significant harm. It also implies attack vectors that are considered "credible;" that is, there is sufficient evidence that the attack vector can be exercised by an active threat actor.

References

Alperovitch, D. (2011, August 2). Revealed: Operation Shady RAT. McAfee, Inc. White Paper.

Greenberg, A. (2018, January 3). A Critical Intel Flaw Breaks Basic Security for Most Computers. *Wired Magazine*. Retrieved from https://www.wired.com/story/critical-intel-flaw-breaks-basic-security-for-most-computers/

Bonardon, O. (2018) Retrieved from https://docbox.etsi.org/Workshop/2018/201806_etsi securityweek/middlebox/s03_joint_efforts/encrypted_traffic_inspection_mcafee_bonorden.pdf

Bureau of Labor Statistics. (n.d.). US Dept. of Labor Statistics for Job Class "Security Analyst." Retrieved from https://www.bls.gov/ooh/computer-and-information-technology/information-security-analysts.htm

Cerbin, W. (2011). Understanding Learning Styles: A Conversation with Dr. Bill Cerbin. Interview with Nancy Chick. UW Colleges Virtual Teaching and Learning Center.

Chandra, B. (2014, May 13). A Technical View of the OpenSSL "Heartbleed" vulnerability, Version 1.2.1. A Security on DeveloperWorks Community Whitepaper. ibm.biz/dwsecurity. Retrieved from https://www.ibm.com/developerworks/community/files/basic/anonymous/api/library/38218957-7195-4fe9-812a-10b7869e4a87/document/ab12b05b-9f07-4146-8514-18e22bd5408c/media

Cohen, Z., Marquardt, A., and Crawford, J. (2018, October 3, 12:44 PM ET). North Korean Hackers Tried to Steal over $1 Billion, Report Says. CNN. Retrieved from https://www.cnn.com/2018/10/03/politics/north-korea-hackers-cybercrimes/index.html

Doyle, J. (1998). *Routing TCP/IP*, Vol. I, Cisco Press, MacMillan Technical Publishing, p. 41.

Ducklin, P. (2014, April 8). Anatomy of a Data Leakage Bug—The OpenSSL "Heartbleed" Buffer Overflow. Naked Security by Sophos. Retrieved from https://nakedsecurity.sophos.com/2014/04/08/anatomy-of-a-data-leak-bug-openssl-heartbleed/

Eadicicco, L. (2014, May 15). Photos of The NSA's Secret Workshop Where It Intercepts Packages and Plants Bugs in Electronics. *Business Insider*. Retrieved from https://www.businessinsider.com/nsa-tao-intercepting-packages-2014-5

Edwards, B. (1989). *Drawing on the Right Side of the Brain.* Tarcher-Perigree.

FBI. (2019, April 22). 2018 Internet Crime Report, Federal Bureau of Investigation, Cyber Division. Retrieved from: https://pdf.ic3.gov/2018_IC3Report.pdf

Fruhlinger, J. (2018). The Mirai Botnet Explained: How Teen Scammers and CCTV Cameras Almost Brought Down the Internet. Retrieved from https://www.csoonline.com/article/3258748/the-mirai-botnet-explained-how-teen-scammers-and-cctv-cameras-almost-brought-down-the-internet.html?

Fuller, M. (2008). *Software Studies: A Lexicon,* p. 170. MIT Press.

Ghaznavi-Zadeh, R. (2017). *ISACA Journal,* Vol. 4. Retrieved from https://www.isaca.org/Journal/Archives/2017/Volume-4/Pages/enterprise-security-architecture-a-top-down-approach.aspx?utm_referrer=&utm_referrer=

Grobman, M. (2016, November 3). Focus Keynote, Chief Technology Officer (CTO), McAfee, Inc. Focus Conference, Las Vegas NV.

Gruss, D., Maurice, C., Fogh, A., et al. (2016). Prefetch Side-Channel Attacks: Bypassing SMAP and Kernel ASLR. Graz University of Technology, G DATA Advanced Analytics. Retrieved from: https://gruss.cc/files/prefetch.pdf

IEEE (2014). Avoiding the Top 10 Software Security Design Flaws. IEEE Center for Secure Design, p. 2. Retrieved from https://cybersecurity.ieee.org/blog/2015/11/13/avoiding-the-top-10-security-flaws/

Intel. (2015). Protect, Detect, Correct: Security Connected for Healthcare Providers. Intel Security. Retrieved from http://www.mcafee.com/us/resources/brochures/br-protect-detect-correct-security-connected-healthcare.pdf

Isaac, M. (2016, October 25). Self-Driving Truck's First Mission: A 120-Mile Beer Run. *New York Times.* Retrieved from https://www.nytimes.com/2016/10/26/technology/self-driving-trucks-first-mission-a-beer-run.html

Ismail, N. (2018, April 24). Global Cybercrime Economy Generates over $1.5TN, According to New Study. *Tech Nation.* Retrieved from https://www.information-age.com/global-cybercrime-economy-generates-over-1-5tn-according-to-new-study-123471631/

Johnson, S. (1836). *The Poetical Works of Alexander Pope, Esq., to Which Is Prefixed: A Life of the Author,* Vol. 1, p. 89. J. Gladding & Co.

Kocher, P., Horn, J., Fogh, A., et al. (2018). Spectre Attacks: Exploiting Speculative Execution. Retrieved from https://spectreattack.com/spectre.pdf

Leyden, J. (2005, August 3, 15:37). Cisco Portal Password Security Compromised. Precautionary Reset Fails to Run Smoothly. Retrieved from https://www.theregister.co.uk/2005/08/03/cisco_password_security_flap/

Lipp, M., Schwarz, M., Gruss, G., et al. (2018). Meltdown: Reading Kernel Memory from User Space. Retrieved from https://meltdownattack.com/meltdown.pdf

Maruoka, A. (2011). *Concise Guide to Computation Theory,* p. 167. Springer-Verlag.

McClue, S. (1999, September 10). Hacking Exposed: Network Security Secrets & Solutions. *Computing*. McGraw-Hill.

McGeehan, R. (2019, April 23). Describing Vulnerability Risks. Medium.com. Retrieved from https://medium.com/@magoo/describing-vulnerability-risks-3a78c2e352d8

Mehta, N. (2014, April 8, 1:08 PM). Twitter.

Michlin, I. (n.d.) DevOps Trainer and Principal Security Consultant at NCC Group, quoted by Robert Lemos. Threat Modeling and DevOps: 3 Lessons from the Front Lines. Tech Beacon. Retrieved from https://techbeacon.com/security/threat-modeling-devops-3-lessons-front-lines

Microsoft. (n.d.) Simplified Implementation of the SDL. Microsoft SDL documentation, p. 6. Retrieved from: https://download.microsoft.com%2Fdownload%2FF%2F7%2FD%2FF7D6B14F-0149-4FE8-A00F-0B9858404D85%2FSimplified%2520Implementation%2520of%2520the%2520SDL.doc&usg=AOvVaw3UCYwxZwcaPbQoTPkFLQ1Q

Microsoft (2014, June 13). The OSI Model's Seven Layers Defined and Functions Explained, Rev. 2. Microsoft Inc. Retrieved from https://support.microsoft.com/en-us/kb/103884)

MITRE. (n.d.). CWE-888: Software Fault Pattern (SFP) Clusters. MITRE Corporation. Retrieved from https://cwe.mitre.org/data/graphs/888.html

NATO. (1969, October). NATO Science Committee. Software Engineering Techniques. Report on a Conference Sponsored by the NATO Science Committee, p. 16. Quote from Edsger Dijkstra, Rome, Italy. Retrieved from http://homepages.cs.nci.ac.uk/brian.randell/NATO/nato 1969.PDF

NIST 800-14 in 1996. Retrieved from https://csrc.nist.gov/publications/detail/sp/800-14/archive/1996-09-03

Ogundeji, O. A. (2015, August 18). Google Launches Android One Smartphone Program in Africa. *PCWorld*. Retrieved from https://www.pcworld.com/article/2972741/android/google-launches-android-one-phone-in-africa.html

Osborne, C. (2018, January 23). Artificial Synapse Creation Makes Brain-on-a-Chip Tech Closer to Reality. Retrieved from: http://www.zdnet.com/article/artificial-synapse-creation-makes-brain-on-a-chip-tech-closer-to-reality/#ftag=RSSbaffb68

Romeo, C. (n.d.) CEO of Security Journey. Quoted by Vijayan, J. 6 DevSecOps Best Practices: Automate Early and Often. Tech Beacon. Retrieved from https://techbeacon.com/security/6-devsecops-best-practices-automate-early-often

Rosen, M. (2008, October 1). 10 Key Skills Enterprise Architects Must Have to Deliver Value. Retrieved from https://www.cutter.com/article/10-key-skills-enterprise-architects-must-have-deliver-value-469471

Schoenfield, B. (2014). Applying the SDL Framework to the Real World. In Ransome, J. and Misra, A. *Core Software Security: Security at the Source*, Ch. 9, pp. 255–324. Boca Raton, FL: CRC Press.

Schoenfield, B. and Quiroga, D. (2017, November 24). Don't Substitute CVSS for Risk: Scoring System Inflates Importance of CVE-2017-3735. Securing Tomorrow McAfee Blog. Retrieved from https://securingtomorrow.mcafee.com/other-blogs/mcafee-labs/dont-substitute-cvss-for-risk-scoring-system-inflates-importance-of-cve-2017-3735/

Schoenfield, B. (2015). *Securing Systems: Applied Security Architecture and Threat Models.* Boca Raton, FL: CRC Press.

Seggleman, R., Tuexin, M., and Williams, M. (2012, February). Request for Comment RFC 6520 "Transport Layer Security (TLS) and Datagram Transport Layer Security (DTLS) Heartbeat Extension." ISSN: 2070-1721. Retrieved from https://tools.ietf.org/html/rfc6520

Shankland, S. (2014, April 8, 2:55 AM PDT). "Heartbleed" Bug Undoes Web Encryption, Reveals Yahoo Passwords. Retrieved from https://www.cnet.com/news/heartbleed-bug-undoes-web-encryption-reveals-user-passwords/

Shankland, S. (2014, April 8, 2:55 AM PDT). Cost of a Retail Data Breach: $179 Million for Home Depot. WebTitan. Retrieved from https://www.webtitan.com/blog/cost-retail-data-breach-179-million-home-depot/

Shostack, A. (2014). Security Engineering: Computers versus Bridges. Adam Shostack and Friends. https://adam.shostack.org/blog/2018/04/security-engineering-computers-versus-bridges/

Stephenson, N. (1995) *The Diamond Age.* Bantam Books.

Swiderski, F. and Snyder, W. (2004, July 14). Threat Modeling. *Microsoft Professional.* Microsoft Press.

Tarandach, I. and Schoenfield, A. (2019, May 30). *Continuous Threat Modeling Handbook.* continuous-threat-modeling/Continuous_Threat_Modeling_Handbook.md, GitHub. Retrieved from https://github.com/Autodesk/continuous-threat-modeling/blob/master/Continuous_Threat_Modeling_Handbook.md)

The Open Group. (2011). An Example of Enterprise Security Thinking Can Be Found in Open Enterprise Security Architecture. Retrieved from https://publications.opengroup.org.G112

The Open Group. (n.d.) The Open Group TOGAF Standard, Version 9.2. Retrieved from https://pubs.opengroup.org/architecture/togaf9-doc/arch/chap03.html

Tipton, H. F. (2000, October 20). *Information Security Management Handbook,* 4th Edition, Vol. 2, p. 581. Boca Raton, FL: CRC Press.

Vaas, L. (2018, February 26). In Fraud We Trust—Cybercrime Org Bust Shows We're Fighting Pros. Naked Security by Sophos. Retrieved from https://nakedsecurity.sophos.com/2018/02/26/in-fraud-we-trust-cybercrime-org-bust-shows-were-fighting-pros/

Vanhoef, M. (2017). Key Reinstallation Attacks: Breaking WPA2 by Forcing Nonce Reuse. [Discovered by Mathy Vanhoef of imec-DistriNet, KU Leuven]. Retrieved from https://www.krackattacks.com/

Williams, C. (2018, January 2). Kernel-Memory-Leaking Intel Processor Design Flaw Forces Linux, Windows Redesign. *The Register*. Retrieved from https://www.theregister.co.uk/2018/01/02/intel_cpu_design_flaw/

Wilson, P. L. (1995, 2004). *Pirate Utopias: Moorish Corsairs & European Renegadoes*. AbeBooks.

Zachman, J. A. (2007). Foreword. In: *Handbook of Enterprise Systems Architecture in Practice*. (P. Saha, Ed.) pp. *xv–xvi*. IGI Global.

Zeigler-Hill, V., Welling, L. M., and Shackleford, T. K. (Eds.). (2015). *Evolutionary Perspectives on Social Psychology Evolutionary Psychology*, p. 231. Springer International Publishing.

INDEX